Afghanistan and Canada

Kabul

AFGHANISTAN AND CANADA

IS THERE AN ALTERNATIVE TO WAR?

Edited by

Lucia Kowaluk and Steven Staples

BLACK
ROSE
BOOKS

Montreal/New York/London

A publication of the Institute of Policy Alternatives of Montreal (IPAM)

Black Rose Books No. MM370

Library and Archives Canada Cataloguing in Publication

Afghanistan and Canada : Is there an alternative to war? / Lucia Kowaluk,
Steven Staples, editors

Includes bibliographical references
ISBN 978-1-55164-329-8 (bound)   ISBN 978-1-55164-328-1 (pbk.)

1. Afghan War, 2001– –Participation, Canadian. 2. Canada–Armed
Forces–Afghanistan. 3. Canada–Military police. 4. Canada–Foreign
relations–1945–. I. Kowaluk, Lucia

DS371.412.A356 2008   958.104'7   C2008-905055-X

Cover image is a painting entitled Afghan Freedom Fighter by John Thompson

**BLACK
ROSE
BOOKS**

C.P. 1258	2250 Military Road	99 Wallis Road
Succ. Place du Parc	Tonawanda, NY	London, E9 5LN
Montréal, H2X 4A7	14150	England
Canada	USA	UK

To order books:
In Canada: (phone) 1-800-565-9523   (fax) 1-800-221-9985
email: utpbooks@utpress.utoronto.ca
In the United States: (phone) 1-800-283-3572   (fax) 1-800-351-5073
In the UK & Europe: (phone) 44 (0)20 8986-4854   (fax) 44 (0)20 8533-5821
email: order@centralbooks.com

Our Web Site address:
http://www.blackrosebooks.net
A publication of the Institute of Policy Alternatives of Montreal (IPAM)
Printed in Canada

Contents

We dedicate this book to our children, Riel Roussopoulos and Juliet Smith-Roussopoulos, Natasha and Orion, and Desmond and Annelise Staples, as we struggle to leave them a world without war.

Acknowledgments

The editors and Black Rose Books would like to thank the following people for their precious collaboration toward the realization of this book project: Martine Eloy, Judith Beryln, Pierre Beaudet, Lyne Chartier, Miriam Green, Ariane Boileau, Martin Lukacs, and David LeBlanc.

Introduction

This book comes out of a deep desire to end Canada's military involvement in a wasteful and costly war – thus helping to end the whole war and finally bring peace to Afghanistan, through a diplomatic resolution of the conflict.

We say, "Let Canada Lead." This can be done in a number of ways. By pressuring all war parties for an immediate ceasefire. By increasing solidarity in practice with the people of Afghanistan: supporting the construction of an education system open to all, supporting the construction of a public health system accessible to all, supporting and enhancing a culture of human rights and civil liberties, in part through a fair judicial system, by engaging in building an Afghanistan economy through fair trade.

Canada should be an example, and in doing so work with other non-combative countries to promote these similar objectives.

This book gives an historical background to the country, a necessary context to understanding how and why Afghanistan is in its current state; explores the real reasons why Canada (under NATO) has been dragged into this conflict; and presents the international conditions and actions immediately required in order to lay the conditions for an acceptable peaceful Afghanistan to exist. Key to this is negotiations at an international round table of all the countries surrounding the country (Pakistan, Iran, Turkmenistan), the countries otherwise concerned and involved (China, Russia, Pakistan, India, and the USA/NATO), and parties (Taliban). Such negotiations have to work out what kind of Afghanistan is minimally acceptable, to ensure a peaceful evolution of the country.

This introduction more fully elaborates the points above by referring to the essays of the book. Each essay will be characterized and woven into the overall purpose of the book, without committing each contributor to the perspective above.

The essays in this book have been gathered with the desire to make available to the reader the information that the editors firmly believe deserves greater attention in the national debate on Canada's combat role in Afghanistan.

We have assembled here a collection of reports, presentations, and articles written by people and organizations who hold important information and viewpoints. In reading the collection, one cannot escape the conclusion that the current war in Afghanistan is wasteful, costly and ineffective. The authors put forward several solutions worthy of consideration. Not all agree on a single alternative, but they are all rooted in the desire to end the war, and for Canada to provide leadership.

The editors of this book, as well as all the writers of the essays included, are individuals who have spent years studying the geographical region of Afghanistan and its neighbours; or studying the issues involved in Canada's participation in fighting wars or in peacekeeping; or actively promoting human rights and/or peace efforts. We believe their credentials are stellar. They are all people who have cooperated with us in producing this book as a gesture of solidarity and commitment to bringing a peaceful settlement to the part of Central Asia that is the subject of our efforts.

THE CONTEXT

D'ABORD SOLIDAIRES, MURRAY DOBBIN, and MICHAEL NEUMANN set the stage with their articles which are lively and heartfelt statements of moral and practical concern. They all lay the moral and political base of the essays that follow. These four articles have in common their sense of moral outrage at the hypocrisy that shrouds the Canadian Government's propaganda justifying its military actions. Each one tears apart a particular angle of the propaganda, leaving the reader wondering "how did we ever believe such nonsense!" These articles set the tone and the basic information that will be followed in all the rest of this book's articles to come.

THE HISTORY AND BACKGROUND

JOHN WARNOCK's article, gives a succinct summary of the history of Afghanistan since the retreat of the Soviet Union, as well as Canada's involvement since 9/11. TARIQ ALI, supplements Warnock's article by describing not only Afghanistan's history, but the history of the whole geographic region.

It is clear from these two well researched articles that the war has been a disaster for the Afghan people, and their attempts to control their own society and their own lives. What we find of specific interest (and more of this in CHESHMAK FARHOUMAND-SIMS' article later) is how many times in the past century the Afghan people have tried to form governments, constitutions and human rights protections, only to be thwarted and controlled by outside invading forces. As Canadians we ignore this history at our peril and the peril of humanity.

ÉCHEC À LA GUERRE (Stop the war) is an eight-year-old Quebec coalition formed in opposition to Canada's involvement in the NATO-led war in Afghanistan. Members of this coalition include peace, human rights, women's, faith-based, community groups and trade unions. They hold public demonstrations, meet with politicians, publish articles, and hold public hearings. In 2006 they published a 50 page document as their position against the war. Well researched and based on the thoughtful consideration of the many individuals who make up the coalition, it gives the reader the framework needed to understand how Canada's involvement in the war evolved. Three years later its facts, its arguments, and its moral position still hold and we present it here as the third article in this background section.

THE CURRENT SITUATION AND CANADA'S ROLE

STEVEN STAPLES, President of the Ottawa-based Rideau Institute (and a co-editor of this book), has been studying the Canadian Military for many years. He has followed its route from a peacekeeping role to a combat role under General Rick Hiller and Prime Minister

Harper. His article, contains the most up-to-date data on the size and scope of the Canadian Military, and the costs to the Canadian tax payer of this military machine, and the war itself .

This article gives the reader real feeling as to what this war is costing and why so much of the financial surplus the Harper Government inherited from the Liberals has been spent and all, without a real debate.

CARE Canada is one of our major humanitarian NGOS and well-respected. STEPHEN CORNISH a key member of the staff, has spent many weeks in Afghanistan over the past eight years. His article, presented in this book, is the second half of a larger article that appeared in *Journal of Military and Strategic Studies*. The article deals with the impossible conundrum facing humanitarian-focused NGOS: namely the attempted alliance between them and the military. Pressured by the military to cooperate as a way of convincing the Afghan population that this war is for their own good, the NGOS find themselves in the position of not being trusted, and therefore unable to carry out useful humanitarian work. This article deals with a very important issue rarely discussed publicly.

This section concludes with three short, sharp articles adding pieces to the puzzle: LINDA MCQUAIG's description of the shameful episode in Canadian history during which the Canadian Military handed over Afghan prisoners to the Afghan military to certain abuse and torture; IRA BASEN's humorous description of the Harper Government's "new" military's PR propaganda efforts; RICHARD PRESTON's short " NOW we know why we're in Afghanistan!"

THE WOMEN'S QUESTION

Thousands of concerned and progressive citizens in Canada and the United States firmly believe that NATO must be in Afghanistan to protect the human rights of Afghan women, many of whom, the whole world knows, are in abusive, cloistered and illiterate states. It is a very persuasive position but it is a mistaken one. CHESHMAK FARHOUMAND-SIMS in a long detailed article tells us why. It covers in fascinating detail the role of women in Afghan society for over a century: the progressive gains made during certain periods, as well as the relapse into abusive periods, and she shows that no periods have been simply black and white. Her conclusions are clear; there are three key reasons for the largely abusive period in which Afghanistan currently finds itself: a particular fundamentalist interpretation of

Islam; a deeply rooted and ancient culture within certain geographical regions (largely rural); and WAR, propagated by outside invasions which increases the patriarchal and authoritarian aspects of the
first two reasons. She is very persuasive and she knows the history of
her culture very well. This section concludes with two short pieces:
an interview with MALALAI JOYA, a feisty, flamboyant, and controversial elected member of the Afghan parliament describing in some
detail abuse she has suffered; and an eye-witness account by a Canadian woman, ROSE MARIE WHALLEY, who visited Afghanistan in
2005, staying in a rural Pashtun village with an extended family. Her
observations round out the effect the war is having on an average
family.

THE GEO-ECONOMIC SITUATION

The current proposal of building a natural gas pipeline from Turk-
manistan to India and Pakistan is first introduced in this section with
a short summary written by JOHN FOSTER and first published in
2008.

John Foster, a retired international energy economist who has
worked for several of the world's large oil companies and development banks, then presents a much longer, thoroughly documented
article on the subject, including maps and graphs. Since he and his
editor and wife Millie Morton, began their research on this crucial
and hardly discussed issue, they have been increasingly distressed by
the scarce publicity about this very important aspect of the NATO
war in Afghanistan which is being developed using Afghanistan as a
bridge. Visits between American and Turkmani diplomats and engineers in both countries are currently taking place, and many Canadian officials – to say nothing of the public at large – are not even
aware of the plans being made. Clearly Canadian citizenry should be
aware that Western control of this vast energy resource is a crucial
reason for the current war. Not only is an important US backed
pipeline being planned, but at least seven other ones, backed by Russia or Iran, or China are in various states of planning.

WHAT CAN BE DONE?

Indeed: what can be done? The editors believe that there is a way out
of this ghastly destructive war and that Canada must lead the way.
Canada is a middle-power country that as a peacekeeper, has always

been highly respected on the international stage. It must return to peacekeeping and use that position to say it does not agree with taking part in the invasion of Afghanistan for all the reasons this book is presenting. It must therefore publicly pressure for an immediate cease-fire which it will be the first to honour; and then will take part in a long-term, all-hands-at the table, negotiated settlement.

It can be done.

WALTER DORN, a faculty member of the Royal Military College, has written a short, pithy factual article arguing for a return to Canada's peacekeeping role.

PIERRE BEAUDET, founder of the Montreal-based NGO, Alternatives, currently teaches International Studies at the University of Ottawa. After describing again how we got into this war, in this article he lays out the pitfalls of calling for a cease-fire, but nevertheless says it must be done as the only humane option open to the international community.

CLAUDE CASTONGUAY, highly respected in Quebec intellectual and Government realms, comes to the same conclusions.

RICHARD PRESTON, in his testimony to the 2007 Manley Commission, makes a very credible case for the desirability and usefulness of establishing a Canadian Government Ministry of Peace, along with a full cabinet position for its Minister.

And finally, PEGGY MASON, known as Canada's former UN Disarmament Ambassador, and as special representative of the UN Secretary-General, strongly comes to the same conclusion: she knows whereof she speaks! She takes the reader step-by-step through the process that can and must be done in order to end the war in Afghanistan, and to allow the Afghan people to build their own society. And whatever her personal opinions may be, the process she describes and promotes must take into account the interests and the agendas of every single player: the US, NATO, the Taliban, the war lords, China, Iran, Pakistan, and Russia, to name only the most prominent. It is a credible scenario and one which the editors support. Canada must lead the way by actively working for a negotiated ceasefire, serious long term negotiations and a withdrawal of troops as soon as possible. All that is required is the political will to do so.

Afghanistan and Canada

Images by Dominic Morissette

A street take-out in Kabul

Kabul

Old Kabul

Outside Kabul

Bamiyan

Election day in Bamiyan

Bamiyan province

Sarubee – a village on the road to Jalalabad

Students sharing a meal

Boys' school

Girls' school

Afghan soldiers

Afghan soldiers

Dr. MaSooda Jalal, the only woman candidate in presidential 2004 election

A candidate in presidential 2004 election

Afghan TV interviewing citizens

Afghan TV interviewing citizens

Demonstration supporting General Dostrum

Afghanistan and Canada
The Context

Putting an End to the "Great War for Civilization"

D'ABORD SOLIDAIRES

INTRODUCTION

Let's Stop Pretending that Canada and the West are Waging a War for Civilization

Nineteen years earlier, the greatest act of terrorism – using Israel's own definition of that much misused word – in modern middle East history began. Typically, on 16 September 2001, no one remembered the anniversary in the West ... the fact that on that date in 1982, Israel's Phalangist militia allies started their three-day orgy of rape and knifing and murder in the Palestinian refugee camps of Sabra and Chatila. It followed an Israeli invasion of Lebanon – designed to drive the PLO out of the country and given the green light by the then US Secretary of State, Alexander Haig – which cost the lives of 17,500 Lebanese and Palestinians, almost all of them civilians. That was more than five times the death toll in the September 11th 2001, attacks. Yet, I could not remember any vigils or memorial services or candle-lighting in America or the West for the innocent dead of Lebanon – no stirring speeches about democracy or liberty or "evil."

No, Israel was not to blame for what happened on September 11th 2001. The culprits were Arabs, not Israelis. But America's failure to act with honour in the Middle East, its promiscuous sale of missiles to those who use them against civilians, its blithe disregard for the deaths of tens of thousands of Iraqi children under sanctions of which Washington was the principal supporter – all these were intimately related to the society that produced the Arabs who plunged New York into an apocalypse fire.

Bush wanted to persuade the world that it had changed forever so that he could advance a neo-conservative war – cloaked in honourable aspirations of freedom, democracy and liberty- that would plunge the Middle East into further chaos and death.

While Bush and Tony Blair prepared their forces for an inevitable attack on Afghanistan – whose Taliban priests predictably declined to surrender their "guest" bin Laden – they went on explaining that this was a war for "democracy and liberty," that it was about men who were attacking civilisation. Bush informed us that "America was targeted for attack because we are the brightest beacon for freedom and opportunity in the world." (p. 1036–7)

It took a while to grasp what was now going on, the extraordinary, almost unbelievable preparation under way for the most powerful nation ever to have existed on God's earth to bomb the most devastated, ravaged, starvation-haunted and tragic country in the world. Afghanistan, raped and eviscerated by the Russian army for ten years, abandoned by its friends – us of course – once the Russians had retreated, was about to be attacked by the surviving superpower. President Bush was now threatening the obscurantist, ignorant, super-conservative Taliban with the same punishment he intended to mete out to bin Laden.

Bush had originally talked about «justice and punishment» and about "bringing to justice" the perpetrators of the atrocities of September 11th. But he was not sending policemen to the Middle East; he was sending B-52s and F-18s and AWACS planes and Apache helicopters. We were not going to arrest bin Laden. We were going to destroy him. And B-52s don't discriminate between men wearing turbans, or between men and women or women and children. None deserved this fate, but after twenty-one years of continuous conflict, the Afghans merited it least of all. (p. 1044)

Fisk, R. (2006) *The Great War For Civilisation. The Conquest on the Middle East*. Harper Perennial.

We have chosen to cite this passage from Robert Fisk's remarkable book, because the author dares to ask the impertinent question "why?" about the attack on the World Trade Center, one of the main causes of the current situation in countries such as Afghanistan and Iraq.

Fisk contends that "since the 1970s the history of the Middle East is almost synonymous with its wars and conflicts: the Soviet war in Afghanistan (1979–1989), the Iran-Iraq war (1980–1988), the Lebanese war (1975–1991), the Gulf war (1991), the American led wars in Afghanistan (2001) and in Iraq (2003), and the interminable Israeli-Palestinian conflict. He maintains that these are the years of the "great war for civilization," caused by the role Western powers have played for decades in a region they consider to be within their sphere of influence – France and the United Kingdom in the early 20th century, and later the United States. Finally, Fisk painstakingly documents the cynicism of the West's Middle East policies; their unconditional support for the most brutal dictators whenever it furthers their current interests (regardless of its effect on women or anyone else); their scorn for the very values they claim to be fighting to uphold: respect for human rights, freedom and democracy.

This situation has prevailed for decades. When Nicaragua was ruled by the bloodthirsty dictator Somoza, the US president was rumoured to have said: "Somoza may be a son of a bitch, but he's our son of a bitch." Today, Human Rights Watch

denounces the double standard of the West ... TheUnited States and Europe tolerate autocrats who pose as democrats in countries such as Pakistan, Kenya, and Russia where human rights are violated ... Washington and the governments of Europe continue to accept the most questionable elections when the winner is a strategic or commercial ally. The United States and Europe also have an increasingly hard time insisting upon respect for human rights when they themselves violate them in waging their war on terror.[1]

And what about Musharraf, in Pakistan? There's a real dictator. Here is a man who suspends human rights, a man who locks up journalists and fires judges who show too much independence. Does Canada denounce him? Not at all. He's our friend. When a dictator is our friend, he is not considered a dictator. In the words of Fisk, he's a tough guy.[2]

A further example of Western politics is found in the significance accorded to US imperialism by many contemporary political leaders, military strategists ... and intellectuals like Michael Ignatieff:

America's empire is not like empires of times past, built on colonies, conquest and the white man's burden ... The 21st century imperium is a new invention in the annals of political science, an empire lite, a global hegemony whose grace notes are free markets, human rights and democracy, enforced by the most awesome military power the world has ever known. It is the imperialism of a people who remember that their country secured its independence by revolt against an empire, and who like to think of themselves as the friend of freedom everywhere. It is an empire without consciousness of itself as such, constantly shocked that its good intentions arouse resentment abroad. But that does not make it any less of an empire, with a conviction that it alone, in Herman Melville's words, bears 'the ark of the liberties of the world.'[3]

It is convictions of this kind that allowed Emperor Bush and his kinglets Blair, Harper and cohorts to bomb Afghanistan, to occupy Iraq, to violate international law, to legitimize torture, and to plunge us into a state of obsession over security (security certificates, presumption of terrorism, etc.), as if all this was a natural by-product of democracy ...

Canadian troops are waging a colonial war of occupation, fraudently labeled as humanitarian in the name of "civilization."

Canada deliberately entered into this infernal round of the war for civilization arm in arm with the Bushes and Blairs of this world, without a thought to the history, that sheds light on how theUnited States became reviled to the point where it saw its innocent citizens cruelly assassinated in September of 2001.

It cannot be denied that this was a barbaric act. No less barbaric, however, is the bombing of Afghanistan, and this unending war, which has already resulted in the death of thousands of Afghans, victims of indiscriminate air strikes and the "preventative" military interventions of the occupying forces.[4] This deplorable situation will likely continue for quite some time, whether Canada pulls out of Kandahar or not, because a number of Western political leaders, citizens, and editorialists, have become imbued with the "mindset convinced of being on the right path and working for the forces of good ... according to the philosophy of good versus evil, a philosophy of being God's deputy ... which mindset is a complete failure and has led America to a dead end."[5]

This way of thinking is echoed by many Canadian soldiers when explaining why they are training for deployment to Afghanistan ... to do good, to fight the Taliban forces who are bad, because Afghans can't get organized. They go to Afghanistan on a "mission," like 21st century missionaries with a paternalism reminiscent of the height of colonialism. It is equally important to point out the underlying racism in this thinking which portrays Afghans as totally devoid of humanity, congenitally averse to democracy, justice, and human rights.

Strangely, those in high places close their eyes to the current regime's grave transgressions of

the values of civilization ... This is why I cry out when I hear our elected officials try to deceive us with talk of democracy in Afghanistan ... The much celebrated, retired General, the tragic Roméo Dallaire, declared, in April, in response to the cry-baby pacifists who grumble against the mission in Afghanistan, that Canada was in Afghanistan to defend our values. Our values? That's a good one ... While we fight crazed Islamic extremists who want to overthrow the regime in place in Kabul, that regime turns a blind eye to serious infringements of the right to a free press, shameless parodies of justice, and more or less openly admitted agreements between drug traffickers and local officials. Where are our values in all this? Oh, I forgot. The Afghan authorities torture the prisoners. And Canadian authorities close their eyes to this barbaric practice. Our values, yeah, sure. The truth is that the West couldn't care less about 'our values' in this region of the world. As long as the regime in place is not hostile, we close our eyes, hoping that freedom and democracy will somehow emerge. Afghanistan is nothing more than another chapter in this cynical tradition ... But I digress. I wanted to tell you that 77 of our soldiers have been killed in Afghanistan defending a regime that puts dissenting journalists to death.[6]

And finally, if at one time many people believed that Canadian troops were sent "to save women" (as one soldier put it) and that the war against the Taliban seemed like "a possible solution to the horror of the life women endured under their regime," a great number have become disillusioned in light of the limited progress in the situation of women. "How naive we are. As if we had ever fought wars to save women ..."[7]

The war of occupation that Canada is waging in Afghanistan with its NATO allies, and with the *a posteriori* blessing of the Security Council, which is totally dominated by the West, is an abusive and mendacious colonial war, waged under the guise of humanitarianism, that helps perpetuate both the chaos and the long train of death, suffering and destruction, for generations of Afghans and Canadians to come.

We say, "NO"to all this, and above all "Not in our NAME"!

Canadian troops and all other NATO forces must be immediately pulled out of Afghanistan.

We entirely agree with the arguments put forward by the Collectif Échec à la guerre in its document Canada's Role in the Occupation of Afghanistan which explains why we urgently need to withdraw Canadian forces from Afghanistan. (This document is published in this book) The same applies to all foreign troops on Afghan soil.

We assert that:

• the military intervention in Afghanistan is illegitimate and illegal in terms of international law;
• the military intervention advances neither democracy nor justice in Afghanistan, but rather reinforces fundamentalism, incites greater opposition and resistance (as did the Soviet occupation, and as does the continuing occupation of Palestine by the Israeli army, from which we refuse to learn) and incites growing anti-Western sentiment;
• the military intervention has the immediate effect of increasing i)the arms trade (which heightens the risk of violence against women) ii) the drug trade and iii) general destruction. It is the traffickers of arms and drugs who benefit from this war, not the people of Afghanistan;
• Canada's participation in this war serves only to further the economic and strategic interests of the US, bent on extending its domination of the Middle East and Central Asia with the help of NATO. This participation seriously undermines Canada's international credibility as an agent of peace and reconciliation;
• the situation of women has nothing to do with the real motives for the war. Their liberation cannot be achieved through the force of arms. If it could be why not deploy Canadian forces wherever the rights of women are violated, like in Pakistan, Saudi Arabia, Iran, China, India (where the cast system oppreses both men and women)? For that matter, why not use them in Canada, where the murder of women by their spouses is not uncommon?;
• the intervention has not improved security in Canada; on the contrary, it has undermined it. Furthermore, our security was never threatened by Afghanistan. The pretence of fighting terrorists (an all-

encompassing word, which has replaced "communism") with conventional armies and by waging a war of occupation is unacceptable.
• The intervention has changed the lives of Canadians for the worse by instituting security measures that target Arabs or Muslims and threaten the civil liberties of all Canadians; promulgating pro-military propaganda, reinforcing chauvinism in Canada; imposing further restrictions on immigration and refugees; and fostering increased racism and discrimination;
• the intervention has transformed Canada into an increasingly militaristic state, glorified the army, and and led to predatory recruitment strategies that take advantage of unemployment and ever-rising tuition fees at post-secondary institutions.

Unlike the Liberal Party of Canada and the Bloc Quebecois, we believe that it is impossible to transform an occupying army into a kind of humanitarian NGO. Doctors Without Borders withdrew from Afghanistan, stating that it was impossible for the local population to distinguish between aid workers and those working for the occupying forces. We don't win hearts with guns in hand. The child that accepts candy from the left hand of a soldier knows full well that the gun in the soldier's right hand could at any moment be used to kill her family, for as one soldier from Quebec put it, "a Taliban can be hiding behind anyone – so the solution is to eliminate everyone!!!"

In presenting his recent motion on Afghanistan, Prime Minister Harper affirmed that "This is a mission under a mandate from the United Nations, with our NATO allies and by request of the democratically elected government of Afghanistan. It is a very important mission for us, for the morale of our troops and for our security."[8] These reasons are unfounded. We are certainly not staying in Afghanistan because we are concerned about the morale of "our boys," but rather to please the members of Bush's "old boys' club" (i.e. NATO).

Silence the guns in order to seek politically negotiated solutions.

One day, we will have to leave Afghanistan. The present situation (as spelled out in the Manley Report, among others) already constitutes a failure which future reports will confirm, whether in 2009, 2011 or even several decades from now. Why not leave now and avoid further needless casualties and suffering caused by our military presence?
Why not:

• silence the guns and employ diplomacy, including the Taliban, in the political solution, whether or not we find this palatable;
• support the civilian population and particularly organizations who actually seek to defend human rights at great personal risk (such organizations do exist);
• substantially increase funding for development projects, ensuring that funds are transferred through non-military channels;
• call for the UN (not simply the Security Council) to take charge of addressing the full spectrum of political work to be done.

We must withdraw our troops if we really want to help the people of Afghanistan.

Only by withdrawing can we achieve politically negotiated solutions that will usher in development brought about by the people of Afghanistan. First and foremost, we must recognize that the Afghans have a right to control their own destiny and are capable of designing and putting into place their own solutions to their problems.

CONCLUSION

The decision to intervene militarily in Afghanistan constitutes a departure from the traditional role Canadians like to associate with their army, namely that of peacekeeper. It is the image of peacekeeper, not hostile aggressor, that Canadians embrace.

We believe that Canada is becoming increasingly militaristic. This is evidenced both by an increase in military spending and by the one-sided pro-Israeli position held by Canada during the Lebanese war and in regards to the plight of the Palestinian people. When waging war, we quickly begin to think that the military solution is the only solution and that without war there will be chaos, when, in fact, war itself is chaos.

The Manley Report brings no new insight into the nature of the quagmire in which Canada and NATO have chosen to become embroiled. It only serves to protract indefinitely this "new Vietnam" in which not only Canadian troops suffer needlessly, but also, and above all, the people of Afghanistan.

We equally believe that the situation in Afghanistan is directly linked to that of Pakistan, of Iran and of Palestine, to name a few. Canada can not claim to defend human rights, freedom, and democracy in Afghanistan while remaining silent about Israel's occupation of Palestinian territory and the systematic violation of Palestinian human rights for over 60 years!

The time has come for Canada to resume its role as a peacekeeper and as a negotiator and to take the lead in breaking with foreign policies held to this day by the United States and rubber-stamped by NATO. Let us hope that the 2008 American presidential election will help put a definitive end to the "great war for civilization" and usher in a new era of sharing the resources of the earth and of peaceful collaboration between peoples.

It's up to us.

NOTES

1 Human Rights Watch denounces the double standard of the West. *La Presse*, 1 February 2008.

2 "So Canada defends this regime!?", Patrick Lagacé, *La Presse*, 24 January 2008.

3 Michael Ignatieff, "The Burden," *New York Magazine*, 5 January 2003, p. 22–7, 50 53–4. Cited in the Preface of Normand Bailla Baillargeon.

4 According to Marc Herold, University of New Hampshire, 3000 to 3400 civilains were killed in Afghanastan between 7 October and 7 December 2001, more than all the vistims of 9/11. Source: Agence France-Presse, August 6, 2007. Since the beginning of the year more than 600 civilians were killed, of which about half were victims of "collateral damage" from the international forces, facts which are making the Western forces increasingly unpopular, and eroding the crediblility of President Karzai. *Le Devoir*, 6 August 2007.

5 "The Disaster of George W. Bush," comments by Nicolas Berubé. In Glenn Greenwald, *A Tragic Legacy*, *La Presse*, 27 January 2008.

6 Patrick Lagacé, op. cit.

7 "We have to get out of Afghanistan," Lise Payette, *Le Devoir*, 18 January 2008.

8 "Afghanistan: the debate will continue until March," *Le Devoir*, 7 February 2008.

War-fighting Role in Afghanistan Betrays Canadian Values

MURRAY DOBBIN

"It is hard to imagine a less honourable 'mission' than this increasingly brutal and unwinnable occupation on which to base such fundamental changes to our country."

Some government policy decisions are so profound in their impact that they can actually change the nature of the country. Medicare was one such policy decision, and so was the signing of the Canada-US Free Trade Agreement. It could be argued that the decision to take on an explicitly war-fighting role in Afghanistan will turn out to be another watershed decision, this one at odds with Canadian values and Canadians' convictions about the military's role in the world and society.

It also is having the effect of transforming both our foreign policy and our foreign aid policy – in both areas tarnishing our international reputation and integrating us into the US and its imperial designs on Middle East oil. In order to justify this colonial occupation, Canada now spends so much of its paltry aid budget on Afghanistan (much of it finding its way into the pockets of corrupt officials) that there is barely any financing left over for other developing countries' needs.

Perhaps most profound of all, the conflict's "war on terror" rationale is being used to justify massive increases in military spending, completely distorting the role of government and the spending priorities of Canadians.

Lastly, the military's role in Canadian politics and culture is being rapidly Americanized, with military spokesmen openly promoting their war-fighting role and taking part in cultural events, and with the media (most notably the CBC) promoting this new expansive role.

It is hard to imagine a less honourable "mission" on which to base such fundamental changes to the country. There are no longer any secrets about the Afghan conflict, nor about Canada's continuing role in it. It is an increasingly brutal occupation, unwinnable in any foreseeable circumstances, threatening to become an even wider regional conflict involving Pakistan, and whose "building democracy" cover story has been debunked by countless sources. The initial invasion was justified on the basis of destroying al Qaeda, a loosely organized force of no more than 300 fighters. The Taliban government, as hideous and deeply reviled as it was, had nothing to do with 9/11.

Any military action which followed the rapid rout of al Qaeda was directed at occupying the country as part of the US plan to control Middle East oil and gas. Even Allan Greenspan, the former head of the US Federal Reserve, admitted earlier this year (2008) that Afghanistan and Iraq were all about oil. The Taliban had broken off negotiations with the US for a pipeline from the Caspian basin. According to Middle East expert Eric Margolis, "In early 2001, six or seven months before 9/11, Washington made the decision to invade Afghanistan, overthrow the Taliban government, and install a client regime that would build the energy pipelines."

Afghanistan is increasingly framed as "the good war" by those who have long since given up portraying the Iraq quagmire as morally justified. Even Barack Obama is now promising to send soldiers from Iraq to bolster the 60,000 NATO and US troops now there and to "win" the war.

But winning in Afghanistan is sheer fantasy. Just ask the British and the Russians. US General Dan McNeill, the former commander of US and NATO forces in Afghanistan, recently stated that he would need 400,000 troops just to pacify the country. Even if every US soldier in Iraq transferred tomorrow, they would still be 200,000 short. The UN has said that its analysis shows one-third of the country is literally a no-go zone, controlled by insurgents, and an additional one-half is "high risk." Even Kabul is not safe, as attacks in and near the capital have increased by 70% since January (2008). Supply lines from Pakistan are under constant attack.

The "hearts and minds" struggle is in even worse shape. With so few troops, occupying forces have to rely increasingly on US air power just to maintain the status-quo – with predictable results: up to 1,000 civilians killed in the past six months (recall this article was written September 2008) with 260 of those in July alone, including a wedding party of 47 slaughtered in Helmand province. The NGOs trying to deal with this catastrophe are now in full panic mode, cutting back their operations. Their network, ACBAR (Agency Coordinating Body for Afghan Relief), representing 100 Afghan and international organizations, issued a statement on August 1 drawing attention to the civilian casualties, the spread of danger to previously secure areas, and increasing attacks on aid agencies and their staff (19 killed since January (2008), twice the total for all of 2007).

But what of the democratically elected government of Hamid Karzai? The man they call the mayor of Kabul – because that is as far as his government's authority extends – is perhaps the best evidence of the real purpose of the occupation, as well as its inevitable failure. The US blithely "appointed" Karzai as interim president and then rigged the political process to ensure that he won the subsequent election. A former consultant for US oil giant Unocal, Karzai was part of negotiations between the Taliban and Unocal for a gas pipeline through Afghanistan to Pakistan and India from the Caspian basin. (See articles in this book by John Foster.) The US was negotiating with the Taliban until four months before 9/11.

Karzai has literally no political base among the competing tribes in the country. His support is exclusively American firepower and cash. Most observers agree that he was elected president primarily because, at least, he was not a warlord. Yet his election was the result of systematic manipulation by the US and by the changing of the 1964 secular constitution to one that declared Islam supreme: no laws could violate "the sacred religion of Islam."

The new Political Parties Law also restricted parties: they could not pursue policies that were "contrary to Islam." Many secular parties were effectively excluded from the parliamentary elections of 2005. These largely unknown details of the Afghan political system are detailed in Jack Warnock's excellent new book: *Creating a Failed State: The U.S. and Canada in Afghanistan*. (The editors also recommend this book; Fernwood Press, 2008.)

Warnock, author of many acclaimed books on international affairs, also details the systematic breaking of the law banning political parties or individual candidates associated with armed groups. He quotes the Afghan Research and Evaluation Unit's analysis of the election results: of 249 members elected to the House of the People, 133 had fought in the internecine Mujahedin war. The Afghan Independent Human Rights Commission concluded that "80% of winning candidates in the provinces and more than 60% in Kabul have links to armed groups."

Following his own election, Karzai appointed some of the most reviled war lords in the country to senior posts – including Abdul Rashid Dostum, known as the "butcher of the north" to be the new army chief of staff. All of this, of course, was done with the approval and connivance of the US. Despite the talk of democracy, the US – with Canada in obsequious support – still holds to its strategic position that it is better to have an Islamist state than a secular one which might actually be committed to modern government: industrial development, social programs, public education, human rights, and the strengthening of civil society. This strategy goes back to the days of Jimmy Carter's administration, the one which created the Mujahedin on the theory that religious fanatics would be the most determined foes of the godless communists then occupying Afghanistan.

Warnock quotes Dan Everts, the former NATO special representative in Afghan, about the deliberate sabotaging of genuinely democratic government: "… the result has been an extremely chaotic parliament. There are 248 talking heads, with very little discipline and little organized deliberations that are meant to produce legislation which the country so badly needs. We deliberately did this." Combined with a constitution that put enormous powers in the hands of the president and you have a political structure designed to ensure American dominance.

The definitive piece of evidence about the real goals in Afghanistan arrived in mid-summer (2008) with the announcement that Afghanistan had signed a major deal to build the pipeline the US has wanted all along. If the reports are accurate, the $8 billion pipeline will go through the southern part of the country – and right through Kandahar. With this final piece of the puzzle in place, Canada's role becomes even more clear: a private protection force for the American pipeline.

Right now, the Canadian military are riding high, arrogant and confident that their new war-fighting role as junior partner to the US empire, and their new billions in spending money, are secure. Maybe.

But the Afghan conflict is set to bleed America, just as it bled the Soviet Union. As time passes, that might just drive the Canadian generals back into their cushy quarters and convince Canadians to demand their money back.

Harper Is Happy to Turn Canada from Peacemaker to War-maker

MURRAY DOBBIN

It is alarming for many Canadians to watch Stephen Harper, the head of a minority government with the support of fewer than 40% of citizens, turn Canada into a nation of war. But that is what is happening.

The roots of Harper's preference for war go to the core of his view of government: maintaining a strong, war-fighting armed forces is one of the few roles that Harper believes government should have. He is fighting a war against a battle-hardened and determined enemy in one of the most fiercely independent nations on Earth. The complexity of Afghan society confounds all but a few who would try to understand it. Yet, for Stephen Harper, understanding Afghanistan seems almost irrelevant. But it *is* relevant, because this is a war that Canada and the West cannot win, any more than Britain and the Soviet Union could before us. And Canada will share disproportionately in its ultimate loss in terms of dead and wounded, billions of dollars wasted, and our international reputation sullied for a long time to come. It will go down in history as one of our country's biggest foreign policy disasters.

Stephen Harper's contempt for Canada and what it became in the decades following the Second World War is firmly on the record. Most of his comments – his sneering dismissal of our egalitarianism and sense of community – relate to social programs like Medicare. He once described Canada as "a second-tier socialistic country, boasting ever more loudly about its social services to mask its second-rate status."

It was not until recently that he revealed his disdain for Canada's three decades of peacekeeping. In a CBC interview conducted as Parliament resumed sitting in September (2006), Harper showed that he relished the fact that Canadian soldiers were war-fighting, and dismissed Canada's peacekeeping history as virtual cowardice: "For a lot of the last 30 or 40 years, we were the ones hanging back." He even mused that the deaths of Canadian soldiers were a boost for the military – cathartic after years of not being able to kill or die like real soldiers. "I can tell you it's certainly engaged our military. It's, I think, made them a better military, notwithstanding – and maybe in some way because of – the casualties."

Utterly blind to how the rest of the world sees the conflict in Afghanistan, Harper told the CBC that Canada's role in Afghanistan is "... certainly raising Canada's leadership role, once again, in the United Nations and in the world community."

You have only to look at Harper's history and his government's "five priorities" to understand why he would get Canada and himself deeper into a conflict he cannot win. For five years, in the middle of his political career, Harper was with the National Citizens Coalition, an extreme right-wing organization that was founded by an insurance company millionaire explicitly to fight public Medicare. Its slogan is "More freedom through less government." It is virtually impossible for Stephen Harper to recognize Canadian leadership in any field – such as Medicare – that he believes Canada should not be involved in. For the Conservative prime minister, the Afghanistan conflict may be literally the first time that Canada has shown real leadership in decades.

Harper can finally be proud of Canada, now that we are making war. It does not even matter to him that more Canadians question the country's commitment to the increasingly distorted mission in Afghanistan (49%) than support the mission (38%). Embarrassed for years about living in a "socialist" country, Harper can now hold his head high where it counts: in Calgary and Washington, DC.

Four of Harper's five priorities following the last election reflect his "less government" imperative. Cutting taxes is critical to creating "less government" because, as long as you have robust revenue (even surpluses), citizens will expect you to deliver those things they desire. Combatting crime is one of the "core" activities of Canada for Harper and all neo-cons. While priority No. 3, cleaning up government, is a noble cause, many experts on the effective running of government say that aspects of his huge Accountability Act will serve to paralyze the federal government. His "child care" grants were transparently designed to ensure that government would not be involved in the provision of child care at all.

In the secretive and tightly controlled world of the Harper government, it isn't always easy to determine who Harper is listening to for advice. But his disdain for government and his enormous intellectual arrogance suggest that bureaucrats, including civilian military officials and the diplomatic corps, are not high on his list. These are the people who would have tried to give Harper an objective analysis of how the Afghanistan conflict was going back in February (2006) when he took over as prime minister. But, given that they were part of a military establishment that was responsible for the peace-keeping culture he detested, he was unlikely to listen to any cautionary advice.

They were part of the problem, not part of the solution.

He was much more likely to listen to those running the US (whom he has admired to the point of worship for many years) and to those Canadian generals who were also rejecting the peacekeeping culture. In fact, Harper's predecessor, Paul Martin, had already signalled a political change.

Jean Chrétien warned about military demands for money: "It's never enough ... They all need more and they all have plans for more." But Martin eagerly listened to the war generals and to Bay Street, who also supported a stronger military integrated into the US war machine. Already the seventh-highest spender in NATO at nearly $14 billion, Martin added $12.8 billion over five years. Conservatives top that by a further $5.3 billion, putting military spending much higher than at any time during the Cold War. Both Martin and Harper were bending over backwards to please George Bush.

Former US Ambassador to Canada, Paul Cellucci, in 2002, made a remarkable admission: the only order he received from the White House when he was appointed was to get Canada to dramatically increase its military spending.

It isn't just the money; it's how it will be spent. As defence analyst

Steven Staples points out: "Without billions of dollars, the military can't afford to buy the high-tech weaponry required for joint operations with the Americans, the most lethal and technologically advanced fighting force in history ... Defence spending fuels military integration [with the US]."

Harper is even more committed to the idea of fully integrated armed forces as part of the Security and Prosperity Partnership, a formal integration agreement between the three NAFTA countries that will see huge areas of government policy "harmonized," including energy, water, drug testing, security, immigration and refugees, and more.

But military integration is the key to other areas of continental integration – such as open borders – that Canadian corporations want. "Security trumps trade," Paul Cellucci said repeatedly in lobbying other political parties and Bay Street against Chrétien's refusal to increase the military budget. They won the money battle, but that's not enough. As Staples says: "Afghanistan is the proving ground for Canada-US military integration." (See article by Steven Staples in this book.)

But of course Harper will not talk about military integration, because that debate would damage an already unpopular engagement. In order to sell Canadians on our war-fighting mission in Afghanistan, the Harper government resorts to language that reduces the debate to an adolescent level. By constantly repeating phrases like "we can't cut and run" and we won't leave "until the job is done," or "we have to support our troops" or we "can't let the terrorists win," Harper hopes to frame the debate so that nothing substantive ever gets discussed. These are the kinds of arguments you find among adolescent boys fighting in schoolyards: too immature and too driven by their testosterone to actually think straight about the consequences of their actions.

It might be productive if every conversation about Afghanistan had to begin with a quotation from Benjamin Franklin: "The definition of insanity is doing the same thing over and over and expecting different results." At least it might lead those discussing the war to delve a little deeper, to examine Afghanistan's social and political structures, its history and, most importantly, the record of the West in creating the current horrors.

As is stands now, we proceed as if Afghanistan was created from nothing on Sept. 11, 2001.

But Afghanistan does have a history. Canada's involvement is part of a 30-year continuum of Western (and Soviet) interference, and it cannot be surgically excised and declared pristine in its motives. So long as we ignore this history, we will have more body bags coming home, thousands of innocent Afghans will die, and homes and whole villages will be destroyed – along with orchards, crops, and other means of survival – by our tanks, mortars, and US "air - support."

Afghanistan was not always a country totally dominated by warlords and reactionary Islamic fundamentalism. This brand of Islam was largely imported into the country as part of the US-inspired Cold War effort to defeat the Soviets. For a brief period, the country had a progressive, secular government which, according to University of Winnipeg professor John Ryan, "affirmed the separation of church and state, labour unions were legalized, health care and education became priorities, women were given equal rights, and girls were to go to school ... A program was being developed for major land reform." [http://tinyurl.com/fvqzt] (See article by Cheshmak Farhoumand-Sims in this book)

That government was put in place following a 1978 military coup that removed an autocratic and unpopular president. Noor Mohammad Taraki, a Marxist (and a university professor, writer and poet) was asked by the army to form a government simply because the Marxists were the only ones who had an actual development program. Tragically for the Afghan people, however, the US was not prepared to allow such a government to exist in the context of the Cold War. The US used the CIA (and the assistance of Saudi Arabia and Pakistan) "to provide military aid and training to the Muslim extremists, who became known as the Mujahedin and 'freedom fighters.'" Barely a year later, Taraki and his closest associates were killed in another coup. It was after this that the Soviets invaded in support of the government.

Years later, Zbigniew Brzezinski, President Jimmy Carter's National Security Advisor, boasted of implementing a plan to tie down the USSR in its own version of Vietnam and to bleed it into submission. According to Ryan: "Brzezinski saw this as a golden opportunity to fire up the zeal of the most reactionary Muslim fanatics – to have them declare a jihad (holy war) on the atheist infidels who defiled Afghan soil." What followed was the recruitment of thousands of non-Afghan Muslims (including Osama bin Laden) into a 10-year jihad, funded by hundreds of millions of US dollars that destroyed much of the country.

In 1992, three years after the end of the Soviet occupation, the government was finally defeated and Afghanistan fell into absolute chaos, inter-tribal warfare, drug smuggling, and mass rape. In 1994, according to Middle East authority Eric Margolis, "a village prayer leader, Mullah Omar, armed a group of 'talibs' (religious students), and set about defending women from rape. Aided by Pakistan, the Taliban stopped the epidemic of rape and drug dealing that had engulfed Afghanistan, and imposed order based on harsh tribal and Sharia religious law."

Oil and gas are part of every US intervention in the Middle East, and the US had no qualms about dealing with the Taliban in the 1990s. Washington began to pour millions into Taliban coffers in the hope of signing a contract with US oil giant Unocal to build a gas pipeline south from the Caspian Basin to Pakistan. The negotiations broke down in the spring of 2001 – just months before 9/11. As for those attacks, they were planned in Germany, carried out by Saudis, and were almost certainly done without the knowledge of the isolationist Taliban. When the US demanded that Osama bin Laden be handed over, the Taliban agreed to turn him over to an international tribunal upon seeing evidence of his guilt. But the US had no such evidence. Instead, they invaded.

The government of Hamid Karzai is constantly touted as having been "democratically elected," and it is fair to say that Afghans voted in the election because they hoped it might make a difference. But the Karzai government is totally dependent for its survival on the US and is heavily influenced by the US oil industry. According to *Le Monde* newspaper, Karzai was a consultant for Unocal during the failed negotiations with the Taliban. Another Unocal consultant, Zalmay Khalilzad, was initially the US envoy to Afghanistan. By May 30, 2002, he had in place a multi-billion-dollar contract for a gas pipeline. (See article by John Foster in this book.)

Afghanistan's democracy is a fraud and operates more as a grim coalition of Mujahedin, warlords, drug-lords, oil company executives, and US agents. Following 9/11, the US recruited and armed its old Mujahedin creation to help in the task of defeating the Taliban, renaming them the "Northern Alliance." Many of the elected MPs stand accused of carrying out massacres, mass rape, torture, and other war crimes. A lengthy 2005 UN report (leaked to the *Guardian* newspaper) documents these atrocities and names those responsible. According to Afghan MP Malalai Joya, an Afghan woman legislator, Karzai has also "appointed 13 former commanders with links to drug smuggling, organized crime, and illegal militias to senior positions in the police force."

This is the context for Canada's involvement in Afghanistan. When Hamid Karzai visited Canada and told the House of Commons and the Canadian people that our troops are desperately needed in his country, he didn't tell the whole story. And who would blame him? But there is no excuse for the soft-peddling of the conflict by the mainstream Canadian media, who remain complicit in the government's misleading description of the "mission" and in covering for Harper's failure to protect Canadian troops.

Even a cursory examination of the facts about our country's disastrous involvement in Afghanistan reveals that the two men most responsible for this continuing nightmare are simply not up to the task of leadership. Stephen Harper and General Rick Hillier, his "butt-kicking" military chief, have demonstrated a level of ineptitude that should have Canadians extremely worried.

This military engagement will go down in Canadian history as one of the most shameful betrayals of Canadian soldiers in our history. Canadian troops are dying because neither their supreme commander nor their prime minister has the courage to acknowledge what is actually happening. They are dying so Stephen Harper can prove himself to George W. Bush. Hillier and Harper keep asking Canadians to "support our troops." But they insist our troops pursue a strategy ensuring more of them will die, and they mislead them about their prospects.

A quick survey of what is happening in Afghanistan puts the lie to every positive statement coming out of the government. First, the notion that we will still be doing development work and nation-building, once Afghanistan is "stabilized," is a cruel hoax. With the approximately 40,000 troops (half of whom are not allowed to fight) now stationed there, this simply will never happen. When the Soviet Union was finally driven out of that country, after 10 years of brutal conflict and 15,000 dead, it had 100,000 troops there, a functioning Afghan government working in cooperation with it, and an additional 100,000 Afghan troops fighting with it.

It is no wonder, as reported by CCPA defence analyst Steven Staples [http://tinyurl.com/kk689], that Canadian soldiers are six times as likely to die in Afghanistan as American troops are in Iraq. No wonder, either, that the Senlis Council [http://tinyurl.com/pg5hw], a Brussels-based security and development policy group, assailed Canada's approach as continuing "... to unquestioningly accept America's fundamentally flawed policy approach in southern Afghanistan, thereby jeopardizing the success of military operations in the region and the stabilization, reconstruction, and development mission objectives."

As a result of this "war on terror" mind-set, General Hillier has shown no interest in counter-insurgency strategy. As continued deadly attacks reveal, the much touted "Operation Medusa" turns out to have been a complete waste of resources, and of Canadian and Afghan lives. In addition, it alienated thousands of Afghans whose "hearts and minds" must be won to give this mission any meaning at all.

Hillier's response to the shocking Canadian deaths was to send 15 Leopard tanks to bolster the troops – exactly the wrong thing to do, according to Gavin Cameron, a specialist in counter-insurgency wars at the University of Calgary's Centre for Military and Strategic Studies: "If you see tanks in your streets, it's hard not to think about it as an army of occupation."

No one in the Canadian military will criticize Hillier for such an inexcusably wrong-headed strategy. But Captain Leo Docherty, of the Scots Guards, the former aide-de-camp to the commander of the British task force in southern Afghanistan, does so indirectly. He resigned in disgust in September (2006), calling a similar campaign in southern Helmand province "a textbook case of how to screw up a counter-insurgency. All those people whose homes have been destroyed and sons killed are going to turn against the British."

According to the Senlis Council, there are between 10 and 15 refugee camps in the provinces of Helmand and Kandahar, with up to 10,000 people in each, the result of Canadian and British conventional war tactics. They are receiving "... little or no help from relief agencies."

The third factor in this endless misery has to do with reconstruction. Canada has now spent over $4 billion on its Afghan mission – 90% of which has been used in the military conflict. But even the development aid that has been spent in Afghanistan by other Western nations is often resented for the way in which it is spent – and wasted. (See article by Stephen Cornish in this book.)

According to University of Manitoba Professor John Ryan [http://tinyurl.com/fvqzt], "… a recent report for the Overseas Development Institute, by Ashraf Ghani, the chancellor of Kabul University and former Karzai finance minister, has stated that in 2002 about 90% of the $1 billion spent on 400 aid projects was wasted." Problems abound – not least the gross disparity in pay for Afghan civil servants ($50 a month) and Afghans who work for Western aid organizations($1,000 a month). The government can barely hold on to its staff. Also, says Ryan: "Where the Afghan government could build a school for about $40,000, an international aid agency undertook the task of building 500 schools, at a cost of $250,000 each." Contracts for reconstruction are handed out to donor country corporations, who take huge fees up front and then hire layer upon layer of subcontractors who make sure they make their profit – leaving substandard construction behind. Says Ryan: "The result is collapsing hospitals, clinics, and schools, rutted and dangerous new highways …"

The Afghanistan conflict is no longer just a fight against the old Taliban. The Taliban has morphed into what many now suggest is a formal jihad – a general call to arms of all Afghans to rid the country of foreigners. Last May, according to the *Toronto Star's* Chris Sands, clerics in Kabul mosques were calling on worshippers to join the Taliban's fight against the Karzai government and NATO troops. The war is now everywhere – even in Kabul.

Even worse, says *Star* reporter Mitch Potter: "Money, as much as any concept of jihad, is the driving force today behind an unholy alliance of religious radicals, drug-running militias, smuggling cartels – and, in many cases, apolitical young Afghans simply looking for work – who have enlisted in the confrontation with foreign troops."

And what is Stephen Harper's response to this reality? "[Canadians] want a Canada that …punches above its weight." It is reminiscent of George Bush's adolescent musing about Iraqi insurgents: "Bring 'em on."

Lastly, Harper chose to ignore evidence available at the time he extended the mission that the US was losing interest in Afghanistan and was totally preoccupied with Iraq. He also ignored the caveats that European members of NATO had placed on what their troops could do in Afghanistan – the same caveats that now leave the NATO commander unable to send more troops into the south. In addition, Pakistan is doing virtually nothing to end the safe haven for the Taliban. The US has now handed its messy war over to NATO. But, despite repeated, desperate pleas for more NATO troops for the south, almost none have been forthcoming.

On September 1 (2006), NDP leader Jack Layton, in calling for Canada to withdraw from its southern Afghanistan mission, stated: "We believe that a comprehensive peace process has to bring all combatants to the table." For this he was vilified in the media. Now the situation is deteriorating so quickly that even hard-liners – including Bill Frist, the hard-right US Senate Majority Leader – are calling for negotiations with the neo-Taliban resistance.

There is an alternative policy that would bring Canada credit. According to retired international affairs professor John Warnock [http://www.actupinsask.org] of Regina, Canada should "withdraw all military forces from Afghanistan and withdraw from all projects being sponsored by the US government and NATO [and then] work within the UN General Assembly to develop a new project for Afghanistan ... completely separate from any US or NATO project." Unrealistic? Not compared to the current policy of desperation and denial.

Canada in Afghanistan:
"a well-intentioned atrocity"

MICHAEL NEUMANN

For many Canadian partisans of The Mission in Afghanistan, Canada is just fighting the good fight. Their attitudes are curiously anachronistic, as if our boys have gone off to stick it to Jerry. There are yellow-ribbon support-our-troops stickers on many cars; there's hometown pride. Embedded correspondents produce little more than a stream of human-interest pieces, as if Afghanistan was some enormous Katrina aftermath. You'd probably find something similar in Norway, Finland, and other Nice Countries that have sent troops over there. Perhaps Americans would feel the same way were the whole Afghanistan question not obscured by the much more spectacular disaster of Iraq.

The opponents of The Mission sound wimpy. They say it's not a peacekeeping operation – so what? Is nothing else ever justified, under any circumstances? They point out that the mission doesn't have popular support. Again, so what? Can't something unpopular be right? They claim it helps the Americans, but the Americans, really, are beyond help, and Canadian assistance isn't about to turn US idiocy into success. They protest that civilians are being killed. True: one might add that 'collateral damage' is a rather abstract way to describe tearing off a child's face and going 'oops.' However all modern wars, because they involve air power, inevitably involve collateral damage, so only a complete pacifist could find this objection decisive. Should we not tell other countries or societies how to run their lives, ever? How about Rwanda?

On top of this, the entire opposition to the Afghan war worships at the altar of Supporting our Troops (Bring Them Home!). This is either hypocrisy or nonsense. If you support the troops, you must support them where they are, not where you might wish them to be. So someone might ask: do you or don't you wish that the troops who are in fact now in Afghanistan remain safe? If you do wish that they remain safe, you wish them to possess that huge military asset, invulnerability. You want their armor and air support and heavy weapons to protect them. This can only mean that you hope they kill any Afghan who threatens their lives. Push come to shove, you want them to win all their battles. This, as an anti-war stance, is nonsense. "Support our troops, bring them home" is not an anti-war slogan, it is mere evasion. But if you don't wish them to remain safe, then you don't really support the troops. You're a hypocrite: you can't support them if you don't hope to keep them from harm. No one I know admits to this attitude.

In other words, there is no serious opposition to the Afghan war, for much the same reason that the opposition to the Iraq war has been so feeble: the 'opponents' of The Mission agree with its promoters that the troops, its cutting edge, should be protected at any cost. Moreover the complaints about The Mission are just that – mere complaints, making bogus appeals to principles which no one holds unconditionally anyway. No one has shown that in these conditions, the principles are so terribly important that The Mission should end.

Yet the West's war in Afghanistan is an outrage – contemptible in its conception and shameful in its execution. If this isn't obvious, it's because the invaders don't seem to be violating any sacred principle or (to give them the benefit of a doubt) acting from bad motives. Instead, The Mission fairly screams that it will fail, and failure, in these circumstances, is a huge, bone-headed crime. The troops who make this crime happen can be viewed with a certain sympathy, but they should never be supported in any way.

CONTEMPTIBLE STRATEGIES

The big justification for The Mission is that we are fighting, as the in-
fantile phrase goes, the Bad Guys, the Taliban. There's something
criminally dishonest about this. Here's an inexact parallel which tries
to get at what's wrong.

Suppose the Taliban are bad like TB, not cancer – you lead an
awful life, but usually you live. Now suppose there's TB in your town.
I come to believe that TB is a scourge of your society, and fighting TB
should be your number one priority. I could eliminate TB in your
town by providing 100mg of a certain drug to each inhabitant, but I
have no intention of allocating resources on that scale. So, on the
cheap, I provide 10mg of the drug per person. This may bring some
temporary relief; it may even cure a very few exceptionally healthy
people, but of course what it won't do is eliminate TB, and those
helped are very likely to get it again, later. I use this distribution of
drugs to justify my military occupation of your town. I kill inhabitants who oppose my TB program, on the grounds that they're an obstacle to curing your society.

The contemptible wrongness of my actions is elusive. I have no
bad intentions or motives; I've violated no inviolable principles. But
there is something repugnantly shoddy about my good intentions.
It's not that I'm trying to do something bad. It's that I'm not really
trying to do something good, only pretending to do so. I pretend, first
of all, to myself. I've embarked on an enterprize that I know will have
terrible costs to others, and which will achieve nothing. This looks a
bit like the sort of gamble we just have to take from time to time. But
it isn't a gamble, because I know my strategy will fail. I choose to ignore this, and pretend my efforts are serious. In short I'm trying to
hold two obviously clashing beliefs. One is that after much struggle I
will succeed; the other is that I've invested much too little in the
'struggle' to succeed. I don't want to relinquish either of them. Academics call this cognitive dissonance.

Willful myopia helps us manage these clashing beliefs. We see our
killings of Afghan civilians as a series of mistakes, of setbacks, and so
they are. But we know these mistakes will continue to happen, and
we refuse even to estimate their eventual, total cost to the Afghan
people. Instead, we go on about our noble sacrifice. That sacrifice includes going thousands of miles to kill others, often as not people
who did us no harm. We make as though we've done their grieving,

often starving, maimed or crippled friends and relatives and neighbours a great big favour. They did not ask for this favour, and the
sacrifice we impose on them dwarfs our own. Our blood-drenched
dishonesty is nothing if not contemptible.

But how do we know we will fail?

FORESEEABLE FAILURE

You can always say: we don't know for sure that we will fail. Well, we
also don't know for sure that 10% of the recommended minimum
dose for the treatment of TB won't cure the patient, but we're sure
enough. We can be about that sure that The Mission will not cure
Afghanistan of its ills, or do much for our own. That's because no one
even proposes troop commitments anything remotely like what we
believe is necessary for success. When the US invaded Iraq, military
people told us that vastly more troops would be needed. If there was
some excuse for dismissing such advice in 2003 – and few would see
any such excuse – there is none now. Once again, military analysts
suggest troop levels orders of magnitude greater than anyone con-
templates. Afghanistan is as large as Iraq; its population is slightly
larger. Its people have more experience in irregular warfare, and its
topography is better suited to guerrilla operations. Its languages and
cultures are, to Western invaders, an even greater obstacle to intelligence gathering than the Arabic of Iraq. Its fighters have a sanctuary
in Pakistan such as the Iraqis can only envy. And no one is going to
push Pakistan around too much, because it has nuclear weapons and
the means to deliver them.

Respectable military thinking holds that, even with allies, The
Mission might take half a million men. A Rand Corporation study in
2003 stated you need 20 soldiers per 1000 inhabitants for that sort
of thing. Based on RAND's population figure for Afghanistan of
27,755,775, this, yields a force of about 500,000.[1] Defense expert
Craig T. Cobane does not dispute the calculation, but adds: "That
number was totally unfeasible and impractical."[2] In 2001, mainstream publications like the Christian Science Monitor and the New
York Times echoed the 500,000 figure. Nothing and no one has discredited this estimate; it's studiously ignored. Current 'coalition'
forces number 30,000 to 50,000.

If no one likes to mention the 500,000 figure any more, it's probably because we also realize that nothing remotely like that number will be provided. The US speaks of increasing its commitment by 3,200 men, not 320,000. (This article was written in 2007) Other countries are at least as cautious; it's not even clear how long they're willing to maintain their current contributions. So no one expects the West to remake Afghanistan on its own. Afghanistan is, in this respect, like the town with TB.

Precisely because Western military planners agree they don't have enough troops, it has always been assumed that, as Musharraf says, we will use the locals as canon fodder, and this is what has been done ever since the Americans invaded in 2001. This of course means that Western powers must cooperate with the local powers that be. And this in turn means that even military 'success' will bring failure of The Mission.

What could possibly count as success? Not simply defeating the Taliban, but creating conditions which ensure that Afghanistan won't host some similar group once the West packs up and leaves. Usually this objective is dressed up as rebuilding the country, eliminating the drug trade, creating a democratic society, and – especially popular in North America – stopping the oppression of women. Perhaps none of this is meant seriously, and the real reason NATO is in Afghanistan is to please the Americans: perhaps European and Canadian governments have terrified themselves by defying America over Iraq. But whatever the objectives, none can be attained. The reason is well known but rarely said out loud: attaining any of them requires real control of the whole country, not the illusion of control maintained with the assistance of various warlords.

The notion that some national army will supplant the warlords is a non-starter, because these same warlords are an essential element in the national government. Nothing they don't want – not least the extinction of their own power – can happen in such circumstances. However much Western troops and their fawning journalists may vaunt the military prowess of Our Side, we are weak, and we cooperate from weakness.

One spectacular sign of this cooperation from weakness is the opium renaissance that has flowered under Western occupation. But the costs of cooperation go far beyond this. Because Western troops are colossally ignorant of the country, they have on several occasions fought innocent people, because anyone can bring destruction to his enemies by labelling them 'Taliban.' More important, military weakness on the ground means reliance on air power, inevitably applied with the wishful thinking that passes for tactical intelligence: a desire to hit the enemy becomes a belief that the enemy has been located, even when those located are civilians. Quite often, civilians are knowingly killed to get at enemy hiding amongst them.

These idiotic practices show no sign of going away. They are accompanied by a failure to provide basic security in the country, and the much more important failure to provide long-term security. Everyone, including the Western powers, knows that sooner or later they will leave, and the same factions that ran the country piecemeal before will run it again. (In most areas, they run things right now.) So the idea of winning hearts and minds is ridiculous. This might not matter in a truly massive military occupation, but it certainly matters in occupation on the cheap. And Western powers will never opt for a massive military occupation because, even then, the prospects of long-term success are uncertain, and the expense colossal. Moreover a full-scale occupation would not only erase any pretense of an independent Afghan government, but involve massive bloodshed. All this might be politically acceptable to secure something really vital, like the Arabian peninsula, but not a backwater like Afghanistan.

What of fighting terror? There can be no long-term gains here either. The Taliban alliance with al Qaeda cannot very well be broken in Afghanistan when it has moved to Pakistan, and even if it could, such alliances would simply reproduce themselves with warlords who remain when the Western troops leave. That's not all. No one even claims that the retention of bases in the region is essential to the operation of anti-Western terrorists, so one wonders on what basis this military occupation can present itself as an important anti-terrorist operation. It seems more likely that the ever popular 'surgical' operations against known individual terrorists are what's needed, and that the invasion is simply an excuse for the inability to mount enough such operations to make any difference. So even if we accept that terror can be fought with military force, the problem seems to be bad intelligence, and that's not solved by troops stomping all over the landscape in a country that for centuries has excelled at confounding occupying armies.

We have seen all this in Iraq. It's all old news. We know that Rumsfeld's bluster about high-tech war on the cheap, with few troops, was a fantasy, and that the conventional, sky-high estimates of what's required reflect reality. We know, whatever we say, that The Mission will fail. It may be a good cause, but that doesn't matter. It doesn't matter because its objectives are out of reach.

We hear a lot about commitment. Canadian Prime Minister Steve Harper, like Blair before him and like Bush, tells us that we've made a commitment to the Afghan people, and we must not leave them in the lurch. It's common to hear this from soldiers, too. This is, at best, self-deception. Suppose I promise to rebuild your bridge and allocate, from the very beginning, one tenth of the manpower and materials necessary to rebuild it. Then I have either made no commitment in the first place – just spoken some words without substance – or I made one without ever intending to keep it. Take your pick. Under either interpretation, this is sleaze masquerading as virtue. If after over five years the West can do no better than this – "Afghan children chew on mud they scratch from the walls of their homes to stave off hunger." – the idea that we will achieve something in Afghanistan is a dream. We know it, and we need to wake up from it.

RESPONSIBILITY

The criminality of The Mission extends beyond our own actions. The West has inserted itself as the dominant military power in Afghanistan. It holds the capital, the airports, and the main transportation routes. It props up a puppet government. It asserts its power everywhere. This makes the West the effective sovereign in the country, which in turn makes the West responsible for every single thing that goes on there. Except for the sort of everyday crime that no society can eliminate, this includes what would have gone on even if the West had not invaded: a ruler is responsible for the security and welfare of those ruled. Instead of fulfilling this responsibility, the West brought all the agony of war, and virtually none of the benefits of civil society, to a country that posed no substantial threat. The invaders did this knowing it was all for nothing, just as the TB criminals knew that.

The Mission, then, is a well-intentioned atrocity, so obviously futile that it shames all who join or support it in any way. They say that ignorance of the law is no excuse: the wilful disregard involved in the creation of a disaster is no excuse either. No rhetoric and no UN or international seal of good housekeeping can ever change this.

Our responsibilities therefore involve opposing The Mission and everything that contributes to its success. This requires real opposition, not support-our-troops cowardice, not human interest reporting, not entertaining 'our brave fighting men and women over there.' If the war is a crime, then Steve Harper and the other Western leaders can't be the only criminals. The mature, competent adults who volunteer for the armed forces and fight in Afghanistan, who actually wreak the death and destruction, have to be criminals as well. This doesn't preclude having sympathy for them. Some of my friends have gone wrong and committed serious crimes, in one case a murder. I still care about them and wish they hadn't made bad choices. But they did, and I didn't try to make them feel good about it.

NOTES

1 "Burden of Victory: The Painful Arithmetic of Stability Operations," By James T. Quinlivan, http://www.rand.org/publications/
2 "A 2003 RAND report noted there were twenty peacekeepers per thousand people in Kosovo. To reach a comparable number in Afghanistan would require 500,000 peacekeepers. That number was totally unfeasible and impractical." Cobane's article appeared in Defense Institute of Security Assistance Management Journal, 6/22/2005, available at http://www.encyclopedia.com/doc/1G1-142421588.html.

Afghanistan and Canada

History and Background

What is Canada Promoting in Afghanistan? A Brief History of its Role

JOHN W. WARNOCK

From the initial attack on the World Trade Center and the Pentagon, the governments of Canada have given unqualified support to the US war on terrorism. In the military area this has meant pledging Canadian Forces to the war in Afghanistan and supporting the US naval forces in the Persian Gulf and the Arabian Sea. In the construction of the new government in Afghanistan, Canada has played an important support role for the US government. But as the US/ NATO counter insurgency war continues to escalate, and the government headed by President Hamid Karzai and the elected legislature continue to lose credibility and support, it is time for a change in policy. The people of Afghanistan want an end to the war, and they want economic and social development, and the democratization of its new political institutions.

REGIME CHANGE

The US assault on Afghanistan began on October 7, 2001. The war was short, given the overwhelming military superiority of the US military and the massive bombing campaign. On November 12 the

Taliban fled Kabul, and the US allies, the Islamist Northern Alliance, assumed the role of defacto government. In early December Kandahar fell and the war was over.

The war having been won, and a new regime installed in Kabul, the US government then called for support from the United Nations. On December 20, 2001 the UN Security Council agreed to sanction the creation of an International Security Assistance Force (ISAF) under Chapter 7 of the UN Charter, an enforcement mandate. The ISAF, completely outside the United Nations, is part of the "coalition of the willing" created by the US government. This "stabilization mission" was to support the UN humanitarian assistance program. Canada was to be part of the ISAF, under British command. This peacekeeping mission changed in July 2006 when Canadian forces in ISAF were shifted to Kandahar to engage in a counter insurgency war in support of US political and military objectives.

Over this period the governments of Jean Chretien, Paul Martin and Stephen Harper all gave unqualified support to the position of the administration of George W. Bush on Afghanistan. In April 2008 a resolution passed the Parliament authorizing Stephen Harper's government to extend Canada's role in the counter insurgency war through 2011. The resolution by the Conservative government received the support of the Liberal opposition headed by Stephane Dion.

PERSISTENCE OF THE TALIBAN

The Afghan people at first welcomed the formation of the Taliban in 1994 and their military campaign to seize power. Between 1992 and 1996 Afghans had experienced the military regime of the Islamist Mujahedin parties, the primary allies of the US government in the proxy war with the Russians. This government, headed by Burhanuddin Rabbani, was an oppressive regime, and civil war and human rights abuses were the order of the day.

Where the Taliban took control, they successfully restored law and order. But soon after seizing power in Kabul it became clear that they were if anything worse than the Mujahedin armies. While the Afghan people expressed opposition to the US bombing campaign, they were pleased to see the Taliban removed from power. Public opinion polls taken in Afghanistan over the last several years all indicate that at least 70% of the population do not want to see the Taliban return to government.

Yet in spite of this widespread public disapproval, and because of the counter insurgency war waged by around 65,000 US/NATO troops and close to 40,000 members of the Afghan National Army, over the past two years the Taliban and their allies have grown in strength and the conflict has spread to all parts of the country, including Kabul. The number of conflicts has doubled in the past year. Why is this happening?

The main problem is the unpopularity of the government of President Hamid Karzai and the national parliament. President Karzai has no base of support in the country; he is seen by all as the puppet of the US government. His government is notoriously corrupt and characterized by nepotism and favouritism. The central focus of the economy is still the production of poppies for opium and heroin, and drug lords have great power and influence locally, in the Karzai government and the legislature.

In February 2008 the US Director of National Intelligence reported to Congress that regional warlords control around 60% of the country. It is widely known that 65% of the members of the national legislature are commanders and warlords. They are stronger than they were in 2001 because of their official status in the Afghan government and the income they receive from the drug economy and the funds they obtain from the economic assistance provided by external donors.[1]

The Afghan government has also failed to deliver on its promised improvements in the life of ordinary citizens. Some parts of the economy are growing, mostly those sectors linked to the large foreign presence in the country. But the vast majority have poor housing and are having a very difficult time finding adequate food. At least 40% of the labour force is unemployed. The average annual income is only around $350. Health care is unavailable to most. Electricity has yet to be restored. Heating in winter is a serious problem. The educational system is lagging, especially for women.

The only legal opposition to President Karzai is the United National Front, based primarily in the national legislature. But this political coalition is completely dominated by the Islamist parties of the right and their warlords. If anything, it has less public legitimacy than the President. The public widely sees their leadership as dominated by war criminals. It is reported that Yunus Qanooni of the

Northern Alliance, and the Speaker in the House of the People, will be their candidate for the presidency in 2009.

THE US GOVERNMENT CREATES A NEW REGIME

In spite of widespread public opposition, the Taliban and their allies have been able to mount a fairly successful war of insurgency. This has been possible because of the very weak public support for the Karzai government. Everyone in Afghanistan knows that President Karzai has long been the puppet of the US government. Furthermore, under the direction of President Karzai and the US government, the democratic forces in the country have been systematically excluded from the new political regime. The Canadian government has played a direct role in support of US policy throughout this process.

The formation of a post-Taliban government began on November 27, 2001 when the US government brought some representatives from Afghanistan together at Bonn, Germany to create an interim government. The Bush administration chose groups aligned to the Northern Alliance, the militant Islamists who have been their close political allies since 1979, and other conservative groups in exile. Five broad groups representing the democratic forces in Afghanistan asked to participate, but they were refused official status and voting rights. These were the Republican Party of Afghanistan, the Afghanistan Freedom and Democracy Movement, the People's Party, the Council of Afghanistan's Tribes, and the Alliance of Peace and Progress Fighters of Afghanistan. This set the tone for everything that followed.[2]

Nevertheless, even this narrow group of right-wing Afghans wanted a constitutional monarchy, a legislature chosen by proportional representation, and a federal state. In the first round of voting for the interim chairman the majority of the representatives at Bonn voted for Abdul Satar Sirat, representing the Rome group which wanted a constitutional monarchy under former King Zahir Shah. Other votes went to Burhanuddin Rabbani, the former Afghan president (1992–96) who represented the Northern Alliance. Hamid Karzai, the US-backed candidate, received no votes! After threats and pressure from US government and UN officials, on December 5 the delegates reluctantly agreed to accept Karzai as chairman of the Interim Administration. He then selected 30 people to constitute the new transitional administration, the large majority being leaders of the Islamist Northern Alliance.

Following the terms of the Bonn Agreement, an interim Emergency Loya Jirga (ELJ), or grand council, was held in June 2002. This strategy had been proposed by Zalmay Khalilzad, President Bush's Special Envoy. The ELJ was to choose an Interim President and a cabinet which would govern Afghanistan until elections were held.

A total of 1500 delegates were chosen from across Afghanistan. While the local warlords, commanders and the regional leaders of dominant ethnic groups had a great deal of influence on who was chosen a delegate, it was a broad cross section of Afghan society. However, the new democratic parties and organizations were again excluded from this gathering.

The delegates protested that many warlords who were not delegates were allowed to enter the tent and pressure delegates. They were also intimidated by the presence of agents from the feared Afghan Intelligence Service. Many warlords were there as delegates, even though they were to be specifically excluded by the rules of procedures governing the ELJ.[3]

The legitimate delegates wanted to reduce the power of the regional warlords and create a representative government. As part of this goal, 900 signed a petition requesting a constitutional monarchy with former King Zahir Shah as head of state. The US government blocked this proposal. For two days they pressured the king, and in the end he agreed not to serve as constitutional monarch and to instead back Hamid Karzai for Interim President. The US and UN officials at the meeting convinced the delegates that if they did not follow the path chosen by the US government there would be no money for reconstruction. Karzai was then reluctantly approved by the delegates as the Interim President. The delegates were well aware of the fact that they were there to rubber stamp US plans. Members of the Northern Alliance dominated the interim administration appointed by Karzai. The process, and the selection of Karzai as Interim President, was praised by Jean Chretien's government.

CREATING A NEW CONSTITUTION

The people of Afghanistan have a strong commitment to the 1964 Constitution, which they hoped would be re-instated after the Taliban were removed from power. It was actually adopted as the operating constitution during the interim period. But the US government had a different plan for the constitution and the structure of government. In addition, the Islamist forces in the Northern Alliance opposed the 1964 Constitution with its separation of church and state.

The 1964 Constitution had been developed through an open, participatory democratic process. There was a national Constitutional Loya Jirga, with locally elected delegates, wide discussion and participation by the public, and decisions were made by democratic consensus. It established a constitutional monarchy, with a two-house legislature, political parties, elections by proportional representation, and an independent judiciary. It declared Afghanistan to be a secular state where laws passed by parliament would have priority over Shariah law. The constitution entrenched historic individual and human rights.[4]

The new process, dictated by the US government and strongly supported by the Canadian government, was in direct contrast. Interim President Karzai and his US, Canadian and UN advisers drafted a new constitution through a very secret closed door process. The general public did not even get a chance to see the draft constitution before it was presented to the Constitutional Loya Jirga (CLJ) on December 14, 2003.

Again, the delegates to the CLJ were unrepresentative of Afghan society and opinion. Of the 500 delegates, 344 were selected at district meetings. Human Rights Watch reported that the selection process was characterized by "vote buying, death threats and naked power politics." Their analysis found that the majority of the delegates to the CLJ were from "voting blocs controlled by military faction leaders."[5]

But even this highly select group opposed the basic structure of the proposed constitution, a highly centralized government with enormous power entrusted to the president. For example, the president has the power to appoint and remove all governors of provinces and mayors of cities. Furthermore, there was strong opposition to the central principle of this new constitution: the creation of Afghanistan as an Islamic state. Article 149 declares that "The provisions of adherence to the provisions of the sacred religion of Islam and the republican regime cannot be amended."

When 48% of the delegates walked out in protest and refused to vote on the draft, they were threatened by Karzai who declared that if they did not approve his constitution he would not run for president. US and UN officials, and "security" personnel from the Northern Alliance, pressured the delegates. No vote was taken yet Karzai declared that the new constitution had been adopted "unanimously." Representatives from the Canadian government played key roles in helping the US government to create this new constitution. The process was praised by Prime Minister Paul Martin and other government officials.

DEMONSTRATION ELECTIONS

Afghanistan was hardly ready for elections after twenty years of constant warfare and a shattered government. Yet President Bush wanted an election to be held prior to the US presidential election in November 2004. The US government ruled out a general election at this time, and a presidential election was held on October 9, 2004. This was in spite of the fact that there was no national government and no functioning provincial or local governments. No political parties were allowed to participate. The laws governing the elections were decrees issued by Interim President Karzai.

The process of registering voters was deeply flawed. But the turnout was quite high at 75% of registered voters. Karzai received 55% of the vote. Dr. Masooda Jalal, the only woman candidate for the office, did not vote, insisting that the election was "massively rigged." But many people voted for Karzai because they feared one of the warlords would win. At least Karzai was not a war criminal. Public opinion surveys found that a large majority of the public wanted the warlords and commanders disarmed and banned from holding office. But this was not to be, and many were again appointed to high posts in government by Karzai. Canadian government officials were deeply involved in this fraudulent "demonstration election." The results of the election, and the "democratic process" was widely praised by the Canadian government.[6]

The election for the parliament, held on September 18, 2005, was if anything worse. Again, no political parties were allowed to participate, which greatly strengthened the regional Islamist forces. Twenty democratic parties were in existence, but they had not been allowed to register. Since they supported a secular Afghanistan, allowing them to participate would be contrary to the constitution, for they were deemed to be promoting an "anti-Islamic" agenda.[7]

President Karzai, working with officials of the US government, mandated the use of the Single Non-Transferable Vote (SNTV) system and banned the use of party lists. This system was supported by the Canadian government, and Elections Canada was directly involved. The goal was to prevent the development of new political parties on the democratic left. President Karzai refused the request by thirty-four political parties for a system of proportional representation. This SNTV system greatly aided the power of regional ethnic war-lords and commanders.

The Joint Electoral Management Body, appointed by President Karzai, included four international members, including one Cana-dian. The electoral regulations prohibited candidates who had ties to armed groups, criminal groups or drug lords. But no action was taken to keep them off the ballot, and they ended up firmly in control of the legislature. Many other allegedly disqualified candidates were appointed by President Karzai to the House of Elders, the upper house.

Of the 249 elected positions to the House of the People (the lower house), over one half were filled by men who had fought in the Mu-jahedin war, and one half were clearly identified as militant Islamists. A number of well-known drug lords were also elected. The large ma-jority of those elected had close ties to regional armed groups. Most of the candidates for office ran as individuals, but around 12% regis-tered under the name of an official party. Voter turnout was very low, estimated at 40% overall and 30% in Kabul.

Thomas Ruttig, a world-renowned expert on the structure of po-litical parties in Afghanistan, stresses that the basic political split in the country is between the new democratic formations, the old left and most of the ethno-nationalists and the Islamist parties on the right. It is between those who want a democratic, secular govern-ment and the conservative forces which want an Islamic republic where Shariah law is the rule. Daan Everts, the special representative from NATO in Afghanistan, declared in December 2007 that the de-cision to ban political parties from the electoral process had resulted in "an extremely chaotic parliament" which had accomplished little. "We deliberately did this," he confessed.[8]

The process of forming a new regime in Afghanistan, and the holding of the demonstration elections, was widely praised by the Canadian government. Canadian government officials directly par-ticipated in this process in support of the policies of the Bush ad-ministration. However, the whole process was fundamentally antidemocratic. It was an exercise of neo-colonial power. The result is a government which has very little legitimacy among the Afghan people. As such it greatly aids the insurgent forces.

GROWING OPPOSITION TO THE US PUPPET REGIME

The report of the UN Secretary General on September 26, 2007 noted the expansion of the war and the very weak support for the Karzai government. Corruption is widespread and there is no confidence whatsoever in the legal system. The Afghan National Army and the Afghan National Police have limited public support. The program for humanitarian assistance has largely been a failure as between 40% and 50% of all external aid disappears inside the present system of government. Since then there have been quite a few similar reports from US and British officials. .

In April 2008 Jan Alekozai from Radio Free Afghanistan spent a month touring eastern Afghanistan assessing the concerns of the local people. The message was the same everywhere: end corruption in the government, terminate warlordism and the private militias, improve the poor status of women in society, and find a political leader willing to promote "real democracy." After this tour Alekozai concluded that in the 2009 presidential election Karzai would only get between 20% to 25% of the vote.[9]

In June 2008, just prior to the Paris meeting of countries who have pledged economic and humanitarian assistance to Afghanistan, Human Rights Watch issued a special appeal to the delegates. They cited the persistence of insecurity, poverty, and the low status of women. They emphasized the widespread human rights abuses and persistent impunity. Not only was the Taliban guilty, so were the warlords, the drug lords and the political allies of the Afghan government. They denounced the passage of the 2007 Amnesty Law for human rights abuses, which, they argued, "could make impunity the law of the land." They noted that the vast majority of Afghans want the war criminals and human rights abusers brought to justice.[10]

In 2005 the Afghan Independent Human Rights Commission (AIHRC) carried out an extensive survey of public opinion on the issue of impunity and human rights violations. They interviewed 4151 people and carried out 200 focus group discussions with 2000 participants over 32 of Afghanistan's 34 provinces. A total of 69%

reported that they or members of their family had suffered human rights abuses under the Communist regime (1978–92), the Mujahedin regime (1992–96) and/or the Taliban regime (1996–2001). These abuses included murder, disappearance, sexual rape, detention and torture, beatings, displacements, confiscation of property, demolition of homes and/or crops, deprivation of the right to work, and restrictions on women.[11]

Furthermore, the AIHRC concluded that "There was no sense among participants that the period since the Bonn Agreement had brought a reprieve in the violations, and numerous participants indicated that they had been subject to recent violations." Participants pointed out that many of the faction leaders of the Mujahedin parties, who were responsible for human rights abuses, were now in the Karzai administration and the parliament. The vast majority want the war criminals and human rights abusers to be brought to justice. They were extremely critical of the US and UN (and Canadian) officials for allowing known criminals to run for political office. But this wide appeal has received no support from the US or Canadian governments.

WHAT CAN BE DONE?

It would seem that there is no alternative to a continuation of the deteriorating status quo. If Barack Obama wins the US presidential election in November 2008, there might be some changes. (Note that this article was written in spring 2008) The Democrats have established Afghanistan as the "good war" and have promised to shift US armed forces from Iraq to Afghanistan. Obama has pledged to increase the US forces by at least two brigades (10,000). If the Democrats win the election and pursue a policy shift it could provide the opening for Canada to withdraw its armed forces.

Yet it is doubtful whether the Canadian government would take this option. At all times the governments of Jean Chretien, Paul Martin and Stephen Harper have given unqualified support to US policy. Our leaders have been fulfilling the role of the "safely predictable ally" in support of the Anglo-American alliance to dominate the world.

However a large percentage of the Canadian public does not agree. It is time for this group of Canadians to stand up and be counted, to pressure the political parties and the Canadian government to break with US policy in Afghanistan. It is time to actively support the people of Afghanistan who want an end to the war and a chance to improve their lives.

An opportunity appeared beginning in 2007 when the Shanghai Co-operation Organization put Afghanistan high on their agenda and called for regional negotiations to settle the conflict and promote reconstruction. The SCO members are China, Russia, Kazakhstan, Kyrgyzstan, Uzbekistan and Tajikistan.[12]

At the April 2008 meeting of NATO at Bucharest the SCO position was advanced by President Islam Karimov of Uzbekistan. He proposed the reconstitution of the Six Plus Two negotiations (held between 1998 and 2001), hosted by the United Nations, which included the six countries on the border of Afghanistan plus the United States and Russia. To this group would be added NATO. This new group would design a general regional plan for establishing peace and democracy in Afghanistan. The United Nations would then replace NATO as the lead organization to direct peace and redevelopment.

Unfortunately, this proposal was rejected out of hand by the US government, which has broader geopolitical interests in the region. Zamir Kabulov, the Russian ambassador to Afghanistan, commented that "The longer NATO stays in Afghanistan, the worse for them."[13] The Harper government stood by the Bush Administration. None of Canada's opposition parties seemed to be aware of this peace proposal. It is fairly certain that it would have the broad support of the majority of Canadians, and it would be welcomed by the Afghan people.

NEGOTIATING WITH THE TALIBAN

It is well known that negotiations are under way with the Taliban. President Karzai's government formally announced this process in September 2007. They have insisted that the insurgents must end the armed operations and accept the basic principles of the present Afghan constitution. In mid-October 2007 the Taliban and their allies responded. They demanded the removal of all foreign armed forces, the release of their supporters being held in prison, and recognition of Taliban control over ten southern provinces, Pashtun provinces where they have their strongest support. These negotiations have reached an impasse.[14]

In contrast, the United National Front (UNF), based in the parliamentary opposition to Karzai, has launched their own negotiations with the Taliban. These negotiations have a better chance to succeed, for both parties are agreed that Afghanistan must be an Islamic state and could end in an agreement to share government power. Changes can be made to the constitution. Yunus Qanooni, who is expected to be the candidate for the UNF in the 2009 presidential elections, has stated that "There is no place for secularism in Afghanistan." NATO and the Canadian government were shocked when the leaders of the Kandahari tribes, supposedly their allies, drew up a manifesto in April 2008 which referred to NATO as "the occupying forces."[15]

Canadian politicians and military leaders are always presenting a polyanna view of the counter insurgency war in Afghanistan. In contrast, many military leaders in the United States and Great Britain present a very different view, describing the expansion of the resistance and the weakness of the Karzai government. In Europe governments are skeptical of the NATO exercise and across all countries public opinion is opposed to active participation in the Afghan counter insurgency war. Outside the Canadian elite, including the mass media, there is a widespread understanding that there has to be a negotiated peace. The SCO proposal for a regional settlement presents the best hope.

Any settlement must have the democratic approval of the Afghan people. It is highly unlikely that they would approve any peace settlement that included the Taliban as members of some sort of coalition government and which included their view of an Islamist state.

Militant Islamist opposition would most likely continue, especially if the Afghan people were to choose to return to the 1964 constitution. However, a counter insurgency war can be won. As the militarists emphasize, this rests on "security, government and development." It is clear that these are not working in Afghanistan and that is why the war is not being won even though the large majority of the population is hostile to the Taliban and their allies.

The Dutch tried the "ink spot approach" in the province of Uruzgan. They confined their peacekeeping to the capital. They did not send forces out into the rural areas to try to seek out and confront the Taliban. They did not use air strikes or artillery, having concluded that civilians are inevitably killed and public support drops. They did not destroy property nor the poppy economy. When attacked by the Taliban, when out of the capital, they pulled back their forces.

This counter insurgency strategy did not work. Of course, it was opposed by the US and NATO military leadership. But it failed because there is little public support in this province for the Karzai government and little economic development is happening which aids the majority. The local people cannot even elect their own governor. But under different circumstances, such a strategy could work.

Under any general peace settlement, administered by a regional coalition and the United Nations, the people of Afghanistan must be given the right to choose their own form of government, their own constitution, open the political process to the new democratic parties, and implement the right to democratically choose their own economic development strategy. The United Nations and the regional countries must make this a reality. Otherwise, armed resistance will continue and Afghanistan will remain one of the poorest countries in the world.

Since 2001 our Canadian governments have given complete support to the US government in Afghanistan. This policy has failed and is doomed to fail in the long run. The challenge for Canada is to take a different position, one which puts the interests of the Afghan people first. The majority of Canadians would surely support an alternative policy on Afghanistan, one which involves shifting from a counter insurgency war that will never be won to promoting a peaceful solution which involves the participation of the United Nations and the democratic forces in that country. In public opinion polls in Canada over recent years a consistent 70% have indicated that they want Canada to return to a role of peacekeeper. Higher majorities want Canada to emphasize humanitarian and economic assistance. The challenge we face is how to convince our elected governments and political parties to join with this majority opinion.

NOTES

1 Deborah Tate, "U.S. Official Says Afghan Government Controls only 30 Percent of Country." *Voice of America News*, February 27, 2008 http://voanews.com; "Afghanistan: Warlordism 'Is Winning' Versus Democracy." *Eurasianet*, April 14, 2008. www.eurasianet.org; Seema Paatel and Steven Ross, *Breaking Point: Measuring Progress in Afghanistan*. Washington, DC: Center for Strategic and International Studies, March 2007. www.csis.org.

2 For a good overview of the process of the US government establishing a new government in Afghanistan see Sonali Kolhatkar and James Engalls, *Bleeding Afghanistan: Washington, Warlords and the Propaganda of Silence*. Toronto: Seven Stories Press, 2006.

3 "Afghanistan: Loya Jirga Off to Shaky Start: Delegates Coerced, Threatened, Spied on." Human Rights Watch, June 13, 2002. http://hrw.org.

4 For a good description of the process for developing the 1964 Constitution, see Louis Dupree, *Afghanistan*. Oxford: Oxford University Press, 1973.

5 John Sifton, "Afghanistan's Warlords Still Call the Shots," *The Asian Wall Street Journal*, December 24, 2003. Sifton is a specialist on Afghanistan with Human Rights Watch. http://hrw.org.

6 Andrew Reynolds and Andrew Wilder. *Free, Fair or Flawed: Challenges for Legitimate Elections in Afghanistan*. Briefing Paper Series, Afghanistan Research and Evaluation Unit, September 2004. www.areu.org.af

7 For a more detailed discussion of the electoral process and Afghan political parties see International Crisis Group, *Afghanistan's Flawed Constitutional Process* , June 12, 2003 and *Political Parties in Afghanistan*, June 2, 2005; Andrew Wilder, *A House Divided? Analysing the 2005 Afghan Elections,* Afghan Research and Evaluation Unit, December 2005; and Thomas Ruttig, *Islamists, Leftists – and a Void in the Center: Afghanistan's Political Parties and Where They Come From*. Konrad Adenauer Foundation, November 27, 2006. These papers are available on line.

8 Interview with Daan Everts. "Afghanistan Needs Muslim Aid Effort." *Al Jazeera English*, December 31, 2007. http://english.aljazeera.net

9 Radio Free Afghanistan interview with Jan Alekozai, *Eurasianet*, April 14, 2008. www.eurasianet.org

10 Human Rights Watch, *Open Letter from Human Rights Watch to the International Afghanistan Support Conference on June 12, 2008*. June 10, 2008. http://hrw.org

11 Afghan Independent Human Rights Commission, *A Call for Justice*. Kabul: AIHRD, 2005. www.aihrc.org.af.

12 While these developments in Central Asia have been completely ignored by the mass media in Canada they are reported in detail at *Asia Times Online*.

13 Igor Torbakov, "Russia and NATO: A Meeting of the Minds on Afghanistan?" *Eurasianet*, April 2, 2008. www.eurasianet.org

14 Barnett R. Rubin, "Afghanistan: Negotiations with the Taliban?" Informed Comment – Global Affairs, October 16, 2007. http://icga.blogspot.com

15 Anand Gopal, "Afghan Opposition Courts Taliban." *Christian Science Monitor*, April 3, 2008. www.csmonitor.com

Afghanistan: Mirage of the Good War

TARIQ ALI

Rarely has there been such an enthusiastic display of international unity as that which greeted the invasion of Afghanistan in 2001. Support for the war was universal in the chanceries of the West, even before its aims and parameters had been declared. NATO governments rushed to assert themselves 'all for one.' Blair jetted round the world, proselytizing the 'doctrine of the international community' and the opportunities for peacekeeping and nation-building in the Hindu Kush. Putin welcomed the extension of American bases along Russia's southern borders. Every mainstream Western party endorsed the war; every media network – with BBC World and CNN in the lead – became its megaphone. For the German Greens, as for Laura Bush and Cherie Blair, it was a war for the liberation of the women of Afghanistan.[1] For the White House, a fight for civilization. For Iran, the impending defeat of the Wahhabi enemy.

Three years later, as the chaos in Iraq deepened, Afghanistan became the 'good war' by comparison. It had been legitimized by the UN – even if the resolution was not passed until after the bombs had finished falling – and backed by NATO. If tactical differences had sharpened over Iraq, they could be resolved in Afghanistan. First Zapatero, then Prodi, then Rudd, compensated for pulling troops out of Iraq by dispatching them to Kabul.[2] France and Germany could extol their peacekeeping or civilizing roles there. As suicide bombings increased in Baghdad, Afghanistan was now – for American Democrats keen to prove their 'security' credentials – the 'real front' of the war on terror, supported by every US presidential candidate in the run-up to the 2008 elections, with Senator Obama pressuring the White House to violate Pakistani sovereignty whenever necessary. With varying degrees of firmness, the occupation of Afghanistan was also supported by China, Iran and Russia; though in the case of the latter, there was always a strong element of *Schadenfreude*. Soviet veterans of the Afghan war were amazed to see their mistakes now being repeated by the United States in a war even more inhumane than its predecessor.

Meanwhile, the number of Afghan civilians killed has exceeded many tens of times over the 2,746 who died in Manhattan. Unemployment is around 60 per cent and maternal, infant and child mortality levels are now among the highest in the world. Opium harvests have soared, and the 'Neo-Taliban' is growing stronger year by year. By common consent, Karzai's government does not even control its own capital, let alone provide an example of 'good governance.' Reconstruction funds vanish into cronies' pockets or go to pay short-contract Western consultants. Police are predators rather than protectors. The social crisis is deepening. Increasingly, Western commentators have evoked the spectre of failure – usually in order to spur *encore un effort*. A *Guardian* leader summarizes: 'Defeat looks possible, with all the terrible consequences that will bring.'[3]

Two principal arguments, often overlapping, are put forward as to 'what went wrong' in Afghanistan. For liberal imperialists, the answer can be summarized in two words: 'not enough.' The invasion organized by Bush, Cheney and Rumsfeld was done on the cheap. The 'light footprint' demanded by the Pentagon meant that there were too few troops on the ground in 2001–02. Financial commitment to 'state-building' was insufficient. Though it may now be too late, the answer is to pour in more troops, more money – 'multiple billions' over 'multiple years', according to the US Ambassador in Kabul.[4] The second answer advanced by Karzai and the White House, but propagated by the Western media generally – can be summed up in one word: Pakistan. Neither of these arguments holds water.

POLITICAL FAILURES

True, there was a sense of relief in Kabul when the Taliban's Wah-
habite Emirate was overthrown. Though rape and heroin production had been curtailed under their rule, warlords kept at bay and
order largely restored in a country that had been racked by foreign
and civil wars since 1979, the end result had been a ruthless social
dictatorship with a level of control over the everyday lives of ordinary people that made the clerical regime in Iran appear an island of
enlightenment. The Taliban government fell without a serious struggle. Islamabad, officially committed to the US cause, forbade any
frontal confrontation.5 Some Taliban zealots crossed the border into
Pakistan, while a more independent faction loyal to Mullah Omar
decamped to the mountains to fight another day. Kabul was unde-
fended; the BBC war correspondent entered the capital before the
Northern Alliance. What many Afghans now expected from a successor government was a similar level of order, minus the repression
and social restrictions, and a freeing of the country's spirit. What
they were instead presented with was a melancholy spectacle that
blasted all their hopes.

The problem was not lack of funds but the Western state-building
project itself, by its nature an exogenous process – aiming to construct an army able to suppress its own population but incapable of
defending the nation from outside powers; a civil administration
with no control over planning or social infrastructure, which are left
in the hands of Western NGOs; and a government whose foreign policy marches in step with Washington's. It bore no relation to the realities on the ground. After the fall of the Taliban government, four
major armed groups re-emerged as strong regional players. In the
gas-rich and more industrialized north, bordering the Central Asian
republics of Uzbekistan and Tajikistan, the Uzbek warlord Rashid
Dostum was in charge with his capital in Mazar-i-Sharif. Allied first
to the Communists, later the Taliban and most recently NATO, General Dostum had demonstrated his latest loyalty by massacring
2–3,000 Taliban and Arab prisoners under the approving gaze of
US intelligence personnel in December 2001.

Not too far from Dostum, in the mountainous north-east of the
country, a region rich in emeralds, lapis lazuli and opium, the late
Ahmed Shah Masoud had built a fighting organization of Tajiks,
who regularly ambushed troops on the Salang Highway that linked

Kabul to Tashkent during the Soviet occupation. Masoud had been the leader of the armed wing of Burhanuddin Rabbani's Jamaat-i-Islami, which operated in tandem with an allied Islamist leader, Abd al-Rabb Sayyaf (both men were lecturers in *sharia* at the law faculty of Kabul University in 1973, where these movements were incubated). Until 1993 they were funded by Saudi Arabia, after which the latter gradually shifted its support to the Taliban. Masoud maintained a semi-independence during the Taliban period, up to his death on 9 September 2001.[6] Masoud's supporters are currently in the government, but are not considered one hundred per cent reliable as far as NATO is concerned.

To the west, sheltered by neighbouring Iran, lies the ancient city of Herat, once a centre of learning and culture where poets, artists and scholars flourished. Among the important works illustrated here over the course of three centuries was a 15th-century version of the classic *Miraj-nameh*, an early medieval account of the Prophet's ascent to heaven from the Dome of the Rock and the punishments he observed as he passed through hell.[7] In modern Herat, the Shia warlord Ismail Khan holds sway. A former army captain inspired by the Islamic Revolution in Iran, Ismail achieved instant fame by leading a garrison revolt against the pro-Moscow regime in 1979. Backed by Teheran he built up a strong force that united all the Shia groups and were to trouble the Russians throughout their stay. Tens of thousands of refugees from this region (where a Persian dialect is the spoken language) were given work, shelter and training in Iran. From 1992–95, the province was run on authoritarian lines. It was a harsh regime: Ismail Khan's half-witted effrontery soon began to alienate his allies, while his high-tax and forced conscription policies angered peasant families. By the time the Taliban took power in Kabul in 1996, support had already drained away from the warlord. Herat fell without a struggle, and Ismail was imprisoned by the Taliban, only escaping in March 2000. His supporters meanwhile crossed the border to Iran where they bided their time, to return in October 2001 under NATO cover.

The south was another story again. The Pashtun villages bore the brunt of the fighting during the 1980s and 90s.[8] Rapid population growth, coupled with the disruptions of war and the resulting loss of livestock, hastened the collapse of the subsistence economy. In many districts this was replaced by poppy cultivation and the rule of local bandits and strongmen. By the early 1990s, three militant Sunni groups had acquired dominance in the region: the Taliban, the group led by Ahmed Shah Masoud from the Panjsher province, and the followers of Gulbuddin Hekmatyar, once Pakistan's favourite, who had been groomed by the Saudis as the new leader. The jihad was long over, and now the jihadis were at each other's throats, with control of the drug trade the major stake in a brutal power struggle. Under Benazir Bhutto's second premiership, Pakistan's military backing for the Taliban proved decisive. But the overthrow of the Mullah Omar government in the winter of 2001 saw the re-emergence of many of the local gangsters whose predations it had partly checked.

ANOINTMENT OF KARZAI

Washington assigned the task of assembling a new government to Zalmay Khalilzad, its Afghan-American pro-consul in Kabul. The capital was occupied by competing militias, united only by opposition to the toppled Taliban, and their representatives had to be accommodated on every level. The Northern Alliance candidate for president, Abdul Haq of Jalalabad, had conveniently been captured and executed in October 2001 by the Taliban when he entered the country with a small group from Pakistan. (His supporters alleged betrayal by the CIA and the ISI, who were unhappy about his links to Russia and Iran, and tipped off Mullah Omar.) Another obvious anti-Taliban candidate was Ahmed Shah Masoud; but he had also been killed – by a suicide bomber of unknown provenance – two days before 9/11. Masoud would no doubt have been the EU choice for Afghan president, had he lived; the French government issued a postage stamp with his portrait, and Kabul airport bears his name. Whether he would have proved as reliable a client as Khalilzad's transplanted protégé, Hamid Karzai, must now remain an open question.

Aware that the US could not run the country without the Northern Alliance and its backers in Teheran and Moscow, Khalilzad toned down the emancipatory rhetoric and concentrated on the serious business of occupation. The coalition he constructed resembled a blind octopus, with mainly Tajik limbs and Karzai as its unseeing eye. The Afghan president comes from the Durrani tribe of Pashtuns from Kandahar. His father had served in a junior capacity in Zahir

Shah's government. Young Karzai backed the Mujahedin against Russia and later supported the Taliban, though he turned down their offer to become Afghanistan's Ambassador to the UN, preferring to relocate and work for UNOCAL. Here he backed up Khalilzad, who was then representing CentGas in their bid to construct a pipeline that would take gas from Turkmenistan across Afghanistan to Pakistan and India.[9]

After his appointment as interim president, the Saudi daily *Al-Watan* published a revealing profile of Karzai, stating that he had been a CIA pawn since the 80s, with his status on the Afghan chessboard enhanced every few years:

Since then, Karzai's ties with the Americans have not been interrupted. At the same time, he established ties with the British and other European and international sides, especially after he became deputy foreign minister in 1992 in the wake of the Afghan Mujahedin's assumption of power and the overthrow of the pro-Moscow Najibullah regime. Karzai found no contradiction between his ties with the Americans and his support for the Taliban movement as of 1994, when the Americans had – secretly and through the Pakistanis – supported the Taliban's assumption of power to put an end to the civil war and the actual partition of Afghanistan due to the failure of Burhanuddin Rabbani's experience in ruling the country.[10]

Karzai was duly installed in December 2001, but intimacy with US intelligence networks failed to translate into authority or legitimacy at home. Karzai harboured no illusions about his popularity in the country. He knew his biological and political life was heavily dependent on the occupation and demanded a bodyguard of US Marines or American mercenaries, rather than a security detail from his own ethnic Pashtun base.[11] There were at least three coup attempts against him in 2002–03 by his Northern Alliance allies; these were fought off by the ISAF, which was largely tied down in assuring Karzai's security – while also providing a vivid illustration of where his support lay.[12] A quick-fix presidential contest organized at great expense by Western PR firms in October 2004 – just in time for the US elections – failed to bolster support for the puppet president inside the country. Karzai's habit of parachuting his relatives and protégés into provincial governor or police chief jobs has driven many local communities into alliance with the Taliban, as the main anti-government force. In Zabul, Helmand and elsewhere, all the insurgents had to do was "approach the victims of the pro-Karzai strongmen and promise them protection and support. Attempts by local elders to seek protection in Kabul routinely ended nowhere, as the wrongdoers enjoyed either direct US support or Karzai's sympathy."[13]

Nor is it any secret that Karzai's younger brother, Ahmad Wali Karzai, has now become one of the richest drug barons in the country. At a meeting with Pakistan's president in 2005, when Karzai was bleating about Pakistan's inability to stop cross-border smuggling, Musharraf suggested that perhaps Karzai should set an example by bringing his sibling under control. (The hatred for each other of these two close allies of Washington is well known in the region.)

NEW INEQUALITIES

Also feeding the resentment is the behaviour of a new elite clustered around Karzai and the occupying forces, which has specialized in creaming off foreign aid to create its own criminal networks of graft and patronage. The corruptions of this layer grow each month like an untreated tumour. Western funds are siphoned off to build fancy homes for the native enforcers. Housing scandals erupted as early as 2002, when cabinet ministers awarded themselves and favoured cronies prime real estate in Kabul where land prices were rocketing, since the occupiers and their camp followers had to live in the style to which they were accustomed. Karzai's colleagues, protected by ISAF troops, built their large villas in full view of the mud-brick hovels of the poor. The burgeoning slum settlements of Kabul, where the population has now swollen to an estimated 3 million, are a measure of the social crisis that has engulfed the country.

The ancient city has suffered cruelly over the past thirty years. Jade Maiwand, the modernized 'Oxford Street' cut through the centre in the 1970s, was reduced to rubble during the warfare of 1992–96. An American-Afghan architect describes how Kabul has been relentlessly transformed:

from a modern capital, to the military and political headquarters of an invading army, to the besieged seat of power of a puppet regime, to the front lines of factional conflict resulting in the destruction of two-thirds of its urban mass, to the testing fields of religious fanaticism which erased from the city the final layers of urban life, to the target of an international war on terrorism.[14]

Yet never have such gaping inequalities featured on this scale before. Little of the supposed $19 billion 'aid and reconstruction' money has reached the majority of Afghans. The main electricity supply is worse now than five years ago, and while the rich can use private generators to power their air conditioners, hot-water heaters, computers and satellite TVS, average Kabulis "suffered a summer without fans and face a winter without heaters."[15] As a result, hundreds of shelterless Afghans are literally freezing to death each winter.

Then there are the NGOs who descended on the country like locusts after the occupation. As one observer reports:

A reputed 10,000 NGO staff have turned Kabul into the Klondike during the gold rush, building office blocks, driving up rents, cruising about in armoured jeeps and spending stupefying sums of other people's money, essentially on themselves. They take orders only from some distant agency, but then the same goes for the American army, NATO, the UN, the EU and the supposedly sovereign Afghan government.[16]

Even supporters of the occupation have lost patience with these bodies, and some of the most successful candidates in the 2005 National Assembly elections made an attack on them a centre-piece of their campaigns. Worse, according to one US specialist, 'their well-funded activities highlighted the poverty and ineffectiveness of the civil administration and discredited its local representatives in the eyes of the local populace.'[17] Unsurprisingly, NGO employees began to be targeted by the insurgents, including in the north, and had to hire mercenary protection.

In sum: even in the estimate of the West's own specialists and institutions, 'nation-building' in Afghanistan has been flawed in its very conception. It has so far produced a puppet president dependent for his survival on foreign mercenaries, a corrupt and abusive police force, a 'non-functioning' judiciary, a thriving criminal layer and a deepening social and economic crisis. It beggars belief to argue that 'more of this' will be the answer to Afghanistan's problems.

AN AFGHAN SURGE?

The argument that more NATO troops are the solution is equally un-sustainable. All the evidence suggests that the brutality of the occu-pying forces has been one of the main sources of recruits for the Tal-iban. American air power, lovingly referred to as 'Big Daddy' by frightened US soldiers on unwelcome terrain, is far from paternal when it comes to targeting Pashtun villages. There is widespread fury among Afghans at the number of civilian casualties, many of them children. There have been numerous incidents of rape and rough treat-ment of women by ISAF soldiers, as well as indiscriminate bombing of villages and house-to-house search-and-arrest missions. The be-haviour of the foreign mercenaries backing up the NATO forces is just as bad. Even sympathetic observers admit that "their alcohol con-sumption and patronage of a growing number of brothels in Kabul … is arousing public anger and resentment."[18] To this could be added the deaths by torture at the US-run Bagram prison and the re-suscitation of a Soviet-era security law under which detainees are being sentenced to 20-year jail terms on the basis of summary allega-tions by US military authorities. All this creates a thirst for dignity that can only be assuaged by genuine independence.

Talk of 'victory' sounds increasingly hollow to Afghan ears. Many who detest the Taliban are so angered by the failures of NATO and the behaviour of its troops that they are pleased there is some op-position. What was initially viewed by some locals as a necessary po-lice action against al Qaeda following the 9/11 attacks is now per-ceived by a growing majority in the region as a fully fledged imperial occupation. Successive recent reports have suggested that the un-popularity of the government and the 'disrespectful' behaviour of the occupying troops have had the effect of creating nostalgia for the time when the Taliban were in power. The repression leaves people with no option but to back those trying to resist, especially in a part of the world where the culture of revenge is strong. When a whole community feels threatened it reinforces solidarity, regardless of the character or weakness of those who fight back. This does not just apply to the countryside. The mass protests in Kabul, when civilians were killed by an American military vehicle, signalled the obvious targets:

Rioters chanted slogans against the United States and President Karzai and attacked the Parliament building, the offices of media outlets and non-governmental organizations, diplomatic residences, brothels, and hotels and restaurants that purportedly served alcohol. The police, many of whom disappeared, proved incompetent, and the vulnerability of the government to mass violence became clear.[19]

As the British and Russians discovered to their cost in the preceding two centuries, Afghans do not like being occupied. If a second-generation Taliban is now growing and creating new alliances it is not because its sectarian religious practices have become popular, but because it is the only available umbrella for national liberation. Initially, the middle-cadre Taliban who fled across the border in November 2001 and started low-level guerrilla activity the following year attracted only a trickle of new recruits from madrasas and refugee camps. From 2004 onwards, increasing numbers of young Waziris were radicalized by Pakistani military and police incursions in the tribal areas, as well as devastating attacks on villages by unmanned US 'drones.' At the same time, the movement was starting to win active support from village mullahs in Zabul, Helmand, Ghazni, Paktika and Kandahar provinces, and then in the towns. By 2006 there were reports of Kabul mullahs who had previously supported Karzai's allies but were now railing against the foreigners and the government; calls for jihad against the occupiers were heard in the north-east border provinces of Takhar and Badakhshan.

The largest pool for new Taliban recruits, according to a well-informed recent estimate, has been 'communities antagonized by the local authorities and security forces.' In Kandahar, Helmand and Uruzgan, Karzai's cronies – district and provincial governors, security bosses, police chiefs – are quite prepared to tip off US troops against their local rivals, as well as subjecting the latter to harassment and extortion. In these circumstances, the Taliban are the only available defence. (According to the same report, the Taliban themselves have claimed that families driven into refugee camps by indiscriminate US airpower attacks on their villages have been their major source of recruits.) By 2006 the movement was winning the support of traders and businessmen in Kandahar, and led a mini 'Tet offensive' there that year. One reason suggested for their increasing support in towns is that the new-model Taliban have relaxed their religious strictures, for males at least – no longer demanding beards or banning music – and improved their propaganda: producing cassette tapes and CDs of popular singers, and DVDs of US and Israeli atrocities in Iraq, Lebanon and Palestine.[20]

The re-emergence of the Taliban cannot therefore simply be blamed on Islamabad's failure to police the border, or cut 'command and control' links, as the Americans claim. While the ISI played a crucial role in bringing the Taliban to power in 1996 and in the retreat of 2001, they no longer have the same degree of control over a more diffuse and widespread movement, for which the occupation itself has been the main recruiting sergeant. It is a traditional colonial ploy to blame 'outsiders' for internal problems: Karzai specializes in this approach. If anything, the destabilization functions in the other direction: the war in Afghanistan has created a critical situation in two Pakistani frontier provinces, and the use of the Pakistan army by Centcom has resulted in suicide terrorism in Lahore, where the Federal Investigation Agency and the Naval War College have been targeted by supporters of the Afghan insurgents. The Pashtun majority in Afghanistan has always had close links to its fellow Pashtuns in Pakistan. The present border was an imposition by the British Empire, but it has always remained porous. It is virtually impossible to build a Texan fence or an Israeli wall across the mountainous and largely unmarked 1,500-mile frontier that separates the two countries.

OLDER MODELS

The current occupation of Afghanistan naturally recalls colonial operations in the region, not just to Afghans but to some Western mythmakers – usually British, but with a few Subcontinental mimics – who try to draw lessons from the older model; the implication being that the British were 'good imperialists' who have a great deal to teach the brutish, impatient Americans. The British administrators were, for the most part, racist to the core, and their self-proclaimed 'competence' involved the efficient imposition of social apartheid in every colony they controlled. They could be equally brutal in Africa, the Middle East and India. Though a promise of civilizational uplift was required as ideological justification, then as now, the facts of the colonial legacy speak for themselves. In 1947, the year the British left India, the overwhelming majority of midnight's children were illiterate, and 85 per cent of the economy was rural.[21]

Not bad intentions or botched initiatives, but the imperial presence itself was the problem. Kipling is much quoted today by editorialists urging a bigger Western 'footprint' in Afghanistan, but even he was fully aware of the hatred felt by the Pashtuns for the British, and wrote as much in one of his last despatches from Peshawar in April 1885 to the *Civil and Military Gazette* in Lahore:

Pathans, Afridis, Logas, Kohistanis, Turcomans and a hundred other varieties of the turbulent Afghan race, are gathered in the vast human menagerie between the Edwardes Gate and the Ghor Khutri. As an Englishman passes, they will turn to scowl on him, and in many cases to spit fluently on the ground after he has passed. One burly, big-paunched ruffian, with shaven head and a neck creased and dimpled with rolls of fat, is specially zealous in this religious rite – contenting himself with no perfunctory performance, but with a whole-souled expectoration, that must be as refreshing to his comrades as it is disgusting to the European.

One reason among many for the Pashtuns' historic resentment was the torching of the famous bazaar in Kabul, a triumph of Mughal architecture. Ali Mardan Khan, a renowned governor, architect and engineer, had built the *chahr-chatta* (four-sided) roofed and arcaded central market in the 17th century on the model of those in old Euro-Arabian Muslim cities – Cairo, Damascus, Baghdad, Palermo or Córdoba. It was regarded as unique in the region; nothing on the same scale was built in Lahore or Delhi. The bazaar was deliberately destroyed in 1842 by General Pollock's 'Army of Retribution', remembered as amongst the worst killers, looters and marauders ever to arrive in Afghanistan, a contest in which competition remains strong. Defeated in a number of cities and forced to evacuate Kabul, the British punished its citizens by removing the market from the map. What will remain of Kabul when the current occupiers finally withdraw is yet to be seen, but its spreading mass of deeply impoverished squatter settlements suggest that it is set to be one of the major new capitals of the 'planet of slums.'[22]

The Western occupation of Afghanistan is now confronted with five seemingly intractable, interrelated problems. The systemic failures of its nation-building strategy, the corruption of its local agents, the growing alienation of large sectors of the population and the strengthening of armed resistance are all compounded by the distortions wrought by the opium-heroin industry on the country's economy. According to UN estimates, narcotics account for 53 per cent of the country's gross domestic product, and the poppy fields continue to spread. Some 90 per cent of the world opium supply emanates from Afghanistan. Since 2003 the NATO mission has made no serious attempt to bring about a reduction in this lucrative trade. Karzai's own supporters would rapidly desert if their activities in this sphere were disrupted, and the amount of state help needed over many years to boost agriculture and cottage industries and reduce dependence on poppy farming would require an entirely different set of priorities. Only a surreal utopian could expect NATO countries, busy privatizing and deregulating their own economies, to embark upon full-scale national-development projects abroad.

NATO'S GOALS

It need hardly be added that the bombardment and occupation of Afghanistan has been a disastrous – and predictable – failure in capturing the perpetrators of 9/11. This could only have been the result of effective police work; not of international war and military occupation. Everything that has happened in Afghanistan since 2001 – not to mention Iraq, Palestine and Lebanon – has had the opposite effect, as the West's own intelligence reports have repeatedly confirmed. According to the official 9/11 Commission report, Mullah Omar's initial response to Washington's demands that Osama Bin Laden be handed over and al Qaeda deprived of a safe haven was 'not negative'; he himself had opposed any al Qaeda attack on US targets.[23] But while the Mullah was playing for time, the White House closed down negotiations. It required a swift war of revenge. Afghanistan had been denominated the first port of call in the 'global war on terror', with Iraq already the Administration's main target. The shock-and-awe six-week aerial onslaught that followed was merely a drumroll for the forthcoming intervention in Iraq, with no military rationale in Afghanistan. Predictably, it only gave al Qaeda leaders the chance to vanish into the hills. To portray the invasion as a 'war of self-defence' for NATO makes a mockery of international law, which was perverted to twist a flukishly successful attack by a tiny, terrorist Arab groupuscule into an excuse for an open-ended American military thrust into the Middle East and Central Eurasia.

Herein lie the reasons for the near-unanimity among Western opinion-makers that the occupation must not only continue but expand – 'many billions over many years.' They are to be sought not in the mountain fastnesses of Afghanistan, but in Washington and Brussels. As the *Economist* summarizes, "Defeat would be a body blow not only to the Afghans, but" – and more importantly, of course – "to the NATO alliance."[24] As ever, geopolitics prevails over Afghan interests in the calculus of the big powers. The basing agreement signed by the US with its appointee in Kabul in May 2005 gives the Pentagon the right to maintain a massive military presence in Afghanistan in perpetuity, potentially including nuclear missiles. That Washington is not seeking permanent bases in this fraught and inhospitable terrain simply for the sake of 'democratization and good governance' was made clear by NATO's Secretary-General Jaap de Hoop Scheffer at the Brookings Institution in February this year (2005): a permanent NATO presence in a country that borders the ex-Soviet republics, China, Iran and Pakistan was too good to miss.[25]

More strategically, Afghanistan has become a central theatre for reconstituting, and extending, the West's power-political grip on the world order. It provides, first, an opportunity for the US to shrug off problems in persuading its allies to play a broader role in Iraq. As Obama and Clinton have stressed, America and its allies "have greater unity of purpose in Afghanistan. The ultimate outcome of NATO's effort to stabilize Afghanistan and US leadership of that effort may well affect the cohesiveness of the alliance and Washington's ability to shape NATO's future."[26] Beyond this, it is the rise of China that has prompted NATO strategists to propose a vastly expanded role for the Western military alliance. Once focused on the Euro-Atlantic area, a recent essay in *NATO Review* suggests, "in the 21st century NATO must become an alliance founded on the Euro-Atlantic area, designed to project systemic stability beyond its borders":

The centre of gravity of power on this planet is moving inexorably eastward ... The Asia-Pacific region brings much that is dynamic and positive to this world, but as yet the rapid change therein is neither stable nor embedded in stable institutions. Until this is achieved, it is the strategic responsibility of Europeans and North Americans, and the institutions they have built, to lead the way ... security effectiveness in such a world is impossible without both legitimacy and capability.[27]

The only way to protect the international system the West has built, the author continues, is to 're-energize' the transatlantic relationship: "There can be no systemic security without Asian security, and there will be no Asian security without a strong role for the West therein."

These ambitions have yet to be realized. In Afghanistan there were angry street demonstrations against Karzai's signing of the US bases agreement – a clear indication, if one was still needed, that NATO will have to take Karzai with them if they withdraw. Uzbekistan responded by asking the United States to withdraw its base and personnel from their country. The Russians and Chinese are reported to have protested strongly in private, and subsequently conducted joint military operations on each other's territory for the first time: "concern over apparent US plans for permanent bases in Afghanistan and Central Asia" was an important cause of their rapprochement.[28] More limply, Iran responded by increasing export duties, bringing construction in Herat to a halt.[29]

There are at least two routes out of the Khyber impasse. The first and worst would be to Balkanize the country. This appears to be the dominant pattern of imperial hegemony at the moment, but whereas the Kurds in Iraq and the Kosovars and others in the former Yugoslavia were willing client-nationalists, the likelihood of Tajiks or Hazaras playing this role effectively is more remote in Afghanistan. Some US intelligence officers have been informally discussing the creation of a Pashtun state that unites the tribes and dissolves the Durand Line, but this would destabilize Pakistan and Afghanistan to such a degree that the consequences would be unpredictable. In any event there appear to be no takers in either country at the moment.

The alternative would require a withdrawal of all US forces, either preceded or followed by a regional pact to guarantee Afghan stability for the next ten years. Pakistan, Iran, India, Russia and, possibly, China could guarantee and support a functioning national government, pledged to preserve the ethnic and religious diversity of Afghanistan and create a space in which all its citizens can breathe, think and eat every day. It would need a serious social and economic plan to rebuild the country and provide the basic necessities for its people. This would not only be in the interests of Afghanistan, it would be seen as such by its people – physically, politically and morally exhausted by decades of war and two occupations. Violence, arbitrary or deliberate, has been their fate for too long. They want the nightmare to end and not be replaced with horrors of a different kind. Religious extremists would get short shrift from the people if they disrupted an agreed peace and began a jihad to recreate the Taliban Emirate of Mullah Omar.

The US occupation has not made this task easy. Its predictable failures have revived the Taliban, and increasingly the Pashtuns are uniting behind them. But though the Taliban have been entirely conflated with al Qaeda in the Western media, most of their supporters are driven by local concerns; their political evolution would be more likely to parallel that of Pakistan's domesticated Islamists if the invaders were to leave. A NATO withdrawal could facilitate a serious peace process. It might also benefit Pakistan, provided its military leaders abandoned foolish notions of 'strategic depth' and viewed India not as an enemy but as a possible partner in creating a cohesive regional framework within which many contentious issues could be resolved. Are Pakistan's military leaders and politicians capable of grasping the nettle and moving their country forward? Will Washington let them? The solution is political, not military. And it lies in the region, not in Washington or Brussels.

NOTES

1 In fact, the only period in Afghan history where women were granted equal rights and educated was from 1979–89, the decade it was ruled by the PDPA, backed by Soviet troops. Repressive in many ways, on the health and education fronts real progress was achieved, as in Iraq under Saddam. Hence the nostalgia for the past amongst poorer sections of society in both countries.

2 Visiting Madrid after Zapatero's election triumph of March 2008, I was informed by a senior government official that they had considered a total withdrawal from Afghanistan a few months before the polls but had been outmanoeuvred by the US promising Spain that the head of its military would be proposed for commander of the NATO forces, and a withdrawal from Kabul would disrupt this possibility. Spain drew back, only to discover it had been tricked.

3 'Failing State,' *Guardian*, 1 February 2008; see also 'The Good War, Still to Be Won' and 'Gates, Truth and Afghanistan,' *New York Times*, 20 August 2007 and 12 February 2008; 'Must they be wars without end?', *Economist*, 13 December 2007; International Crisis Group, 'Combating Afghanistan's Insurgency,' 2 November 2006.

4 *New York Times*, 5 November 2006.

5 Pakistan's key role in securing this 'victory' was underplayed in the Western media at the time. The public was told that it was elite Special Forces units and CIA 'specialists' that had liberated Afghanistan; having triumphed here they could now be sent on to Iraq.

6 Masoud had been a favourite pin-up in Paris during the Soviet–Afghan war, usually portrayed as a ruggedly romantic, anti-Communist Che Guevara. His membership of Rabbani's Islamist group and reactionary views on most social issues were barely mentioned. But if he had presented an image of incorruptible masculinity to his supporters in the West, it was not the same at home. Rape and the heroin trade were not uncommon in areas under his control.

7 The stunning illustrations were exquisitely calligraphed by Malik Bakshi in the Uighur script. There are 61 paintings in all, created with great love for the Prophet of Islam. He is depicted with Central Asian features and seen flying to heaven on a magical steed with a woman's head. There are also illustrations of a meeting with Gabriel and Adam, a sighting of Houris at the gates of Paradise, and of winebibbers being punished in hell. European scholars have suggested that an early Latin translation of the poem may have been a source of inspiration for Dante.

8 Afghanistan's ethnography has generated a highly politicized statistical debate. The 6-year survey carried out by a Norwegian foundation is probably the most accurate. This suggests that Pashtuns make up an estimated 63 per cent of the population, along with the mainly Persian-speaking Tajiks (12 per cent), Uzbeks (9 per cent) and the mainly Shia Hazaras (6 per cent): WAK Foundation, Norway 1999. The CIA Factbook, by contrast, gives 42, 27, 9 and 9 per cent respectively. The tiny non-Muslim minority of Hindus and Sikhs, mainly shopkeepers and traders in Kabul, were displaced by the Taliban; some were killed, and thousands fled to India.

9 The CentGas consortium, incorporated in 1997, included UNOCAL, Gazprom, Hyundai and oil companies from Saudi Arabia, Japan and Pakistan. In late 1997 a Taliban delegation received full honours when they visited UNOCAL HQ, hoping to sign the £2bn pipeline contract. According to the *Sunday Telegraph* ('Oil Barons Court Taliban in Texas,' 14 December 1997): 'the Islamic warriors appear to have been persuaded to close the deal, not through delicate negotiation but by old-fashioned Texan hospitality. Dressed in traditional *shalwar kameez*, Afghan waistcoats and loose, black turbans, the high-ranking delegation was given VIP treatment during the four-day stay.' The proj-

ect was suspended in 1998, as the Taliban were split on to whom to award the pipeline project: Mullah Rabbani preferred the offer from the Argentine company Bridas, while Mullah Omar was strongly in favour of the American-led deal. But US–Taliban contacts continued till mid-2001 both in Islamabad and New York, where the Taliban maintained a 'diplomatic office' headed by Abdul Hakim Mojahed.

10 BBC Monitoring Service, 15 December 2001.

11 The late Benazir Bhutto made the same request for American protection on her return to Pakistan, but in her case it was vetoed by Islamabad.

12 Barry McCaffrey, 'Trip to Afghanistan and Pakistan,' US Military Academy Memorandum, West Point, NY 2006, p. 8.

13 Antonio Giustozzi, *Koran, Kalashnikov and Laptop: the Neo-Taliban Insurgency in Afghanistan*, London 2007, p. 60. The corruption and brutality of the newly established Afghan National Police is also widely credited with turning the population against the Karzai government.

14 Ajmal Maiwandi, 'Re-Doing Kabul,' presented at London School of Economics, 11 July 2002.

15 Barnett Rubin, 'Saving Afghanistan,' *Foreign Affairs*, January–February 2007.

16 Simon Jenkins, 'It takes inane optimism to see victory in Afghanistan,' *Guardian*, 8 August 2007.

17 S. Frederick Starr, 'Sovereignty and Legitimacy in Afghan Nation-Building,' in Fukuyama, ed., *Nation-Building Beyond Afghanistan and Iraq*, Baltimore 2006, p. 117.

18 Barnett Rubin, 'Proposals for Improved Stability in Afghanistan,' in Ivo Daalder et al, eds, *Crescent of Crisis: US–European Strategy for the Greater Middle East*, Washington, DC 2006, p. 149.

19 Rubin, 'Saving Afghanistan.' op. cit.

20 Giustozzi, *Koran, Kalashnikov and Laptop*, pp. 42, 69.

21 'Per capita income was about one-twentieth of the level then attained in developed countries … Illiteracy was a high 84 per cent and the majority (60 per cent) of children in the 6 to 11 age-group did not attend school; mass communicable diseases (malaria, smallpox and cholera) were widespread and, in the absence of a good public health service and sanitation, mortality rates (27 per 1,000) were very high.' Dharma Kumar and Meghnad Desai, eds, *Cambridge Economic History of India*, vol. II: c.1757–c.1970, Cambridge 1983, p. 23.

22 Mike Davis, 'Planet of Slums,' *New Left Review*, 26, March–April 2004, p. 13.

23 The 9.11 Commission Report, New York 2004, pp. 333–4; 251–2.

24 'Must they be wars without end?' op. cit. footnote 3.

25 'Afghanistan and NATO: Forging the 21st Century Alliance,'
29 February 2008; available on Brookings website.

26 Paul Gallis, 'NATO in Afghanistan,' CRS Report for Congress,
23 October 2007.

27 Julian Lindley-French, 'Big World, Big Future, Big Nato,' *NATO Review*, Winter 2005.

28 Rubin, 'Proposals for Improved Stability in Afghanistan.' op. cit

29 In response to Karzai's pleas, Teheran proposed a treaty that would prohibit foreign intelligence operations in each country against the other; hard to see how Karzai could have signed this with a straight face.

Canada's Role in the Occupation of Afghanistan

ÉCHEC À LA GUERRE

INTRODUCTION

This document reflects the reading, thinking, and discussion among members of the Échec à la Guerre collective. It represents a revision of an earlier draft to incorporate the many comments made by individuals and member groups. The document is divided into 5 sections and a total of 18 questions. There is some logic to the order in which the questions are presented, but the answers are largely independent of each other, making it easy for you to explore them in any order that is convenient for you.

Before getting into these specific questions, here is a summary of the collective's overall position on the war in Afghanistan:

• The war in Afghanistan is not a just war; the invasion of Afghanistan was never authorized by the Security Council and cannot be justified by invoking self-defence.

• "Reconstruction" and "democracy-building" in the Afghan context are pure propaganda at worst, self-congratulatory rationalization at best. After five years of foreign intervention in Afghanistan, the country is in a disastrous situation that bears no relationship to the stated good intentions of the countries involved.

• In reality, the goal of this war has always been to install a regime favourable to US interests and those of its allies. It is part of a broader offensive – the so-called "war on terror" – whose real purpose is to expand the US empire into Central Asia, the Middle East, and Eastern Europe.

• Canada is participating in this strategy in order to preserve and deepen its strategic partnership with the United States, and several large Canadian corporations expect to benefit.

• For all these reasons, the collective is calling for the withdrawal of Canadian troops from Afghanistan.

The following questions and answers have not been endorsed by all the decision-making bodies of our member groups, but we believe that they represent a useful contribution to the debate on continued Canadian military involvement in Afghanistan. They also offer a coherent and systematic agenda for opposition to this war of occupation.

–The *Échec à la Guerre* Steering Committee

SECTION 1: AFGHANISTAN: A LEGITIMATE MILITARY INTERVENTION?

QUESTION 1: Was the invasion of Afghanistan a legitimate act of self-defence by the United States after the 9/11 attacks?

No, for several reasons. First, self-defence, in both international law and domestic law (in Canada, the Criminal Code), must be clearly distinguished from the use of force for revenge or punishment; states, like persons, must not act as vigilantes. Second, in criminal law, self-defence may be invoked in the face of an imminent threat of death or grave bodily harm. In general, the threat must be immediate[1] and the response must not be pushed beyond what is reasonably required to repel that threat. Therefore, in general, self-defence may not be invoked to justify physical retaliation to an attack a few weeks after it occurs. The appropriate course of action in that case would involve police work, legal proceedings, and so forth.

In international law, the concept of self-defence is recognized by the *Charter of the United Nations*:

Article 51. Nothing in the present Charter shall impair the inherent right of individual or collective self-defence if an armed attack occurs against a Member of the United Nations, until the Security Council has taken measures necessary to maintain international peace and security. Measures taken by Members in the exercise of this right of self-defence shall be immediately reported to the Security Council and shall not in any way affect the authority and responsibility of the Security Council under the present Charter to take at any time such action as it deems necessary in order to maintain or restore international peace and security.[2]

Article 1 of Resolution 3314 of the UN General Assembly (1974) defines aggression:

Aggression is the use of armed force by a State against the sovereignty, territorial integrity or political independence of another State, or in any other manner inconsistent with the Charter of the United Nations, as set out in this Definition.

The resolution provides several concrete examples of acts that would be considered instances of aggression, including invasion, blockade, bombardment, or "[t]he sending [of armed groups] by or on behalf of a State" against another state.

In the case of the 9/11 attacks, the concepts of self-defence and aggression simply do not apply. Afghanistan could not be considered an aggressor state since the attacks were neither perpetrated by it or its agents nor planned on its territory (the planning took place in Germany). As well, in early October 2001 when it launched its war on Afghanistan, the United States was not, to anyone's knowledge, facing an imminent threat of new attacks.

Furthermore, it was not until three years later, on 29 October 2004, that Osama bin Laden acknowledged al Qaeda's authorship of the attacks. Before that time, the United States had not demonstrated his or al Qaeda's guilt, much less that of Afghanistan, in any appropriate forum. The United States even rejected the Taliban's offer to extradite bin Laden to Pakistan for trial so that the US could present their evidence against him.

In both international and domestic law, self-defence certainly cannot be invoked to justify a later attack on a person or country who is merely presumed or claimed to be an aggressor.

The US aggression against Afghanistan in October 2001 more closely resembles the new doctrine of "preventive war" which the White House subsequently made official in its National Security Strategy of September 2002. With this doctrine, the US claims the right to attack unilaterally, "preventively," any country perceived as a serious threat to its vital interests or those of its allies. This doctrine was used as a cover for the invasion of Iraq and will likely serve the same purpose in any future aggression against Iran, Syria, or other countries. Under international law, such acts and "strategy" are totally illegal and illegitimate. All they are is the doctrine of "might makes right" dressed up in fancy language.

QUESTION 2: Was the Afghanistan war authorized by the United Nations?

The war in Afghanistan was devised and directed by the United States. It was led by a coalition of countries, mainly NATO members (including Canada), who on 4 October 2001 invoked Article 5 of the North Atlantic (Washington) Treaty. Under this provision, an armed attack against any NATO country is considered an attack against them all.

There is no UN Security Council resolution authorizing the United States, whether alone or in coalition with other countries, to attack Afghanistan. Between 11 September and 7 October 2001, when the bombardment of Afghanistan began, the UN Security Council adopted only two resolutions concerning the 9/11 attacks. Resolution 1368 of September 12 "unequivocally condemns in the strongest terms the horrifying terrorist attacks ... and regards such acts, like any act of international terrorism, as a threat to international peace and security." The preamble to this resolution recognizes "the inherent right of individual or collective self-defence in accordance with the Charter." Though, as we have seen, the terms of the Charter do not apply to the Afghan war, this language in the preamble of the resolution allowed the United States to claim legitimacy for its actions. Then, on 28 September 2001, the Security Council adopted Resolution 1373, which sets forth certain anti-terrorism measures that all states must apply. Neither Resolution 1368 nor Resolution 1373 even mentions the word "Afghanistan."

In the aftermath of September 11, the United States capitalized on an outpouring of international sympathy to acquire carte blanche for war under the rules of international law. The Security Council, whose official mandate is to prevent war, allowed the United States and its "coalition" to prepare and declare one. The Security Council, of course, is no neutral body. Of its fifteen members, the five permanent ones (the United States, the United Kingdom, France, Russia, and China) have veto power, impairing the Council's capacity to prevent a war being conducted by any of the five. The ten remaining Council members are chosen from the UN member countries for rotating two-year terms. In practice, these ten rotating members are pressured by the United States to vote in its favour. Since the end of the Cold War, the Security Council has been dominated by the American agenda, even though Russian and Chinese interests have occasionally obstructed it.

In this context, it took more than five weeks after the bombardment of Afghanistan commenced before the Security Council took a position on the war conducted by the United States and its "coalition." Yet Resolution 1378 (14 November 2001) does not even mention it. Instead, it condemns the Taliban and supports "the efforts of the Afghan people to replace the Taliban regime"! Likewise, Resolution 1383 (6 December 2001) simply ratifies the Bonn Agreement signed the day before, providing for temporary arrangements among the "coalition" countries, the representatives of their Afghan allies (in the country and in exile), and the UN Secretary-General's special representative.[3] In addition, with Resolution 1386 (20 December 2001) the Security Council authorized, "as envisaged in Annex 1 to the Bonn Agreement, the establishment for 6 months of an International Security Assistance Force" (ISAF). The previous day, the United Kingdom had officially offered to take command of ISAF, and Canada assumed this role later.

And if this is not bad enough, not only has the US Operation Enduring Freedom continued to this day, but after nineteen resolutions the Security Council has yet to set any guidelines whatsoever for the military invasion of Afghan territory or to call its authors to account. Meanwhile, the Council repeats *ad infinitum* its deep attachment to Afghan sovereignty. Two years after the invasion, the words "enduring freedom" finally appeared in Resolution 1510 (13 October 2003). While authorizing the expansion of the ISAF mandate outside of Kabul and its environs, this resolution calls on ISAF "to continue to work in close consultation with the Afghan Transitional Authority and its successors and the Special Representative of the Secretary

General as well as with the Operation Enduring Freedom." This clause appears in each subsequent 12-month renewal of ISAF authorization, effectively giving carte blanche to the US military intervention in Afghanistan.

QUESTION 3: The UN Security Council has ratified the Afghanistan war – doesn't that make it legitimate?

The question of after-the-fact legitimacy is more difficult to resolve since it is quite true that the UN Security Council never officially disapproved or denounced the war in Afghanistan (or the war in Iraq, for that matter); quite the contrary. Nevertheless, we believe that the war is neither legitimate nor legal under international law, the only appropriate system of law for deciding such matters.

The UN Charter clearly states that the primary role of the United Nations is to prevent war, and to propose other means of resolving conflicts between nations. Even if one accepts the idea that the United States was trying to prevent new terrorist attacks by attacking Afghanistan,4 the Security Council violated its mandate by failing to consider possible non-military solutions once the bombardment began.

This failure by the Security Council is unfortunately not an isolated case. In fact, it is no exaggeration to say that the United Nations has been undergoing a severe crisis since the end of the Cold War. The absence of a second superpower to act as a counterweight to the US has created a new situation at the UN – and especially on the Security Council, which is often reduced to ratifying the US empire's wars, in violation of the UN charter. This happened with:

• the UN Security Council resolution of the fall of 1990 giving advance authorization to the Gulf War;
• the resolutions renewing the genocidal sanctions on Iraq for twelve straight years;
• the resolutions ratifying the *fait accompli* consisting of the illegal March 2003 "coalition" invasion of Iraq – a June 2004 resolution even welcomed the end of the Iraq occupation!

On several occasions since the end of the Cold War, the UN's fundamental mission has been derailed. It has become an instrument for approval of the US empire's wars of expansion. In fact, former US Permanent Representative to the UN John Bolton allowed as much:

There is no such thing as the United Nations. There is only the international community, which can only be led by the only remaining superpower, which is the United States, when it suits our interest and we can get others to go along ... When the United States leads, the United Nations will follow. When it suits our interest to do so, we will do so. When it does not suit our interests we will not.[5]

Just as it is possible for governments to pass laws violating their own country's constitution or bill of rights – laws whose legality and legitimacy can then be challenged with reference to these fundamental legal instruments – the Security Council, under pressure from the United States, is increasingly passing resolutions that violate the spirit and the letter of the UN Charter. In these cases it is our duty to defend international law and denounce such resolutions, not to accept that they grant legitimacy to illegal acts.

QUESTION 4: With a regime like the Taliban that trampled on human rights, and especially women's rights, wasn't military intervention justified?

In addressing this question, it is important to keep in mind the troubling fact that civilians are the main victims of war. Civilians suffer both directly, as war casualties, and indirectly, as people who have to live in a destroyed environment without means of subsistence. Using war to "help" people whose rights are being violated is obviously not something to be taken lightly.

Furthermore, countries who plan wars in order to capture resources, conquer territory, or in other ways advance their strategic interests or hegemonic designs never lack for noble-sounding pretexts: self-defence, defending civilization, rescuing threatened national minorities, and so on. After no weapons of mass destruction had been found to justify the invasion of Iraq, the Bush administration argued that it was legitimate to overthrow a brutal dictatorship in order to free the Iraqi people. But to allow any country to make war entirely on its own grounds means throwing out international law and replacing it with "might makes right."

True, there are situations in which concerted, disinterested international intervention may be warranted. The need to learn the lessons of the Rwandan genocide is often cited in this connection, and the 2005 *World Summit Outcome* contains the following point on the international responsibility to protect civilians:

139. The international community, through the United Nations, also has the responsibility to use appropriate diplomatic, humanitarian and other peaceful means, in accordance with Chapters VI and VIII of the Charter, to help protect populations from genocide, war crimes, ethnic cleansing and crimes against humanity.[6] In this context, we are prepared to take collective action, in a timely and decisive manner, through the Security Council, in accordance with the Charter, including Chapter VII,[7] on a case-by-case basis and in cooperation with relevant regional organizations as appropriate, should peaceful means be inadequate and national authorities manifestly fail to protect their populations from genocide, war crimes, ethnic cleansing and crimes against humanity. We stress the need for the General Assembly to continue consideration of the responsibility to protect populations from genocide, war crimes, ethnic cleansing and crimes against humanity and its implications, bearing in mind the principles of the Charter and international law. We also intend to commit ourselves, as necessary and appropriate, to helping States build capacity to protect their populations from genocide, war crimes, ethnic cleansing and crimes against humanity and to assist those which are under stress before crises and conflicts break out.[8]

Two remarks are relevant here. First, these provisions did not apply to Afghanistan, where there was no ongoing genocide or ethnic cleansing. Second, the invocation of Chapter VII to cover the use of force for humanitarian purposes falls under the aegis of the Security Council, which is dominated by the United States and not the General Assembly. Given the historical status of war as a pillar of US foreign policy, it is to be expected that these new provisions will be vehemently invoked where the US has a strategic interest in invading another country, and will be ignored otherwise.

Perhaps this remark seems cynical, but it is in fact a fair conclusion to be drawn from US foreign policy in general, and from its Afghanistan policy in particular. The United States has maintained close ties to many brutal regimes over the years, selling them arms that are then used to oppress their populations. In the specific case of Afghanistan, the US government never expressed any concern about human rights and women's rights in that country until they became a useful pretext for war. The US government's historical flip-flopping on Afghanistan is revealing.

During the Cold War, the United States supported the Mujahedin – the precursor to most of the armed groups now making up the Northern Alliance – against the Soviet invasion and the pro-Soviet government in Kabul.[9] Dissatisfied with continuing instability caused by constant clashes between the warlords who had overthrown the government, the CIA and the Pakistani intelligence services began to finance and train – the Taliban, of all people! This support continued uninterrupted until the Taliban took power in 1996 and all the way through to 2001. After 9/11, the US restored its favour to the Northern Alliance and the warlords in its effort to overthrow the Taliban. But their new allies – that is, their old Cold War allies – are very much the equal of the Taliban as regards human rights violations and oppression of women (see questions 6 and 7).

SECTION 2: AFTER FIVE YEARS OF FOREIGN MILITARY INTERVENTION IN AFGHANISTAN, WHAT IS THE SITUATION?

We do not deny that some groups of Afghan citizens may have experienced improved living standards; for example, there appears to be expanded access to education for girls in Kabul, and local development projects have been carried out in certain villages and neighbourhoods.

But in Afghanistan, if the reports of the Senlis Council,[10] WOMANKIND Worldwide, and Afghan member of parliament Malalai Joya are to be believed, the general situation has not improved, in stark contrast to the public statements of the occupying powers (including Canada).

In addition, even if living standards had improved for everyone, one would still have to ponder the objectives of the foreign intervention. Is it a matter of installing a local government favourable to Western (and particularly US) interests or of genuinely supporting Afghan self-determination? If the first of these is true, the intervention would not be justifiable even if it led to short-term improvements.

QUESTION 5: Has the foreign intervention contributed to democracy building in Afghanistan?

The voter turnout rate in the Fall 2004 presidential elections was high, around 75%. According to the Senlis Council, polls showed that people wanted to give Hamid Karzai a chance and to see if the central government would improve their daily lives. As well, the

Northern Alliance and the other warlords had no particular stake in these elections, since the president's authority did not extend beyond Kabul and their regional interests were not threatened.

But the parliamentary elections of September 2005 were an entirely different matter. According to the 2006 report of Human Rights Watch (HRW),[11] the last electoral campaign was marked by a very low turnout rate (only 36% in Kabul) and by much intimidation of voters and candidates. More than half the members of the new parliament are linked to armed groups or have a history of human rights violations. When MP Malalai Joya, from the conservative province of Farah, denounced this result in parliament she received over 100 death threats for her pains. She claims that 70% of the parliament is composed of warlords and their agents. With results like these and no improvement in rural living conditions, the rural population rapidly became disenchanted. Speaking before the NDP Federal Convention in September 2006, Joya said:

The US government did remove the medieval-minded regime of Taliban and their al Qaeda masters. But instead they brought back the "Northern Alliance" to power who are brothers-in-creed of the Taliban and as brutal and anti-democracy as Taliban and even worse.

   … Kathy Gannon, an expert in Afghanistan justly states that "the US is not interested in peace in Afghanistan. The people who killed thousands, who patronized the drug business are in charge of the country."

   … [The] US can work with pro-American fundamentalists, but oppose only anti-American fundamentalists. This is the reason that people make mockery of the "war on terror."

   … Hope you have realized from the small parts of problems that I just shared, that my country is still in chains of bloody and terrorist fundamentalists. The situation in Afghanistan and conditions of its ill-fated women will never change positively, as long as the warlords are not disarmed and both the pro-US and anti-US terrorists are removed from the political scene of Afghanistan.[12]

QUESTION 6: Has the human rights situation improved?

One cannot seriously claim a significant improvement in the human rights situation in a country where notorious criminals sit in parliament with impunity and prisoners are tortured.

In March 2006, Amnesty International (AI) launched a worldwide campaign against torture and ill-treatment in the "war on terror." Concerning Afghanistan, the organization wrote:

Since 2001, thousands of Afghans and some non-Afghans have been arbitrarily detained, held incommunicado (without access to the outside world) and subjected to torture and other cruel, inhuman or degrading treatment or punishment by US forces and by armed groups acting under US control ...

Amnesty International is not aware of any investigations by the Afghan government into cases of deaths in US custody. Nor is the organization aware of any efforts by the Afghan government to put an end to torture and ill-treatment by individuals – including members of armed Afghan groups – working under the control of US forces in Afghanistan ...[13]

Likewise, the 2006 HRW report indicates that groups allied with the United States, today well represented in the Afghan parliament, are largely responsible for human rights violations:

Despite the insurgency's growing strength, the majority of Afghans cited the numerous regional warlords as the greatest source of insecurity. In some remote areas, there are still no real governmental structures or activity, only abuse and criminal enterprises by warlords, many of whom were brought to power with the assistance of the United States after the Taliban's defeat.

Armed clashes between rival factions decreased in 2005, but in many areas warlords and their troops continue to engage in arbitrary arrests, illegal detentions, kidnapping, extortion, torture, murder, extrajudicial killings of criminal suspects, forced displacement, and rape of women, girls, and boys.[14]

Malalai Joya makes a related point:

President Hamid Karzai, instead of relying on people to bring the criminal warlords to trial, appoints these criminals to higher posts. For instance, this year he appointed 13 former commanders with links to drug smuggling, organized crime and illegal militias to senior positions in the police force.[15]

And here is Christine Delphy on the relationship between this war and human rights progress:

Wars waged for purposes of control and exploitation will never advance human rights. This bombing in the name of civilisation has also consigned to oblivion many of the principles on which that civilisation prides itself. The allies, complicit first in the slaughter of Mazar-i-Sharif and other crimes[16] and now in the US manoeuvres, have disregarded the Geneva Conventions. The US is inventing new pseudo-legal categories, such as the "unlawful combatants" of Guantanamo Bay, who are not covered by any form of law – national or international, common law or the rules of war. The freedom of the individual, pride of our democracies, is a dead letter, international law mortally wounded, the great body of the United Nations in its death throes. Only genuine and peaceful cooperation between nations will advance human rights and that is not on the agenda. It is up to us to put it there.[17]

QUESTION 7: Has there been any progress on the status of women? Can the occupation of Afghanistan be justified by the need to protect women's rights?

A war to liberate Afghan women? A concern for women's fate under the Taliban has been invoked in hindsight by the occupation forces to justify their bombardments, their war, and their presence in the country. "The American flag flies again over our embassy in Kabul ... today women are free," declared Georges W. Bush in January 2002, several weeks after bombardments by the "coalition against terrorism" had hounded these oppressors of women out of power. "The 'coalition against terrorism' went to war to liberate Afghan women ... Strange reasoning. The Mujahedin now restored to power by the allies are no better than the Taliban ..."[18]

    In March 2003 on International Women's Day, the Canadian organization Rights and Democracy wrote the following to US Secretary of State Colin Powell: "Warlordism threatens the security and stability of the entire country, as well as the fundamental human rights of women, who continue to suffer under renewed discriminatory edicts imposed by powerful provincial warlords, echoing the Taliban-era repression of women." In December 2002, Human Rights Watch reported some troubling facts that led the organization to conclude: "Warlords have replaced the Taliban with similar attitudes toward women."

US WARMAKING AND WOMEN'S RIGHTS:
A HISTORICAL PRIMER

Few governments have women's interests at heart. "The United States doesn't give a damn for women's rights in Afghanistan, Kuwait, Saudi Arabia or anywhere else. On the contrary, it has knowingly and deliberately sacrificed Afghan women to its own interests. What is the origin of the Mujahedin? Back in 1978, even before the Soviet invasion, the tribal chiefs and religious authorities declared a holy war on Nur Mohammed Taraki's Marxist government, which had decreed that girls were to go to school and prohibited the levirat[19] and the sale of women. Never were there so many women doctors, teachers and lawyers as there were between 1978 and 1992."[20]

An awareness of the pall likely to be cast on women's rights did not give the United States any qualms about backing the Mujahedin against the local and Soviet communists. And when the Communists were gone, to quell the chronic instability caused by fighting between warlords, the US did not hesitate to back the Taliban: "The ground was well prepared for the arrival of the Taliban, spiritual heirs to the Mujahedin. They were equally anti-Communist and even more fundamentalist."[21]

From 1996 to the fall of the Taliban in September 2001, the United States and its NATO allies did nothing to protect Afghan women. On the contrary, this was up to the women themselves, along with NGOs and feminists from around the world. There were constant protests, calls for international action, and even clandestine efforts to help Afghan women.

Western governments turned a blind eye to women's suffering in Afghanistan until the events of 9/11 provided a pretext to redress the Taliban's obstinate refusal to deliver the proposed trans-Afghan natural gas pipeline into the hands of US interests. Suddenly, the Bushes of this world were listening to Afghan women; suddenly, the leaders of the "Axis of Good" were commenting on the atrocities. The US-led anti-terrorism coalition came up with a new regime-change scenario: back the Northern Alliance against the Taliban. What does a cynical game of musical chairs like this have to do with Afghan women's interests?

Improvements in the status of Afghan women after five years of occupation, girls' access to education and women's participation in politics, are often presented as major achievements of the foreign intervention. These achievements have indeed been targeted by the Tal-

iban and other Afghan forces, with the burning of several schools
and the assassination, on 25 September 2006, of Safia Ama Jan, a
feminist activist and provincial director of the Ministry of Women's
Affairs in Kandahar.

There has unquestionably been some progress. The situation
under the Taliban was so horrible that any progress, however minimal, is a significant gain. Some women, mainly in Kabul, have gone
back to school, some have found jobs with NGOs, and a few have
traded the *burqa* for the *chador*. Article 22 of the Afghan constitution recognizes gender equality; women make up more than 25% of
parliamentarians (a constitutionally enshrined quota); a working
group on violence against women was formed by presidential decree
after a long campaign by the Ministry of Women's Affairs and the
United Nations Development Fund for Women (UNIFEM); the legal
age for marriage was set at 16 for girls and 18 for boys; and so forth.
But, according to WOMANKIND Worldwide,[22] this progress is on
paper only.

Rigorous analysis of the situation shows that the status of women
in Afghanistan is just as problematic as it was under the Taliban, and
that the mechanisms set up by the new government not only reinforce
patriarchy, but also keep women subjugated. In its 30 May 2005 report, *Afghanistan: Women Still Under Attack – a Systematic Failure
to Protect*, Amnesty International (AI) writes:

Husbands, brothers and fathers are the main perpetrators of violence in the
home but the social control and the power that they exercise is reinforced by
the authorities, whether of the state or from informal justice systems ...

Violence against women is widely tolerated by the community and widely
practiced. It is tolerated at the highest levels of government and judiciary.
Abusers are rarely prosecuted; if cases are prosecuted, the accused are often
exonerated or punished lightly. Impunity seems to exist for such violence.
The authorities seldom carry out investigations into complaints of violent attacks, rape, murders or suicides of women.[23]

More recently, WOMANKIND Worldwide issued a devastating
verdict on the NATO forces, who are supposed to be restoring peace
and security to the country and protecting women's rights. It stated
that:

• Violence of all kinds is on the rise, including:

crimes of honour;
murders of women aid workers;
attacks on women elections workers;
perpetuation of severe forms of domestic abuse;
trafficking and prostitution;
"astronomical" rise in cases of self-immolation;
high rates of child marriage;
kidnapping of young women;
minimal protection from rape and assault.

• The WOMANKIND Worldwide Report summarizes the situation as follows: "The true scale of violence experienced by women has not been reported in the Western media, precisely at a time when interest (and therefore funding) in Afghanistan is beginning to steadily dissipate."
• The Ministry of Women's Affairs operates at low capacity and with minimal influence on government policy; most women's aid programs have not achieve their objectives.
• The practical needs of women and girls, such as access to clean water, education, healthcare and livelihoods, remain unmet.
• Even more troubling, the security situation in several provinces is worse than it was under the Taliban in 2001: "Insecurity remains the overwhelming challenge characterizing all aspects of daily life for Afghan women. Alongside insecurity is grinding poverty, the two perpetuating each other."
• "The failure of the realization of international standards of human rights for Afghan women, at its root, is about the lack of rule of law in Afghanistan." Traditional law continues to dominate the legal system, a situation more or less unchallenged by the central government.

The Report concludes: "It is imperative that the media, donor governments, international organizations and the Afghan government acknowledge the lack of progress in the domain of women's rights and immediately take action in key areas (education, legal system, security services, healthcare, and livelihoods) to transform paper rights to rights in practice."

Malalai Joya speaks in similar terms:

I must tell you that unfortunately there has been no fundamental change in the plight of Afghan people. When the entire nation is living under the shadow of gun and warlordism, how can its women enjoy very basic freedoms? Unlike the propaganda raised by certain Western media, Afghan women and men are not "liberated" at all.

... Suicide among Afghan women is increasing rapidly; according to a recent UNIFEM survey, 65% of the 50,000 widows in Kabul see suicide as the only option to get rid of their miseries and desolation and that a majority of Afghan women are victims of mental and sexual violence.

... Under the Taliban, the vice and virtue department became a notorious symbol of arbitrary abuses, particularly against Afghan women and girls but today the Afghan cabinet once again decides to reestablish this dreadful department instead of focusing on more acute needs of Afghan society.

... Those who speak for justice are threatened with death; on May 7, 2006, I was physically attacked by pro-warlord and drug-lord MPs in the parliament just for speaking the truth – crimes of Northern Alliance. One of them even shouted "prostitute, take and rape her!"[24]

CAN THE NATO-LED WAR IN AFGHANISTAN BE JUSTIFIED IN THE NAME OF WOMEN'S RIGHTS?

We don't think so. Regime change is not enough. What is needed to achieve *de facto* and *de jure* equality between women and men is a profound transformation of Afghan society – something no army in the world can accomplish.

We do not believe that women's status can genuinely improve in a country at war and under foreign occupation, in which soldiers fire at anything that moves, women and children included, on the pretext that Taliban fighters are hiding behind every civilian; in a country where the modest homes and meagre subsistence livelihoods of ordinary people are often destroyed by "counterinsurgency" operations or brutal poppy eradication campaigns.

We think that the presence of NATO forces is contributing to the popularity of the Taliban, making them into heroes in the eyes of some, and confirming to the majority of men that they have a right to dominate women.

We do not think that it is up to the Western powers to impose their conception of women's liberation in the name of some Western civilizing mission, as past colonial governments forcibly unveiled Arab women in Algeria and banned *sati*[25] in India.

We think that it is up to Afghan women to secure their own liberation. They need our solidarity, not our weapons.

We should listen to feminist voices that have spoken up against "humanitarian wars" fought in the name of women's rights – voices like those of Christine Delphy and Malalai Joya:

Even if a greater measure of freedom were to be won, would that make the war right? When it comes to human rights, the question is whether anything can be worse than war. At what point does war become the best option? To say that the war may be good for Afghan women is almost to say that it is better for them to die in the bombing, cold or starvation than to live under the Taliban. The West has decided that death is preferable to slavery – for Afghan women. This would be a truly heroic decision if Western lives, not those of Afghan women, were in the balance.

The cynical way in which the "liberation of Afghan women" has been used as a pretext shows the arrogance of the West in assuming the right to do as it will with the lives of others. That arrogance informs the Western attitude towards Afghan women and the attitude of rulers to their subjects.

Let us propose a simple rule of international, and individual, conduct: no one shall have the right to take decisions, especially heroic decisions, when others have to suffer the consequences. Only those who pay the price of war can say whether it is worth it. In this case, those who decided on war are not paying the price and those who are paying the price had no part in the decision. At present the women of Afghanistan are on the road, living in tents or camps, in the millions. There are a million more refugees outside the country than there were before the war and a million displaced persons in the country itself.[26] Many may die and there is no guarantee that their sacrifice will win them any additional rights. Is it, in any case, proper to speak of sacrifice when they had no choice?

The allies should, in common decency, stop proclaiming that these women are being forced to endure all this suffering for their own good, and pretending that they are being denied the right to decide their own fate, even the right to live, in the name of freedom. But there is reason to fear that this theme is a real hit. There is a long list of countries to which the coalition against evil has vowed to bring good. And of course, any resemblance to past history (events too remote to mention) or colonial wars is pure coincidence.[27]

Christine Delphy

The Canadian policy-makers must know that warlords of the Northern Alliance are equally responsible for the plight of Afghan people and the current tragedy in Afghanistan.

I am well aware of the hardships, challenges, and death from anti-democracy forces, but I trust my people. One day they may kill me as they have guns and power and support of the US government, but they can never silence my voice and hide the truth.

Malalai Joya September 9, 2006

QUESTION 8: Is Afghanistan a more stable country since 2001? Has the security situation improved?

Security in Afghanistan is worse than it has ever been, with a growing number of civilian victims and a much higher number of attacks against foreign troops, including Canadian troops, who have been fighting in Kandahar since February 2006.[28] All serious observers agree that the resistance is on the rise and engaging in new tactics. The influence of the Taliban is growing in the south and southeast and they have created alliances with other nationalists and tribal forces against the occupation. In the rest of the country, regional commanders (warlords) have consolidated their power by usurping the political process and controlling the drug trade. Peacebuilding is nowhere in sight; on the contrary, Afghanistan appears to be settling in for a long war and the number of foreign soldiers is reaching new heights.[29]

Since the overthrow of the Taliban – who had eradicated poppy growing in the areas under their control – Afghanistan is once again the world's largest supplier of illegal opium (90% of world production, according to the UN). The drug trade is the most flourishing industry. While the United States has allied itself with drug barons in the northern and central parts of the country, who are well represented in the Afghan parliament, it has used a brutal military approach to eradicating poppy growing by peasants in the south and southeast, for whom this represents a livelihood. The results of this military campaign are disastrous, with thousands of hungry refugees crowded into 10–15 camps in the provinces of Helmand and Kandahar; popular resentment against foreign troops is growing, and new support for the resistance is appearing every day.

QUESTION 9: Is the foreign intervention in Afghanistan helping to fight terror and reduce the danger of attacks against Canada?

Before answering this question directly, we want to dissociate ourselves from the propagandistic use of the word "terror" in the everyday discourse of politicians and the Western media. For one thing, we do not feel it is fair to automatically apply the word "terrorism" to any armed resistance against foreign military occupation, ours included. For another, we want to dissociate ourselves from the selective use of a term that never seems to apply to what our own armies do. In our view, "shock and awe" campaigns, missile showers, the use of cluster and phosphorus bombs, napalm, depleted uranium weapons, and all the rest have caused "collateral damage" amounting to tens if not hundreds of times as many civilian victims as the tragic attacks on New York, Madrid, and London. These, too, are acts of terrorism.

Having made this distinction, we believe that the impact of the foreign military occupations of Afghanistan and Iraq is diametrically opposed to what they claim to achieve.

The inevitable brutality of these interventions is bound to raise the ire of the civilian population against foreign troops, making more and more people join the resistance and carry out attacks. This implacable logic has not escaped the military command itself, as witness this quote from Canadian Major General Andrew Leslie, explaining that Canada's military intervention in Afghanistan could last twenty years: "Every time you kill an angry young man overseas, you're creating fifteen more who will come after you." A similarly revealing statement was made by British Chief of Staff General Dannatt to the effect that the presence of British soldiers in Iraq only exacerbates security problems rather than solving them.[30]

In ideological terms, the foreign military occupation is clearly giving a boost to religious fundamentalism in both Afghanistan and Iraq. And what about possible terrorist attacks against Canada? Canada's military intervention in Afghanistan appears to be making these more probable; at least, that is the opinion of the majority of the Canadian public, and even of the Canadian Security Intelligence Service (CSIS):

Finally, it is worth remembering that Canada was specifically mentioned by Osama bin Laden as being among the "designated targets" for terrorist action because of our role in Afghanistan after 9/11.[31]

SECTION 3: THE REAL REASON FOR THE WAR: EXPANSION OF
THE US EMPIRE

QUESTION 10 : What are the real reasons for instigating the war in
Afghanistan and, more generally, the "war on terrorism?"

The war in Afghanistan has both immediate and strategic objectives:

• Immediate objective: to overthrow a government hostile to the
United States and put into place an Afghan government favourable
to US interests in the region.

   The Taliban refused, among other things, to grant the construction of the trans-Afghan natural gas pipeline between Turkmenistan
and Pakistan to US interests, i.e. to UNOCAL, of which President
Hamid Karzai had been a consultant. According to Michael Meacher, who was Minister of the Environment in the Blair administration
from May 1997 to June 2003, the United States was already contem-
plating a military intervention against Afghanistan before September
11, 2001:

The BBC reported (September 18, 2001) that Niaz Niak, a former Pakistan
foreign secretary, was told by senior American officials at a meeting in Berlin
in mid-July 2001 that "military action against Afghanistan would go ahead
by the middle of October." Until July 2001 the US government saw the Taliban regime as a source of stability in Central Asia that would enable the construction of hydrocarbon pipelines from the oil and gas fields in Turkmenistan, Uzbekistan, Kazakhstan, through Afghanistan and Pakistan, to
the Indian Ocean. But, confronted with the Taliban's refusal to accept US
conditions, the US representatives told them "either you accept our offer of
a carpet of gold, or we bury you under a carpet of bombs" (Inter Press Service, November 15, 2001).[32]

   On December 27, 2002, an agreement was finally signed between
Hamid Karzai and Turkmeni and Pakistani government representatives: a $3.2 billion project!

• Strategic objectives: to install US military bases not only in
Afghanistan but also in several other countries in Central Asia,
through which the United States can "project its strength" in the entire region (formerly the exclusive domain of the Soviet Union, situ-

ated in China's backyard). Currently, for example, while the Bush administration's tone against Iran becomes shriller, the United States army can rely on military bases on either side of that country.

With respect to the "war on terrorism" more generally, this is how we see things.[33]

- After the end of the Cold War, natural resources and regional markets, which were previously under the control or influence of the Soviet Union, "opened up" to the cupidity of the world's major economic powers: the United States, Europe, Japan and China, as well as Russia, which tried to maintain as much influence as it could.
- Economic competition is intense and the United States cannot be certain of dominating the world economy. US military superiority, on the other hand, is unrivalled and uncontested, so the temptation to gain through force of arms what cannot be won through purely economic competition is very strong. Control of access to Iraqi oil is the most notable recent example of this.
- The neo-conservative ideologues of the Project for a New American Century clearly sensed the key role US military supremacy would play in carrying out their "project." In *Rebuilding America's Defenses*,[34] they wrote that the United States must dramatically increase military spending so as to make it impossible for other countries to catch up, thus placing the US in a position to be able to lead major wars on several fronts at the same time. There was only one problem: without a new Pearl Harbour, the US population would never be willing to accept such a major reallocation of resources to the military. The September 11 attacks then took place, providing the ideal pretext for inflating military expenses to an incredible extent in order to wage "endless war" against the forces of the Axis of Evil.
- This very real war, in which our government is sinking more and more public resources, is accompanied by a whole series of so-called "security" or "anti-terrorist" measures and laws which severely undermine civil liberties and put in jeopardy fundamental principles of justice such as the presumption of innocence, the right to a fair trial, the prohibition against torture.[35]
- The war is also fought in the area of language, creating new expressions which attempt to justify flagrant violations of international law, civil liberties and the principles of fundamental justice: "preventative war," "enemy combatant," "Islamo-fascism." In order to make people forget that this war kills and wounds a great number of

civilians who are bystanders to the conflict, the official accounts of military operations speak only of killing "terrorists," "insurgents" or "Taliban." In Afghanistan, the dead are invariably referred to as "Taliban."

In short, the "war on terrorism" is the smokescreen used to obscure the current thrust of US imperial expansionism, principally through force of arms. According to our analysis, the war in Afghanistan was the official opening volley of this "endless war" and should certainly not be disassociated from it .

SECTION 4: CANADA'S INTERVENTION IN AFGHANISTAN AND THE "WAR ON TERRORISM"

QUESTION 11: How has Canada participated in these wars since they began?

Since October 2001, Canadian participation in the war in Afghanistan and in the "war on terror" has been more extensive, and often more offensive, than most people realize. Canada has participated in a number of missions or operations: Apollo, Altair, Sirius, Athena, Archer, Argus, and others. According to information available on the *Canadian Armed Forces* (CAF) website, "since October 2001, Canada has deployed 22 warships and more than 18,000 Army, Navy, and Air Force personnel in the international campaign against terrorism." The Polaris Institute in Ottawa estimates that to date (recall that this document was written in 2006) Canada has spent approximately $4.1 billion on all of these operations. What follows is some information about the biggest operations (Apollo, Athéna, Archer, Task Force Afghanistan) the CAF have participated in:

• Operation Apollo (October 2001 to December 2003): Approximately three weeks after the September 11 attacks, on October 4, 2001, Article 5 of the North Atlantic Treaty (the Treaty of Washington) was invoked under which "… an armed attack against one or more of them [NATO countries] in Europe or North America shall be considered an attack against them all." Three days later, Operation Apollo was set up to support the American Operation Enduring Freedom, to which Canada committed a large number of naval, air and land forces.

Naval forces included several Canadian frigates deployed in the Arab-Persian Gulf for 6-month periods; at the height of the mission, in January 2002, "the Canadian naval operating group had six warships and approximately 1500 Navy personnel." In February 2003, Canada even took command of the international naval force in the Arab-Persian Gulf.

Air Force involvement included strategic and tactical air transport, long-range patrols and helicopter detachments, most often in direct contact with the naval deployment.

Army forces mainly included (for the first 6 months in 2002) the deployment in Kandahar of approximately 750 soldiers of the 3rd Battalion Princess Patricia's Canadian Light Infantry Battle Group (3 PPCLI) for tasks ranging from airport security to combat, in support of the United States' 187th Brigade Combat Team. Testifying before the Senate on November 19, 2002, Lieutenant-Colonel Pat Stogran, former commander of this Battle Group, stated that:

In addition to our defence of the Kandahar airfield, we embarked on three large-scale, battalion-sized offensive operations in pursuit of the al Qaeda, one such operation being the first combat air assault in the history of the Canadian army into the Sha I Kot Valley, in March 2002. Sub-elements of the battle group also conducted numerous operations of smaller scale, both defensive and offensive in nature.[36]

The return to Canada of Canadian soldiers was coordinated with the planned rotation of American troops, which meant using United States air transport resources. It should be noted that the CAF members assigned to Operation Apollo reported to the commander of Canadian Joint Task Force South West Asia (CA JTFSWA) whose headquarters is the Canadian National Command Element (NCE), which has about forty members and is stationed with the ... US Central Command (CENTCOM) at MacDill Air Force Base, in Florida.

• Operation Athena (August 2003 to November 2005): deployment of a major contingent to Kabul – five successive six-month rotations, involving a total of 6,000 soldiers – as part of the International Security Assistance Force (ISAF), which is under NATO authority. From February to August 2004, Rick Hillier, the Canadian Chief of Staff of Joint Operations, was in command of ISAF, which at the time had 6,500 soldiers from 35 countries, with the largest contingent composed of 2,000 Canadian soldiers. It is important to remember that this major Canadian military deployment had been announced in February 2003, when the United States was preparing to launch its war against Iraq. By providing major support to the United States on another war front, this seemed to compensate for the fact that Prime Minister Jean Chrétien was about to announce that Canada would not participate in the invasion of Iraq. On November 29, 2005 the last Canadian materiel in Kabul were transferred to Kandahar and Camp Julien was officially handed over to the Afghan Defence Ministry.

• Operation Archer and Task Force Afghanistan: From February 2006 to July 31, 2006, under Operation Archer, more than 2,000 CAF troops were deployed in southern Afghanistan, in the Kandahar region, where they once again came under the command of the United States' Operation Enduring Freedom, as was the case with Operation Apollo. ISAF, however, whose mission at first was to ensure security only in the Kabul region, had had its mission gradually expanded to cover the 13 provinces of the North, West and now the South of Afghanistan. Since the end of July 2006, Canada's 2300 soldiers in Afghanistan have once again come under ISAF. This change in command structure, from Enduring Freedom to ISAF – doesn't change anything in the direct combat role that is now the main task of Canadian soldiers in the Kandahar region. In September 2006, NATO asked its member states to increase their resources in ISAF, and Canada announced that it would send 125 more soldiers (from the Valcartier base in Quebec, which provided most of the soldiers deployed in the summer of 2007).

QUESTION 12: Hasn't Canada's participation been constructive, since it was part of NATO's International Security Assistance Force, which was authorized by the Security Council?

ISAF's mandate, until it was expanded to the southern provinces (Kandahar and Helmand), was essentially a "stabilization" and "security" mandate that did not include "anti-insurgency," brush clearing activities, or confrontation with armed opposition forces, including Taliban and others. Canadian military operations were mostly policing (such as patrols or training of Afghan security forces). It wasn't until the start of 2006, while Canadian troops were deployed in Southern Afghanistan, that they took on an overtly offensive role directly under the command of the US Operation Enduring Freedom.[37]

In light of the increasing number of casualties among Canadian soldiers, and of concerns expressed by the public, many voices, both in Canada and abroad, blamed the new situation on the change of command. These voices called for the Canadian intervention to revert to the authority of ISAF, and for NATO to assume command of operations in southern Afghanistan. These analysts present the mandate as having two different approaches – "anti-insurgency" vs. "stabilization and security." On the one hand there is the American approach, brutal and destined to fail; the other approach, European and Canadian, is less aggressive, more focused on help and development, and more likely to succeed. Without calling for the withdrawal of the Canadian troops, these analysts would like to see a return to the original mandate.

The reality of operations command offers no hope of this happening. In fact, in the summer of 2006, command passed from Operation Enduring Freedom to ISAF, without any change in the mandate of the Canadian troops and their combat operations in the Kandahar region. Moreover, this had been predicted in the House of Commons by the Conservative Minister of Defence, Gordon O'Connor.

Furthermore, the different methods applied from the start in Central and Northern Afghanistan, and especially in Kabul, do not really represent different approaches, but different contexts. In Kabul, the Hamid Karzai government and foreign forces have long met with little resistance, which is not the case in the south, where tasks and methods were therefore different, more "constabulary" than "anti-insurgency." As resistance increases in Kabul, and this has already started, the blind and brutal methods will begin again, because that is the usual evolution of foreign military occupations. For the defenders of the American war agenda, these two approaches are complementary, rather than contradictory. Among the four main challenges identified by the Project for a New American Century (PNAC) in their report, *Rebuilding America's Defences,* is the capacity to conduct several major wars simultaneously, as well as the necessity of taking on the "policing operations" that these wars entail. At first, NATO's role in Afghanistan was limited to the latter tasks, but that no longer seems to be the case.

We believe that the distinction made by some analysts between the motivations and methods of the United States and those of NATO can be misleading. NATO's intervention in Afghanistan has been placed under the command of the "Supreme commander of the allied forces in Europe" who is traditionally appointed by the United States. This command's mission is to support the United States' objectives in 93 countries in Europe, Africa and the Middle East. Until recently, the "supreme commander" was General James L. Jones, of the Marine Corps, who directed operations in Vietnam, in Bosnia and in Iraq. His designated successor is General Bantz Craddock, who was the main military adjutant for Secretary of Defence Donald Rumsfeld, from 2002 to 2004, before being named Chief of Southern Command (the Caribbean and Latin America) for the United States army, where he supervised the prison in Guantanamo Bay, which he has always defended against critics.

As we indicated in answering question 3, we believe that by not denouncing the war and by accepting the American intervention in Afghanistan as a *fait accompli,* the Security Council did not uphold the Charter of the United Nations. Authorizing ISAF and NATO's command of that force are part of this breach.

QUESTION 13: Did the 2006 election of the Conservative government in Ottawa lead to the change in the mandate of the Canadian Armed Forces in Afghanistan?

No. Moving the mission of the Canadian troops from Kabul to Kandahar was a decision of Paul Martin's Liberal government.

Overall, since the early 1990s, there has been a major change in the international role as well as a progressive integration of the Canadian army with that of the United States and its offensive operations around the world. This has happened without public debate and, to a large extent, without public awareness. It was hastened following the attacks of September 11, 2001, but only made official in 2005 with the Martin government's International Policy Statement (IPS), whose "3D" approach, linking diplomacy, defence and development, marked the new militaristic turn in Canadian foreign policy.[38] Afterwards, of course, the minority Conservative government raised the stakes in this new orientation, and under its mandate, the result of this change has become obvious. But it didn't instigate the change.

• Even if it seems paradoxical, the role of the Canadian army abroad has become increasingly combative since the end of the Cold War:
    • quasi-secret participation of the Canadian Air Force in the last two weeks of the Gulf War bombings in 1991;

• open participation of the Canadian Navy in the maritime blockade of Iraq;[39]
• participation in the intervention in Somalia, where Canadian soldiers tortured a young Somali to death;
• Canadian Air Force participation in the 78 days of NATO bombings of Yugoslavia in 1999;
• participation in the bombings and the land force invasion of Afghanistan in 2001.

Without actually expressing it as a doctrine, for over 15 years, Canada has generally chosen to participate in the military interventions of the world's only superpower.

• After the end of the Cold War, military budgets declined until 1998–1999, and then rapidly increased[40] following recriminations from the military, political and economic *milieux;* complaints about "our army" no longer having the means to accomplish its role were heard, without any debate about this role, which was changing radically.
• In 2005, Paul Martin's Liberal government announced the largest increase in the Canadian military budget since the Second World War: an increase of $12.8 billion over 5 years. That same year, the Martin government's International Policy Statement (IPS) indicated that this money would be used to increase regular forces by 5,000 soldiers, and reserve forces by 3,000 soldiers, as well as to purchase various equipment that would double the Canadian army's rapid intervention capacity abroad.[41] In July 2005, it was announced that Canadian troops in Afghanistan would be moved from Kabul to Kandahar, and that in February 2006, 1,400 additional soldiers would be sent to this area. This news was accompanied by statements from the new Chief of Defence Staff Rick Hillier, who was happy to be able to hunt down the terrorist "scumbags" and finally see the Canadian army play its true role of "being able to kill people."
• Since it came to power, the minority Conservative government has announced military expenditures of $5.3 billion, in addition to the $12.8 billion announced by the Liberal government in 2005. The goal is to recruit 13,000 additional regular forces soldiers and 10,000 additional reserve forces. As well, in 2006, the Senate Standing Committee on National Security and Defence – mostly composed of Liberal senators – recommended practically doubling the Canadian military budget to $25 and even $35 billion a year!

• It was only recently that people in Canada learned of a major change in the role of the Canadian army abroad, but the change is even more profound than most people might suspect. On August 31, 1999, 1,149 Canadian soldiers were participating in official UN peacekeeping missions around the world. This represented 10.6% of the 10,801 peacekeepers in 11 different missions. Fifteen years later, on August 31, 2006, only 56 Canadian soldiers were participating in UN peacekeeping missions, representing only 0.08% of the 66,786 peacekeepers deployed in 16 different missions, while international demand continues to rise:[42] in other words, 6 to 7 times more peacekeepers internationally than there were 15 years earlier, and Canada contributed one twentieth of what it used to!

• This change in the role of the Canadian army in the world, and the higher participation in wars alongside the U.S. army, are accompanied by increasing integration of the Canadian army with the US army, in terms of both equipment and military training and command. Even when the Chrétien government decided that Canada "would not participate" in the war against Iraq, Canadian soldiers were closely linked to the planning for this war at the US Central Command base at MacDill Air Force Base, in Florida, and later in Qatar; and in 2004, Canadian Brigadier General Walt Natynczyk was the second in command of all American occupation troop in Iraq.

QUESTION 14: Notwithstanding government propaganda, what are the true motives of Canada's participation in the war in Afghanistan?

The Canadian army was sent into this war without public or parliamentary debate. We believe that this initial decision as well as the decision to further increase the role of the Canadian army in Afghanistan is based on a two-level dynamic: the progressive deepening of the economic, ideological and military partnership with the United States; and the immediate profits to be made by a certain number of corporations in Canada.

DEEPENING THE CANADA-UNITED STATES PARTNERSHIP

Remember that following the end of the Cold War, the United States launched a war against Iraq (1991) and proclaimed the dawn of a "new world order" – an order characterized by championing neo-liberal globalization and a more bellicose foreign policy. Pressures then increased on allied countries to adopt the same "threat analysis," and participate in US military interventions. In answering the previous question, we outlined the progressive transformation of Canadian foreign policy and the corresponding change in the role of the Canadian forces – changes that have been made without public debate.

The day after the attacks of September 11, 2001, George W. Bush declared "either you are with us or you are with the terrorists." Moreover, the former American ambassador to Canada, Paul Celluci, revealed that the only guideline he had received upon taking up his post in 2001 was to ensure that Canadian military expenditures increased very significantly. He repeated to anyone who listened that the United States believed "security to be more important than commerce."

The message was clear: if Canada did not adopt the same "security" agenda as the United States, commercial relations between the two nations could suffer. Within this context, economic and political leaders in Canada decided to do everything to keep their access to the United States market, including identifying more closely with the "war on terrorism." In January 2003, the Canadian Council of Chief Executives (CCCE)[43] launched its *North American Security and Prosperity Initiative* in which it takes a position favouring the "intelligent border," the secure supply of Canadian energy resources to the United States, ballistic missile defence, increasing military expenditures, as well as the interoperability of Canadian and American armed forces.

In April 2004, in a policy document entitled *New Frontiers: Building a 21st Century Canada-United States Partnership in North America*, the CCCE stated:

In such a world, Canadians must think hard about what we will need to do to defend ourselves. But as global citizens, we also must continue to think about how we can contribute effectively to peace and security around the world. The way that we and other countries respond to the relentless threat of terrorism and rogue states has vital implications for global economic growth just as it does for Canada's future both as a trade-dependent economy and an immigrant-based society. In short, for Canada and for the world as a whole, economic security and physical security have become inseparable.

When the pressure of public opinion forces the Government of Canada to take decisions that do not please the Bush administration, it tries to compensate by intensifying Canadian military participation in Afghanistan. An early instance of this saw Brian Tobin, a former federal minister and premier of Newfoundland, writing a letter to the *Globe and Mail* (February 5, 2003) just as Prime Minister Chrétien was about to announce that Canada would not participate in the invasion of Iraq:

The US needs to free up key logistical and military assets on the ground in Afghanistan for the coming campaign in Iraq. Canada can, and should, offer to fill the gap.

One week later, Ottawa announced that Canada would take command of the International Security Assistance Force (ISAF) and send 2000 soldiers to Afghanistan.

A second example occurred shortly after Prime Minister Paul Martin's announcement that Canada would not participate in "ballistic missile defence." On March 21, 2005, there was a meeting of his most senior ministers, PMO officials, and General Rick Hillier, the recently appointed Chief of Defence Staff. Hillier proposed that Canada deploy 1,000 soldiers in Kandahar under the authority of the US Operation Enduring Freedom. Faced with reservations, Hillier traded on the Martin government's desire to be a player on the international stage alongside the United States. Scott Reid, Paul Martin's communications director, stated:

There was a strong current [within the Department of Foreign Affairs] that evaluated our strategic interests as a function of our relationship with the United States. Often, policy was presented to us with the proviso that 'this issue is important for the White House.' And what is important for the White House cannot be taken lightly, because the people there will take it personally ...[44]

In Canada, the government cannot publicly state that the reason for its military involvement in Afghanistan is that it wishes a closer partnership with the United States. Yet, in Washington, subway advertisements purchased by the Canadian embassy there push this very message quite clearly among American decision-makers. These ads portray Canadian soldiers in Afghanistan with the following message:

Canadian troops in Kandahar, Afghanistan. Boots on the ground.
U.S.-Canada Relations – Security Is Our Business.

CANADA – US PARTNERSHIP: A BUSINESS OPPORTUNITY

This strategic orientation for an economic and military partnership
with the United States presents golden business opportunities for certain corporations in Canada in the form of military contracts, contracts for the trans-Afghan pipeline or for other projects in the region. Consider two major contracts announced in 2005: first, the
$849 million contract for Bell Helicopter, in Mirabel, for basic as-
sembly of 368 helicopters for the United States army; and the $750
million contract to build new light armoured vehicles. The main contract for the first phase of the latter project, worth $100 million, was
awarded to Oerlikon in Saint-Jean-sur-Richelieu.

Some key sectors of the Canadian economy, such as oil and natural gas, and armaments, have also benefited substantially. In September 2004 and in November 2005, two business delegations from
Western Canada, headed by Jean Chrétien,45 met with President
Niyazov of Turkmenistan. In addition to the trans-Afghan pipeline,
a $3 billion project which, it seems, will be routed through Kandahar,
are the modernizing of the Seyidi refinery and gas exploration in
Turkmenistan. The Seyidi refinery is the second largest in Turkmenistan, and the Israeli company, Merhav, has been invited to set up
a consortium to modernize it: a project worth more than $1.5 billion
US. Canadian companies with interests in this region of the world include PetroKazakhstan,46 Buried Hill Energy and Thermo Design
Engineering.

... AND HUMAN RIGHTS

During his second visit, Mr. Chrétien hailed the immense progress
made by Turkmenistan since its independence. He also stated that
President Niyazov had succeeded in setting up a unique development
model that took into account both the country's enormous potential
and its favourable geopolitical situation.47 Yet, he doesn't seem to
have considered the 2006 report by Human Rights Watch (HRW).
According to HRW, under the late president for life, Saparmurat Ni-
azov, Turkmenistan was one of the most repressive and closed coun-

tries in the world, characterized by backward policies, particularly on culture, education and health. For example, (i) a Turkmeni law equates criticizing any presidential policies with high treason; (ii) the study of the *Ruhnama*, a "new holy book" written by the late President himself, is replacing other disciplines in the school and university curricula; (iii) the President's February 2005 proposal "to close all libraries, with the exception of the central library and those attached to universities." Already, over 100 libraries have been closed.[48]

SECTION 5: WHAT DOES ÉCHEC À LA GUERRE PROPOSE?

Our movement against war and militarism is part of the progressive movements of Canadian civil society and especially of Quebec. Many citizens who have mobilized for this purpose are also involved in various struggles, such as those against neoliberalism, poverty, the oppression of women, racism and other forms of discrimination, and the destruction of our planet.

Although our governments are the product of general elections and claim to act in the people's best interest, our movement must often wage prolonged struggles before the interests and will of the majority are really considered. In these struggles, we even have to counter the disinformation our governments often spread about the human consequences of their projects and policies. If this is our experience here at home on issues that concern us, why should we believe in our governments' professed good intentions regarding wars being waged far from our borders? In examining what we can do as progressive movements, why would we include the government and the Canadian army in this collective "we"? Why would we consider them our partners or, even worse, the agents of our duty to act in solidarity?

QUESTION 15: "Don't we have a responsibility not to abandon the Afghan people and to continue helping them rebuild their country?"

When citizens of good faith ask this question, our first response is to point out the ambiguity of "we." Who are we talking about? About "we" citizens opposed to war ... in partnership with the US Army? Or in a broader partnership with NATO? Or in a more limited partnership with only the Canadian Army? Because, in the final analysis, we are being sold military intervention as a way to "help rebuild."

This is a strange perspective when we recall the words of the Chief of the Defense Staff, Rick Hillier: "We are not the Public Service of Canada. We are not some other department. We are the Canadian Forces and our job is to be able to kill people."[49]

Linking the question of military intervention to reconstruction reveals a lack of knowledge of the reality itself, because in the past five years, the net result of the war and foreign intervention in Afghanistan has not been to help the Afghan people rebuild their country, as the Senlis Council has observed:

Five years of international presence in the country aimed at increasing the living standards of the Afghan population have failed to make any measured improvements in the accessibility and quality of health and educational services in most of Afghanistan, beyond the confines of Kabul.[50]

This isn't surprising when we know that for all foreign interveners, the amounts invested in military spending are ten to fifteen times greater than those allocated to development assistance. This is also true for Canada. In 2006–07, Canadian military intervention in Afghanistan cost $1.4 billion, while $100 million was allocated to "assistance" for that country. Are we rebuilding a little, the better to destroy? When Canadian military officials describe the satisfactory progress of Operation Medusa by explaining that the troops are advancing after intense bombardments, "football field by football field," can we claim to be helping the Afghan people rebuild their country?

We should also ask ourselves serious questions about the real impact and the true nature of the small share of expenditures that goes to "assistance." Here is what Malalai Joya has to say about this:

Ironically, this is happening in a country that has received $12 billion while another $10 billion more were pledged at the London conference last year. But this money will mainly fill the pockets of the warlords to better suppress our nation more severely.

Similar concerns were expressed by Jean Mazurel, French representative of the World Bank in Kabul, in a September 2006 interview with Radio Canada journalist Sylvain Desjardins. He gave the example of a school that would cost $200,000 to build, but for which only $50,000 of the initial budget would be left after all the middlemen took their cut. He also affirmed that a large part of the "assistance" went to pay for expert services and products from the donor countries, without any impact on the population's immediate welfare. In a *Time Magazine* article on May 30, 2006, Rachel Morarjee reported the testimony of a Kabul mechanic to explain why, during the riots in Kabul the previous day, the angry crowd had even looted and burned the offices of NGOs:

People were angry with the NGOs because they are using lots of money for themselves. The only people who get any benefit from them being here are the people who are working for them, said Isatullah, a mechanic.

In conclusion, we will add three points. First, we must mention the fact that the question "Don't we have a responsibility not to abandon the Afghan people and to continue helping them rebuild their country?" often comes out of the mouths of our government officials. Since they aren't really concerned about the plight of people here – and still less about the Afghans – and are diverting the budgets of our social programs to military spending, how dare they lay a guilt trip on the progressive movements of civil society who are fighting every day for people's interests here and abroad?

Secondly, the idea that we are responsible for solving the problems of other societies unfortunately smacks of the colonialism still present in our Western societies.

Finally, we should remember that military intervention is involved. The role of armies isn't to do humanitarian work or to rebuild the countries they occupy. The examples of Iraq and Afghanistan are conclusive on this point! According to the World Bank, it would cost $27.5 billion to rebuild Afghanistan's obsolete and destroyed infrastructure. Yet from 2002 to 2006, the NATO countries – led by the United States – gobbled up more than three times that amount in military spending for Afghanistan. We must reject the 'army/development assistance' and 'army/humanitarian assistance' amalgams, because they are deceitful and in no way produce the promised results. Moreover, this confusion of roles seriously endangers the lives of genuine humanitarian workers by erasing the distinction, in the view of the resistance, between these workers and the military occupation forces. Above all, this confusion of roles is only a way to make war acceptable to the Canadian public, by masking the totally devastating effects it has on the society that suffers it. (See Stephen Cornish article in this book.)

QUESTION 16: Will a withdrawal of Canadian troops from Afghanistan favour the Taliban's return to power? Will it plunge the country into civil war?

It is important to remember two things concerning the Taliban that the supporters of Canadian military intervention in Afghanistan tend to conceal. Interference by the United States in Afghanistan's internal affairs was largely responsible for bringing the Taliban to power and keeping them there. The imperative of preventing the Taliban's return at any price is valid only if the forces currently in power are significantly different, particularly on the issues of religious fundamentalism and respect for human rights, especially women's rights. Yet as we have seen, this isn't really the case.

Obviously we can't predict the future. However, we believe that a solution exists in the short or medium term that would bring peace, democracy and development to a country as poor and as devastated as Afghanistan is today – a country which, over the past three decades, has experienced two foreign invasions and interminable internecine wars, often fuelled by foreign countries. Above all, we do not believe that such a solution can be imposed from outside this society, especially not militarily.

Based on most of the international civilian observers and even on Western military sources, we know that five years of occupation and "reconstruction" have not produced the promised positive results. On the contrary, people in Afghanistan have less and less confidence in the central government and the foreign military forces that support it. The Taliban's influence is rising and they have succeeded in making an alliance with other forces opposed to foreign occupation. The United States and its allies, including Canada, can say that they want to "win hearts and minds" in Afghanistan, but the opposite is what is happening now. And probably the opposite will continue to happen as the number of foreign troops increases and as these troops intensify their brutal and blind oppression of Afghan opponents.

Sooner or later, all the foreign troops currently occupying Afghanistan will leave the country. They will leave because the armed resistance, despite the repression, will have gained in scope and effectiveness, because the Afghans will grant it more support – out of confidence, vexation or fear – and because the citizenry of the occupying powers will be less and less accepting of the human and financial costs associated with military intervention. The question of power in Afghanistan will then be settled according to the balance of forces that exist at that time among the various social, political and military elements of society.

When that time comes, if the Taliban hold military power, they will acquire political power *de facto*. But if they don't, compromise and power-sharing formulas may be possible, finally echoing the wish expressed by the vast majority of people in Afghanistan to put an end to war and the way of arms – unless, ignoring this aspiration, another period of internecine wars begins among the various armed factions. Whichever alternative prevails, we do not believe that the current war between the foreign armies, the Northern Alliance and other warlords, on one side, and the Taliban and their allies, on the other, is of a nature to favour the development of authentically democratic forces in Afghanistan.

The danger, often mentioned, that the withdrawal of foreign troops will result in the outbreak of a civil war, appears to be a hypothetical doom and gloom scenario to make us forget the very real doom and gloom the occupation currently imposes on the people of Afghanistan. It is based on a premise we consider false, namely that maintaining foreign troops in Afghanistan would help mitigate the risk of civil war in that country which it is in fact exacerbating.

The same arguments are resorted to by people in the United States when attempting to justify the continued occupation of Iraq, even by those who consider the initial invasion "an error." Yet, year after year, the number of victims of sectarian attacks and assassinations in Iraq has increased, parallel to the growing number of foreign soldiers killed. In fact, intercommunity attacks in Iraq have reached such proportions that it is perfectly reasonable to talk about civil war, a situation that even then Secretary General of the United Nations, Kofi Annan, publicly acknowledged on December 3, 2006.

Far from being surprising, this is to be expected. The presence of foreign troops in a country they have invaded, far from calming internal divisions, generally exacerbates them and creates a widening gulf between the forces opposing this presence at any price and those allied with or profiting from it one way or another.

QUESTION 17: Why don't we ask for a change of mandate and/or mission for the Canadian troops in Afghanistan?

To understand the situation currently prevailing in Afghanistan, we drew on various sources, including the Senlis Council, WOMANKIND Worldwide, Human Rights Watch and Amnesty International. These organizations, like many others in Quebec, in the rest of Canada and elsewhere, are not necessarily calling for the withdrawal of foreign troops from Afghanistan. Most often, concerning Canadian forces, they call for a review of the troops' role in the sense of "peacekeeping" or "protection of the civilian population." They also sometimes call for the command of foreign troops to be assumed by the United Nations instead of NATO and, in some cases, for replacement of the existing foreign forces with a new military force coming mainly from Muslim countries.

Such proposals generally are based on a desire to move the current situation in the direction of peace and the interests of the Afghan people. They could be pertinent if this really involved peacekeeping and the protection of the civilian population, in a country where the belligerents had at least accepted to observe a ceasefire and negotiate. But foreign invasion, war and military occupation are involved here, which not only make these proposals unrealistic, but also maintain illusions as to the nature of and reasons for Canadian military involvement in Afghanistan.

CHANGE OF MANDATE AND/OR MISSION FOR THE CANADIAN TROOPS

Such a call is unrealistic and maintains illusions because:
- it disregards the concrete conditions on the ground, particularly the resistance;
- it disregards the balance of power within NATO;
- it tends to consider the current mandate to be an aberration;
- it refuses to analyze the reasons for this war beyond the proclaimed intentions.

To expound briefly on each of these aspects:

- It is impossible to call for a change of mandate while disregarding the concrete conditions on the ground. To the extent that it involves deployment of troops in a sector where the local population is suspicious of them, and where armed resistance is intense, the very logic of maintaining this presence makes it necessary to "hunt insurgents," rely on informers, who may have various motives, burst into homes, thereby terrorizing their occupants, carry out military operations aimed at the elimination of armed opponents and resulting in civilian deaths that will be described as "blunders" and "collateral damage."

The alternative, according to some, would be to withdraw from these regions and concentrate on areas where less warlike operations of "protecting development" are possible, gradually expanding these areas. And how will these areas be expanded? Apparently, peacekeeping and reconstruction will win the "hearts and minds" of the Afghans in these areas and this will undermine the resistance. But once again, this scenario ignores an essential player: the resistance itself. Afghan forces opposed to the occupying military presence will target foreign troops wherever they are, and will do this increasingly as their number and preparedness permit. The quieter areas will become hotter and the mandate and/or mission of the occupation troops will have to change accordingly.

• NATO's intervention in Afghanistan isn't a leaderless activity in which each army can choose to do whatever it wants, wherever it likes. From the outset, the United States, who decided on this war, chose to support and arm the Northern Alliance and other warlords, bring them to power and then extend their power to the entire country. Despite the official propaganda about democracy and reconstruction, this is the general mission NATO is performing in Afghanistan and the mandates of the participating armies can only be defined in terms of the resulting tasks.

In a period when armed resistance is growing in Afghanistan and when the United States, in difficulty in Iraq, has to deploy additional troops to that country, there is enormous pressure for other NATO contingents to take over from the American troops in "hunting the Taliban." Canadian troops have been thus engaged since February 2006 and Canadian political and military circles are now pressing other NATO countries to adopt the same mandate and assume "their share" of the costs of these operations.

• The current mandate of the Canadian troops isn't a mere accident which is staining Canada's reputation as a promoter of peace, which it can easily remove by returning to its previous mandate. Over the past fifteen years, Canada's military role abroad has been evolving in the opposite direction from peacekeeping.[51] More recently, using the pretext of the September 11, 2001 attacks, a more militaristic Canadian foreign policy, closely tied to that of the United States, has been explicitly adopted in the highest Canadian economic, political and military spheres.

• The call for a change of mandate disregards the fundamental question of the reason for this war and the interests it really serves, beyond the good intentions professed by the United States and its allies.[52] It is based on the explicit premise that the Government of Canada's intentions are the same as ours but that – by error or by capitulation to outside pressure – it went astray in the new means chosen to fulfill its good intentions. In our opinion, this is very naïve, to say the least, because this war is one of foreign domination and control and any suggestion of different means cannot suddenly transform it into its opposite.

CHANGE OF COMMAND OF THE FOREIGN TROOPS FROM NATO TO THE UN

In the current context, this demand is no more realistic than a change of mandate or mission:

• Such a decision falls under the mandate of the Security Council; yet immediately after the invasion of Afghanistan, it was the United States itself that drove the Council's various resolutions on this subject, resolutions that obviously did not criticize the war, that ratified the establishment of the ISAF and then the extension and broadening of its mandate under NATO command; no other country on the Security Council to date has ventured to propose any changes to these resolutions.

• The only alternative would be for the United Nations General Assembly (UNGA) to take matters in hand in a sort of disavowal of the Security Council's current direction; this is theoretically possible, but very unlikely since it would require a majority of countries to openly confront the US orientation, which few governments find it in their interest to do. In practice, in Canada, our task would be to call on the Government of Canada to intervene in this way, which is contrary to its current policy.

• Finally, this demand maintains the prevailing illusions concerning the role of the UN on issues of war and peace, when these questions are under the jurisdiction of the Security Council where the United States often manages to make its own policies prevail. It would be necessary to start talking openly about this reversion to UNGA.

QUESTION 18: So what responsibilities do we have to the Afghan people?

The many discussions around this question often take place as if we had the solutions to the problems of Afghan society and the responsibility for implementing them. We believe that it is necessary to break with such an approach and base our work on real solidarity with the Afghan people in their struggles for self-determination. In her address to the NDP Convention in September 2006, Afghan Member of Parliament Malalaï Joya affirmed:

I think that no nation can donate liberation to another nation. Liberation should be achieved in a country by the people themselves. The ongoing developments in Afghanistan and Iraq prove this claim. I think if Canada and other governments really want to help the Afghan people and bring positive changes, they must act independently, rather than becoming a tool to implement the wrong policies of the US government. They must align themselves to the wishes and needs of the Afghan people.[53]

To affirm the principle of self-determination is first to recognize that the Afghans are responsible for their own destiny and can very well conceive and implement their own solutions to their problems. It must also be recognized that foreign interventions, in Afghanistan or elsewhere, have rarely been based on respect for this principle, but rather on a will for control and domination contrary to the interest of the peoples it claims to help. The current war in Afghanistan and Canadian intervention in this war are no exception.

The courses of action we present are twofold: on the one hand, what to do specifically concerning Canada's military intervention in Afghanistan; on the other hand, what to do more generally concerning Canadian foreign policy.

CONCERNING THE WAR IN AFGHANISTAN:

1. We call for the withdrawal of Canadian troops from Afghanistan. This withdrawal is not equivalent to abandoning the Afghan people since, from our perspective, it means withdrawing part of a foreign army of occupation. This is our primary responsibility to the Afghan people in their long and difficult struggle for self-determination. The presence of Canadian troops in Afghanistan is part of the increasingly militaristic orientation of Canada's foreign policy, and we reject it on this basis.

2. As long as Canadian military intervention lasts in Afghanistan, we must:

• deconstruct the Government of Canada's misleading discourse concerning the progress made in Afghanistan on "good governance," human rights, women's rights;
• demand accountability and insist on the truth concerning Canadian military intervention: number of Afghan victims caused by our intervention, use of prohibited munitions, number of prisoners transferred and under what agreements,[54] costs of the intervention;
• develop direct ties between civil societies, with Afghan individuals and organizations who do not accept either the logic of repressive fundamentalism or that of foreign armies;
• identify and denounce, within Quebec and within Canadian society as a whole, the promoters of the war in Afghanistan and their interests.

CONCERNING CANADA'S FOREIGN POLICY:

3. We reject the increasingly militaristic orientation of Canada's foreign policy, the deepening of the military partnership with the United States, and the almost total integration of the Canadian Army into the United States Army that results from this.

We demand that a real public debate be held on the role of the Canadian forces and on reducing military spending. We demand the end of government subsidies to Canadian companies in the international arms trade. We oppose military recruiting, which is intensifying everywhere in universities, colleges and secondary schools and

which specifically targets young people from disadvantaged sectors
of our society.

4. We demand an in-depth review of Canada's foreign policy so that
it is really geared to justice and sharing of wealth, particularly concerning official development assistance. We denounce the shift to
"security" adopted by the government and the fact that part of this
assistance is now diverted for military purposes. We not only call for
the immediate achievement of the objective of allocating 0.7% of
Canada's GDP to development assistance, but also for assistance that
is really disbursed and managed transparently, free of any obligation
to the donor country and devoted to projects determined by people
in the countries for which it is intended. Afghanistan, ranked 175th
of 177 countries according to the United Nations Human Development Index, should be one of the main countries to receive the increased real assistance.

NOTES

1 There are special circumstances in which the immediacy of the threat
   need not be invoked; for example, in a case of domestic abuse or where
   a prisoner's life is threatened in a correctional facility. But these are people in vulnerable positions that are in no way analogous to the status of
   the United States on the world stage.

2 See the United Nations website: http://www.un.org

3 The Bonn Agreement (December 5, 2001) provided for the implementation of a temporary government led by Hamid Karzai, the holding of
   an emergency session of the Afghan parliament (Loya Jirga) in 2002,
   the establishment of a transitional authority, and the adoption of a
   national constitution before the holding of national elections.

4 And this is not at all certain, since any number of other objectives may
   have guided the US in this case.

5 Speech delivered in February 1994, at the Global Structures Convoca-
   tion, in Washington, when John Bolton was Deputy Secretary of State for
   international organizations, quoted in Phyllis Bennis, *Calling the Shots,
   How Washington Dominates Today's UN*, Olive Branch Press, 2000.

6 The emphasis is ours.

7 Chapter VII of the UN Charter concerns the use of force by the "international community."

8 These considerations were reaffirmed by Security Council Resolution 1674 of 28 April 2006.

9 Note that the secular regime of the day guaranteed women's access to education.

10 See two recent reports by the Senlis Council, a European think tank that does not oppose the foreign occupation of Afghanistan: *Canada in Kandahar: No Peace to Keep* (28 June 2006) and *Five Years Later: the Return of the Taliban* (5 September 2006).

11 See http://hrw.org/wr2k6/.

12 Malalai Joya, speech to NDP Federal Convention, Québec City, 9 September 2006 (http://www.npd.ca/page/4329, viewed 29 November 2006).

13 See http://web.amnesty.org/library/index/engASA110052006?open&of=eng-2as (viewed 29 November 2006).

14 See http://www.hrw.org/english/docs/2006/01/18/afghan12266.htm (viewed 29 November 2006).

15 Joya, speech to NDP.

16 Robert Fisk, "We are the war criminals now," *The Independent*, London, November 29, 2000. Consult also the Human Rights Watch website, www.hrw.org and the Amnesty International website, www.amnesty.org

17 Christine Delphy, "Free to Die," trans. Barbara Wilson, *Le Monde diplomatique*, March 2002 (http://www.rawa.org/lemonde-d.htm, viewed 29 November 2006).

18 The rule requiring a childless widow to marry her deceased husband's brother.

19 Delphy, "Free to Die."

20 Ibid.

21 WOMANKIND Worldwide, *Taking Stock Update: Afghan Women and Girls Five Years On*, October 2006 (http://www.un-instraw.org/revista/hypermail/alltickers/fr/att-0801/Afghan_Women___Girls_Five_Years_On-WOMANKIND_Report.doc).

22 See http://web.amnesty.org/library/index/engasa110072005.

23 Joya, speech to NDP.

24 The Indian rite, abolished in 1829, whereby a widow had to immolate herself on her husband's funeral pyre.

25 See www.hcr.org and www.msf.org

26 Delphy, "Free to Die."

27 Of the 44 Canadian soldiers who had died in Afghanistan by 29 November 2006, 36 died within the last nine months of the period.

28 There are currently (2006) approximately 38,000 foreign soldiers in Afghanistan, including 20,000 US soldiers. Several thousand members of the US contingent are to be replaced by a larger number from other NATO countries.

29 Interview with *Daily News*, 12 October 2006.

30 Presentation by Jim Judd, Director, Canadian Security Intelligence Service, to the Subcommittee on Public Safety and National Security, 22 February 2005.

31 See http://www.csis-scrs.gc.ca/en/newsroom/speeches/speech 22022005.asp (viewed November 29, 2006).

32 Michael Meacher, "This War on Terrorism is Bogus," *The Guardian*, September 6, 2003. See http://www.guardian.co.uk/comment/story/0,,1036571,00.html. Also see the articles by George Arney of the BBC http://news.bbc.co.uk/1/hi/world/south_asia/1550366.stm and by Julio Godoy of Inter Press Service http://www.commondreams.org/headlines01/1115-06.htm (consulted November 29, 2006).

33 We refer readers who would like to know more about the Échec à la guerre Collective's point of view on this major question to the following previously-published documents : *La guerre contre le terrorisme : une arme de destruction massive,* March 2004 (http://www.echecala-guerre.org/publications.htm); and also *Appel à la société québécoise et canadienne : Rejetons le partenariat militaire avec les États-Unis,* September 2005 (http://www.echecala-guerre.org/docs/declaration_0606_f.pdf).

34 See http://www.newamericancentury.org/RebuildingAmericasDefenses.pdf.

35 See on this subject the publications of the *Ligue des droits et libertés*: http://www.liguedesdroits.ca/ .

36 See http://www.parl.gc.ca/37/2/parlbus/chambus/senate/deb-e/018db_2002-11-19-E.htm?Language=E&Parl=37&Ses=2 (consulted on November 29, 2006).

37 If this declaration is true regarding most of the Canadian military assets in Afghanistan, it remains that most of the time part of the Canadian intervention has been clearly offensive…and secret, notably regarding part of mission Apollo, mentioned in the previous question. But there is more. Joint Task Force 2 (JTF-2) the CAF special operations unit, was sent to Afghanistan soon after the attacks of September 11, 2001. It

participated in the attack in Bora Bora in December 2002, and more than once transferred prisoners to the custody of United States forces.

38 See http://www.itcan-cican.gc.ca/ips/menu-en.asp

39 Taking part in the worst sanctions ever imposed by the United Nations, responsible for the death of more than one million people in Iraq, mostly children.

40 The 1998–99 military budget, set at $9.4 billion and overrun by 9.3%, was the lowest point in this decline. The military budget in 2007 was approximately $15 billion.

41 For more information, see *Appel à la société québécoise et canadienne: rejetons le partenariat militaire avec les États-Unis* (http://www.echecalaguerre.org/Declaration.htm).

42 Data taken from Steven Staples, *Marching Orders: How Canada abandoned peacekeeping – and why the UN needs us now more than ever*, a report ordered by The Council of Canadians, October 2006.

43 The CCCE is a group of chief executives from approximately 150 large Canadian corporations, which together, control most of the exports, investments, training and research and development within the Canadian private sector."

44 Bill Schiller, "The Road to Kandahar," *Toronto Star*, September 9, 2006, p. F1; as quoted in Steven Staples, op. cit. p. 5.

45 Former Prime Minister Chrétien was acting as an advisor for Bennett Jones, a law firm based in Calgary, which specializes in energy issues. He was also at the time the international relations advisor for PetroKazakhstan, also based in Calgary, which has major interests in Kazakhstan and in the Caspian Sea region.

46 There have been several acquisitions in the oil and gas sector, especially regarding these projects in Central Asia. PetroKazakhstan has since been sold to Chinese interests and Unocal, purchased by Chevron.

47 For more information, see http://www.newscentralasia.com/modules.php?name=News&file=print&sid=876 et http://www.newscentralasia.com/modules.php?name=News&file=print&sid=1560 (consulted November 29, 2006).

48 For more information, see http://hrw.org/english/docs/2006/01/18/turkme12244_txt.htm.

49 *Globe and Mail*, July 15, 2005. See http://www.theglobeandmail.com/servlet/ArticleNews/TPStory/LAC/20050715/AFGHAN15/TPNational/TopStories

50 http://www.senliscouncil.net/modules/publications/014_publication/

51 See Question 13.

52 See Questions 10 and 14.

53 Malalai Joya, op. cit.

54 We must denounce the fact that Canadian troops hand over their prisoners to the Afghan authorities under an agreement that does not oblige the Afghan government to transmit their names to independent Afghan human rights organizations and does not prohibit their transfer to third parties!

Afghanistan and Canada
Current Situation and
Canada's Role

How Much Is this War Costing Canadians?

STEVEN STAPLES

AND

DAVID MacDONALD

Prime Minister Stephen Harper reiterated on September 10, 2008, that Canada's mission in Afghanistan will conclude at the end of 2011 with the withdrawal of all Canadian troops. This has sparked a new debate on the cost of the war.

Earlier last year (2008), the Parliament of Canada passed a Conservative government motion to extend Canada's military mission in Afghanistan beyond its current end date of February 2009 to December 2011 – an additional 34 months.

It is astonishing that Parliament voted to extend the war, without a serious estimation of the financial cost of such a decision.

But on March 13, 2008, 198 Members of Parliament favoured the motion and only 77 opposed it. The motion recommended:

Canada should continue a military presence in Kandahar beyond February 2009, to July 2011 ... [and] the government of Canada notify NATO that Canada will end its presence in Kandahar as of July 2011, and, as of that date, the redeployment of Canadian Forces troops out of Kandahar and their replacement by Afghan forces start as soon as possible, so that it will have been completed by December 2011 ...

Main Findings

OUR AFGHANISTAN WAR CALCULATIONS

Values in Billions	What is the cost of the war so far (to Mar 2009)?	How much more will is cost to extend the war to Dec 2011?	What will be the total cost of the war by Dec 2011?
Ammo, equipment, fuel... (aka Incremental Cost)	$ 4.8 (DND)	$ 2.7 (DND)	$7.6
+ troops salaries (aka Full Cost)	$ 6.5 (DND)	$ 3.7 (DND)	$10.3
+ health care for wounded soldiers	$ 0.5 (VAC)	$ 0.5 (VAC)	$ 1.0
+ disability and death benefits	$ 0.3 (VAC)	$ 0.3 (VAC)	$ 0.6
+ aid projects in Afghanistan	$ 1.0 (CIDA)	$ 0.4 (CIDA)	$ 1.3
(The total for all Government of Canada spending...)	$13.2	$ 7.5	$20.7
PLUS economic loss from wounded or killed soldiers[1]	$ 4.1	$ 3.6	$ 7.6
= Total Approximate Cost of the Afghanistan War	$17.2 billion	$11.1 billion	$28.4 billion

Note: Totals may not add due to rounding

The military mission, according to the government's motions, is required to achieve some very laudable goals. The government's motion states that

the ultimate aim of Canadian policy is to leave Afghanistan to Afghans, in a country that is better governed, more peaceful and more secure and to create the necessary space and conditions to allow the Afghans themselves to achieve a political solution to the conflict ...

Whether these goals can be achieved and by what means is the subject of intense public debate. But everyone recognizes that working towards achieving these goals will require Canada and its people, especially members of the Canadian Armed Forces, to pay a price trying.

The Government of Canada has not produced a public estimate of the cost of extending the mission by 34 months, from February 2009 to December 2011, beyond their FY2008–09 estimates ending March 2009. However, the future extension of the mission will resemble the size and scope of the military mission that has been conducted since February 2006, when Canada established a Provincial Reconstruction Team and a battle group based at Kandahar Airfield in the southern province of Kandahar.

Since the initial Kandahar deployment, the size of the Canadian contingent has grown by several hundred soldiers plus additional equipment, including Leopard tanks.

The government's motion proposing the extension of the mission envisions a similar deployment and more equipment, notably helicopters and unmanned aerial vehicles. As well, there has been a public discussion of the deployment of armed Griffon helicopters. These measures would impact the cost of the mission.

Nevertheless, it is reasonable to take the last two years of Canada's Afghanistan military operations in Kandahar as the basis for a projection of costs to December 2011.

In 2006 a new, unique mission was established for Canada, marked by the redeployment from Kabul to restive Kandahar in February of that year.

This new counter-insurgency mission is quite different from the previous International Security Assistance Force in Afghanistan (ISAF) mission in Kabul from 2003 until late 2005 and different as well from Canada's minor role in Operation Enduring Freedom during the initial invasion and post-Taliban government period of 2001–02.

COSTING METHODOLOGY

To fully cost the Afghanistan war, several components must be considered. Spending by the Department of National Defence is the most obvious expenditure. In this case, equipment and salaries are treated separately. Veterans Affairs Canada is responsible for the lifetime health care, disability and death payments for casualties in Afghanistan. Humanitarian aid is a critical component to the reconstruction of Afghanistan and it is provided by the Canadian International Development Agency. The costs from the Departments of National Defence, Veteran's Affairs Canada and the Canadian International Development Agency make up the costs to the federal government of the Afghanistan campaign.

There are also private costs of killed and injured soldiers which are born by them, their families and communities. These private costs are only partially offset by Veteran's Affairs Canada's payments. The full economic cost is the addition of government costs and private costs.

COSTS FOR THE DEPARTMENT OF NATIONAL DEFENCE
THE AFGHANISTAN MISSION(S)

Canada's military mission in Afghanistan is actually composed of several different operations, as defined by the Canadian Forces (CF). For the purpose of this study, Canada's military mission is calculated by combining the costs of the following missions, described by the Department of National Defence:

APOLLO: Canadian "military contribution to the international campaign against terrorism," including the war in Afghanistan. Naval units also took part in Operation APOLLO, "to prevent al Qaeda and Taliban members from escaping the area of operations in merchant ships and fishing boats operating from Pakistan and Iran," among other purposes. Canada concluded the APOLLO mission in 2002–2003 with much of it being transferred to ALTAIR.

ACCIUS: Canadian contribution to the United Nations Assistance Mission in Afghanistan (UNAMA). Canada contributed one Lieutenant Colonel from November 2002 to June 2005.

ATHENA: Canadian contribution to ISAF. Canada participated from October 2003 to October 2005 and from July 31, 2006, to the present. The current number of Canadian personnel is approximately 2,300. (March, 2009)

ARCHER: One of Canada's contributions to US Operation Enduring Freedom Afghanistan. Canada participated from August 2005 to July 31, 2006.

ARGUS: Canadian Strategic Advisory Team providing support to the Afghan government.

ALTAIR: The Canadian Navy contribution to the US Operation Enduring Freedom in Afghanistan.

The Department of National Defence (DND) publishes the cost of each of its international operations in its annual Report on Plans and Priorities, produced for each federal government fiscal year (from April 1 to March 31 the following year). DND calculates the cost of missions using two methods: Full Cost and Incremental Cost.

FULL COST AND INCREMENTAL COST

"Full Cost" as defined by DND includes:

• civilian and military salaries
• overtime and allowances
• petroleum, oil and lubricants
• spares
• contracted repair and overhaul services
• depreciation and attrition costs of all equipment involved

"Incremental Cost" as defined by DND is the cost incurred by DND over and above what would have been spent on personnel and equipment if troops had not been deployed. It is derived from the Full Cost by subtracting salaries, equipment depreciation and attrition, and other sums that would otherwise have been spent on exercises or absorbed as part of normal activities.

Both methods are legitimate measurements, and should be considered. The Incremental Cost, which is typically roughly half the amount of the Full Cost, is frequently cited in the public debate. Some politicians and commentators probably prefer this figure because it minimizes the financial impact on government coffers of unpopular wars.

Both Full and Incremental costs apply only to the Department of National Defence. The costs of the campaign to other related departments such as Veterans Affairs Canada and CIDA will also be examined here.

Proponents of incremental costing suggest that soldiers "would have to be paid anyway." This is partially true. However, Canada's recent focus on recruiting soldiers to increase the number of troops in the Canadian Forces, and their associated increased cost, is in part a response to the need to expand in more, longer-term international missions (arguably in response to the terrorist attacks of September 11, 2001, and the subsequent War on Terror). Neither the Incremental nor the Full Cost of the war incorporate increased spending on recruitment. Relying on incremental cost alone likely underestimates the broader costs born throughout the military of such a large operation.

The Full Cost is equally useful because it includes the "labour" required to undertake the mission, and captures the opportunity costs of choosing one mission over another. For instance, if salaries are paid to soldiers in Afghanistan, it follows that these funds are not available to pay for soldiers for another mission in Darfur as peace-keepers, for example.

A useful analogy would be the sticker price of a new car. The Incremental Cost would only calculate the cost of the rubber, steel and plastic to build the car, and omit the labour costs of building the car. General Motors would not be a viable manufacturer for very long if its dealers ignored the full cost of building autos when quoting a price to customers.

DND FIGURES[2]

According to the Department of National Defence Report on Plans and Priorities (RPP) from FY2002–03 to FY2008–09 (the most recent report available), the Full Cost of the Afghanistan mission to the end of March 2009 will be $11.4 billion. Of that, the Incremental Cost (which excludes salaries) will be $4.8 billion.

The current phase of Canada's involvement in Afghanistan is by far the most expensive. For comparison, the last two years of Canada's mission in Kandahar cost almost as much as the previous six years in Afghanistan combined.

The cost of the mission almost doubled between FY2005-06 and FY2006-07. In one year the Full Cost jumped from $1.1 billion to $2.0 billion. Of that, the Incremental Cost likewise went from $422 million to $814 million per year. Between FY2006–07 and FY2007–08, the Full Cost of the mission again jumped by almost 30%, from $2.0 billion to $2.6 billion, while the Incremental Cost went from $814 million to $1.1 billion.

The estimated Full Cost of the first three years in Kandahar is therefore $7.2 billion. At the current Full Cost spending levels, of $2.57 billion per year, Canada is spending $214 million a month. The Incremental Cost of three years in Kandahar is $3.0 billion. At the current Incremental Cost spending levels of 1.0 billion a year, Canada is spending $90 million per month.

The extension of the current mission until December 2011 will require 28 more months at full strength, and a subsequent dénouement of military operations over the final six-month period, according to the government motion passed by Parliament.

If one assumes that the final winding-down costs during the last six months would be half of the full-strength costs, the Full Cost of the mission extension beyond April 2009 to December 2011 would be $6.4 billion, including $2.7 billion in Incremental Cost.

This will bring the total Full Cost of Canada's military role in Afghanistan from 2001 to 2011 to $17.8 billion, and the Incremental Cost to $7.6 billion.

COSTS FOR VETERANS AFFAIRS CANADA

Veterans Affairs Canada (VAC) is responsible for both health care and disability benefits for veterans. It provides pensions for disabilities when a CF member is injured and survivorship benefits if a CF member is killed. VAC also provides for the health care of wounded or disabled veterans.

VETERANS' HEATH CARE[3]

Veterans Affairs Canada does not break down the costs of health care by conflict. However, given casualty figures and estimates of lifetime treatment cost for common battlefield injuries, it is possible to estimate the lifetime cost of a soldier's injury to VAC.

The Department of National Defence does not release injury figures although it does compile a list of soldiers killed. It also does not reveal the types of injuries that Canadian Forces personnel suffer. The injury figures used in this report have been compiled using news reports. News outlets do cover but may not even know of all injuries in Afghanistan. As such, the figures used here will likely lead to an underestimate of the number of injuries. Also, due to the lack of data for the types of injuries suffered, it is assumed in this report that what Canadians are experiencing in Afghanistan is comparable to the American injury types incurred during the Iraq war.

The health care costs have already been partially offset by VAC spending although the above estimate of $1 billion is significantly above what VAC appears to have committed.[4] The health care costs based on injury rates suggest that $530 million had already been incurred in future health care costs to the end of 2008. With the mission extension to the end of 2011, those costs will climb another $472 million to $1.0 billion.

At this point health care costs are running at approximately 10%

TABLE 1: HEALTH CARE COSTS[5] (US data in US dollars)

Type of Injuries	Wounded suffering injury	Number suffering this injury 2001–11	Lifetime treatment costs	Total Cost in millions
Severe Head Injury	20%	377	$600,000 to $4.3 million ($2.6 mil avg)	$981
Amputation	6%	113	$58,000 to $ 158, 000 ($108, 000 avg)	$12
Injury resulting in inability to return to duty (excluding brain injury and amputation)	24%	453	$20,000	$9.1
Injured but able to return to duty	50%	943	0 (forces are treated then released	0
Total	100%	1,886		$1,002

of the operational cost spent on the conflict in Afghanistan. Although this may appear high, similar studies in the US have estimates that stand significantly higher as a proportion of the operational cost.[6] As well, Canada is incurring significantly higher casualties as a proportion of their overall troop commitment than other nations.[7] If anything, this suggests that the above estimate of health care costs may be too low; however, without more detailed data from Veterans' Affairs Canada it is difficult to say by how much.

VETERANS' DEATH AND DISABILITY PAYMENTS[8]

Veterans Affairs Canada adjusted its budget upwards by $80 million in 2006-07 to compensate for an unforeseen increase in their projected death and benefits. It was during 2006 that Canada moved its operations to the volatile Kandahar region where its casualties increased from approximately ten a year to over three hundred a year. The $80 million likely represents the value today of all future disability and death payments for those Canadian Forces personnel who were killed or disabled in 2006–07.

Given that estimate and the assumption that it varies with the number of soldiers killed and wounded, Veterans' Affairs Canada would have already spent $294 million on future disability and death payments to the end of fiscal year 2008–09. If present casualty rates continue, death and disability payments will increase another $260 million, for a total cost of $555 million from 2001 to the end of 2011.

COSTS FOR CIDA

The Canadian International Development Agency (CIDA) has significantly redirected its aid from other countries to the reconstruction of Afghanistan. If the government's goal is to ensure that Afghanistan becomes "better governed, more peaceful and more secure," it will be difficult to achieve without significant humanitarian aid from CIDA.

CIDA funding for Afghanistan has increased fivefold, from only $50 million in FY2001-02 to $250 million by FY2006–07. Canada has pledged to spend $1.2 billion on aid projects in Afghanistan by 2011.[9] This commitment will make it by far the largest aid project that CIDA is engaged in.

Since the invasion of Afghanistan in 2001, CIDA has spent $965 million on its Afghanistan projects to the end of fiscal year 2008–09.[10] If spending levels are projected to meet the $1.2 billion goal by the start of 2011, then Canada will spend another $360 million in development aid between FY2009 and December 2011 to reach $1.325 billion, topping its original goal by maintaining similar funding levels for an additional year after the pledged period.

TOTAL GOVERNMENT COSTS

Considering all government expenses to FY2008–09, including DND, VAC and CIDA, the operation in Afghanistan has already cost $13.2 billion. The cost to Veterans' Affairs Canada of both health care and payments for death and disability makes up 6% of the total, or $824 million. CIDA is contributing 7% of the total, or $965 million, by the end of fiscal year 2008–09, while the Department of National Defence accounts for the remaining 87%, or $11.4 billion.

If current spending and casualty trends continue, the final Government of Canada costs by the end of 2011 are likely to be much higher. Government costs are likely to reach $20.7 billion by the end of the mission. Between the end of this fiscal year and the end of

TABLE 2: VALUE OF LOST PRODUCTIVITY[11]

Types of Injuries	Injuries suffered	VSL included	Total 2001 to FY08-09 ($mil)	Total FY09-10 to 2011 ($mil)	Total 2001–11 ($mil)
Loss of Life		100%	$935	$792	$1,727
Severe Brain Injury	30%	100%	$1,748	$1,556	$3,305
Other Serious injuries (includes amputation)	20%	40%	$1,014	$902	$1,916
Less serious injuries	50%	10%	$371	$330	$702
Total	100%		$4,069	$3,581	$7,649

2011, veterans' health care costs and disability benefits will increase another $733 million to reach $1.6 billion by December 2011, or 8% of the total costs. CIDA, for its part, will spend over $1.3 billion by December 2011 or 6% of the total costs. As before, the Department of Defence will have contributed the largest amount, totalling over $17.8 billion, or 86% of the government spending.

FULL ECONOMIC COSTS

While government costs are large, topping $20.7 billion for the planned length of the Afghanistan mission, they only represent the costs to the federal government. The full economic costs should include costs incurred by CF members, their families and the larger community. The full accounting of the Afghanistan mission should include these private costs in addition to the government costs estimated above.

It is not possible, nor appropriate, to put a price on a human life. However, economists can estimate the approximate value that a person would have contributed to the economy over his/her productive life. The calculation of these lost wages is the "Value of a Statistical Life," or VSL.

For instance, a Canadian Forces member who was killed in Afghanistan could have otherwise worked at a job for the rest of his life. His income might have supported a spouse and a family. It would also have been spent in a local economy, helping it to grow. While removing one person may not make a large economic impact at a national level, it certainly makes a difference at a local or family level. There are real losses to those who depend on someone who is killed or disabled. It is these local costs that the VSL estimates.

If current trends continue from the past three years in Kandahar, it is likely that before the proposed withdrawal in 2011, 1886 Canadians will be injured and 193 will be killed. These figures nearly double the 998 injured and 97 soldiers killed to date (March 2009).

It is possible to determine the economic impact of having a Canadian soldier struck down in his or her prime. As well, while others may be injured yet survive, disability may prevent them from reaching their full potential after the conflict. Severe brain injury may prevent a Canadian Force member from ever working again or an amputation may restrict his or her ability to take home as much income as (s)he otherwise would have. As such, injuries and disabilities have a real economic impact on returning veterans and should be included in a full accounting of the Afghanistan mission.

Canada does provide disability and survivor benefits; in this section those benefits are deducted from the economic costs as they partially compensate for injury. As well, the breakdown of injuries is based on Table 1 above, examining health care costs.[12]

The increased survival rate of those with severe brain injury is a result of improved battlefield care. However, these types of injuries are severe and often mean that survivors will likely never return to work. Therefore, severe brain injury cases are estimated at the full VSL.

Other serious injuries result in survivors not being able to return to active duty, as their impairments are too severe. In this case, many can and do return to work outside of the military. However, there will likely be some long-term effects from these types of severe injuries. In this category, 40% of the VSL is included to reflect these long-term effects.

Half of those injured will return to active duty. In this case their injuries do not restrict them from continuing to work. However, there will likely be some residual effects of that injury, whether physical or mental. In this final category, 10% of the VSL is included to reflect at least some decreased capacity to work.

The cost of so many young men and women being either killed or disabled is significant. The future private loss has already reached $4.1 billion. Considerably higher casualty rates today, compared to the start of the mission mean that between 2009 and 2011 private

AFGHANISTAN + UN PEACEKEEPING (Current year in millions)

Fiscal Year	Full Cost of Afghanistan Operations	Incremental Cost of Afghanistan Operations	Afghanistan Operations	UN Peacekeeping Full Cost
2000-01	$0	$0		$94.1
2001-02	$510.8	$216.0	Apollo	$73.4
2002-03	$709.3	$233.6	Accius, Apollo, Athena	$35.3
2003-04	$1,166.9	$600.6	Accius, Athena, Altair	$35.0
2004-05	$717.0	$389.9	Accius, Athena, Altair	$34.2
2005-06	$1,098.5	$421.6	Accius, Archer, Athena, Altair	$23.7
2006-07	$2,030.2	$813.7	Archer, Argus, Athena, Altair	$8.5
2007-08	$2,590.1	$1,086.0	Archer, Argus, Athena, Altair	$9.4
2008-09e	$2,565.7	$1,084.8	Archer, Argus, Athena, Foundation	$15.6
2000-01 to 2008-09	$11,388.5	$4,846.2		
Average Past 2 Years	$2,577.9	$1,085.4		
April 2009 to December 2011				
2009-10e	$2,577.9	$1,085.4		
2010-11e	$2,577.9	$1,085.4		
Full strength (April 2011– June 2011)	$644.5 $644.5	$271.4		
Wind-down / half strength (July 2011- Dec 2011)	$271.4			
2011-12e (adjusted for 9 months)	$1,289.0	$542.7		
2001-02 to December 2011	$17,833.3	$7,559.7		
April 2009 to December 2011 (extension)	$6,444.8	$2,713.5		

Source: DND Reports on Plans and Priorities

MISSION CASUALTIES: CALCULATIONS & ESTIMATES (Casualties, injuries & deaths)

Calendar year	Casualties (Injuries & deaths)	Injuries	Deaths
2002	13	9	4
2003	5	3	2
2004	9	8	1
2005	10	9	1
2006	300	264	36
2007	412	382	30
2008e	354	323	31
2002 to 2008	1103	998	105
Average past 2 years (2007–08)	355	323	32
Extend mission to December 2011			
2009e	355	323	32
2010e	355	323	32
Full strength (Jan 2011–June 2011)	178	162	16
Wind-down / half strength (July 2011–Dec 2011)	89	81	8
2011e	266	242	24
February 2009 to December 2011 (extension)	977	888	89
Total 2001 to Dec 2011	2080	1886	193

Source: Department of National Defence (http://www.forces.gc.ca/site/focus/fallen/index_e.asp), Globe and Mail

costs will almost equal the costs incurred in the first six years of the mission. Private costs are projected to reach $7.6 billion by December 2011.

By combining government spending with private costs, a broader picture of the overall economic costs is reached. With all types of costs considered, including those costs that fall on injured or killed soldiers and their families, the total for the nine-year Afghanistan mission will be $28.4 billion. Military costs still make up slightly less than two-thirds of the full economic cost. Other items, primarily private loss to soldiers and their families, make up the other 37% of the full economic cost. The loss of private income due to injury alone represents 22% of the full economic cost or $5.9 billion. The private loss due to the death of young men and women will total $1.7 billion or 6% of the total.

THE ABANDONMENT OF PEACEKEEPING BY CANADA

The costs of the Afghan campaign will be tremendous when all government and private costs are included. Extending the campaign to the end of 2011 will dramatically increase those costs as equipment and people are worn down and high casualty rates continue. Not only is the cost of the Afghanistan mission extremely high, it is also crowding out spending on Canada's traditional uses for its military – peacekeeping.

Canada's military has been withdrawing from peacekeeping for some time. The mission to Afghanistan has quickly completed the Canadian retreat. As the cost of the Afghan campaign increased, the much smaller contribution to UN missions shrank dramatically.

Over the course of the Afghanistan mission, DND spending on UN missions dropped 90%, from $94.1 million in FY2000–01 to a low of $8.5 million in FY2006–07, the lowest level in at least a decade. DND spending has recovered slightly since FY2006–07 to an estimated $15.6 million in FY2008–09. In the same period that DND spending on UN missions increased from $8.5 million to $15.6 million, DND spending on Afghanistan increased over $500 million, from $2.0 billion to $2.6 billion.

Canada's withdrawal from peacekeeping has not been driven by a decline in the UN's need for trained personnel. In fact, it has come at a time of historic need for the UN. The UN Missions in Liberia (UNMIL), Sudan (UNMIS) and the Democratic Republic of Congo (MONUC) were extremely demanding, so much so that by the end of 2006, the number of personnel working in UN peacekeeping missions hit a 16-year high of over 80,000 people.

The increasing needs of the UN is in contrast to DND's vanishing contribution to UN peacekeeping. The same year the peacekeepers in the field hit new highs Canada's peacekeeping spending hit rock bottom, at only $8.5 million including equipment and personnel. While the need for highly skilled Canadian personnel has never been higher for UN missions, Canadian contributions have never been lower. In July 2008, total Canadian personnel contributions to UN operations were a mere 167, ranking Canada 53rd of 119 contributing nations, between Slovakia at 52nd and Malawi at 54th.

The Afghanistan campaign has not only been extremely expensive, it has essentially abandoned Canada's 50-year commitment to UN peacekeeping. While low levels of peacekeeping spending may continue for some time, the reorientation of the Canadian military is clear. For all intents and purposes, DND spending on peacekeeping missions has stopped. DND peacekeeping funding has been consumed by the much more combat-oriented Afghanistan mission.

Recent DND spending lays bare the fact that the Department is much more willing to spend on militaristic campaigns like the one in Afghanistan than it is to spend on UN peacekeeping missions of the kind that Canadians prefer. When push comes to shove, DND will cut peacekeeping contributions in favour of militaristic solutions.

As DND buries Canada's 50-year involvement in peacekeeping, a more ominous version of international military intervention has arisen in its place. Pearson's vision of the Canadian military supporting the United Nations in negotiating solutions has been replaced by an Americanized vision of militaristic solutions imposed by the force of arms.

CONCLUSIONS

Independent reports suggest that the situation in Afghanistan is precarious, and even though it has been dragging on longer than the Second World War, the lives of most Afghans remain unimproved, despite the Herculean effort by the international community.

The cost and risk of extending the mission as it is today must be set against the prospect of achieving our goals. Alarmingly, the government has not published its estimate for the cost "in treasure and blood" of extending the military mission until December 2011.

However, as this study has found, the cost will be extremely high. The extension of the war's military cost is $6.4 billion, creating a total military bill of $17.8 billion by the end of 2011. When veterans' health care and disability benefits are included along with the cost of CIDA's reconstruction, taxpayers are left with a bill of $20.7 billion.

However, examining merely the government's cost ignores the private costs to families and community of lost and injured soldiers. Once the full economic costs are included, the total value of the Afghanistan mission so far balloons to $17.2 billion. To run the mission at the present pace until December 2011 will require an additional $11.1 billion, for a full economic cost of $28.4 billion for the nine-year mission.

While extremely expensive for the military, the Afghanistan campaign has also meant the effective cancellation of Canadian peacekeeping. Military spending on Afghanistan has almost completely crowded out peacekeeping spending.

During the campaign in Afghanistan, DND spending on peace-keeping dropped over 90% to a possible all-time low of only $8.5 million in FY2006–07. The very same year, DND increased spending on the Afghanistan campaign by $1.0 billion. This dramatic spending contrast spells the likely end of peacekeeping in the Canadian military.

If the Harper government believes that the mission can be successful, then the additional cost of extending the $11.1 billion mission and the effective cancellation of all UN missions may be a worthwhile endeavour in the pursuit of peace and stability in Afghanistan.

But if there is any doubt, then a new strategy for Afghanistan must be adopted to quickly bring an end to the conflict.

NOTES

1 Economic loss is net of disability payments.

2 Department of National Defence Report on Plans and Priorities plus author's calculations.

3 All values in this section are Net Present Value.

4 VAC RPPs suggest $15 million in new health care spending in 2006–07, and the budget was increased again by $34 million in 2007–08.

5 Table reproduced from Wallsten and Kosec, *The Economic Cost of the War in Iraq* (AEI, 2005), with author's calculations.

6 Bilmes, Stiglitz, *The Economic Costs of the Iraq War: An Appraisal Three Years after the Beginning of the Conflict* (ASSA, 2006).

7 Staples, Steven, and Bill Robinson, *Canada's Fallen: Understanding Canadian Military Deaths in Afghanistan* (Rideau Institute, Sept. 2006).

8 All values in this section are at Net Present Value of payments at the time of payment.

9 CIDA Report on Plans and Priorities, 2008–09.

10 *Canadian Forces in Afghanistan: Report of the Standing Committee on National Defence*, 2007, and projections based on the commitment of $1.2 through 2011. Assuming 2012 will maintain the same spending levels as previous years.

11 All figures are net of VAC disability and death payments which partially offset lost wages.

12 Wallsten and Kosec, *The Economic Cost of the War in Iraq* (AEI, 2005). As above, DND does not release injury statistics and so it is assumed that Canadian forces in Afghanistan are experiencing similar injury patterns as American forces in Iraq.

The Challenges to Aid: Humanitarian and Development Work in the "War on Terror"

STEPHEN CORNISH

INTRODUCTION

The post-Cold War period saw the emergence of the doctrine of "humanitarian intervention," which boldly promised that military interventions could promote the goal of humanitarian assistance to persecuted and unprotected populations. The doctrine was embraced by increasingly politicized aid organizations, which began advocating for international military intervention in countries suffering grave humanitarian crises, while working ever more closely with the intervening governments to deliver assistance and conduct more comprehensive development work.

Classic humanitarians had always found such blurring of lines between humanitarianism and war-making anathema. Known today as "minimalists," these humanitarian organizations worked on the principle that populations have a right to assistance without discrimination, which is enshrined in international humanitarian law and the Geneva Conventions. They steadfastly maintained their neutrality, impartiality and independence, helping win the consent both of belligerent armies and victimized communities.

But the apparent success of NGO assistance to the Kurdish population of Iraq in the aftermath of the UN-sanctioned US intervention in 1991 convinced some that military and humanitarian objectives could function together. UN Secretary-General Boutros Boutros-Ghali underlined the interest in such an integrated approach in the 1992 Agenda for Peace, in which "the UNSG called for the mobilization of political, military and aid assets in a coherent manner to build peace and security."

But humanitarian catastrophes in Bosnia, Somalia, and Rwanda, which highlighted the unwillingness of states to put their soldiers in harm's way for humanitarian causes, offered food for thought to boosters of the "coherent" approach. Some major aid organizations decided to set standards of conduct and reaffirm independence, in order to ward off the overt politicization of aid and the co-optation of humanitarian assistance. Under their 1995 Red Cross Code, agencies would work with governments only if their own goals were respected.

Other humanitarian organizations, however, wanted to move beyond minimalism or "mere humanitarianism," developing a more active approach to conflict resolution that would tackle the root causes of war and strife and contribute to long-term peace and development. British and American organizations in particular began to look favourably on military interventions, which they believed could set the stage for "maximalist" development work. Whereas classic humanitarians "worked in the conflict," perfecting aid delivery and reaffirming independence, they wanted to "work on the conflict," planning ambitious "peacebuilding" programs and eagerly taking a seat at the table among governments.

With little agreement over contentious but key operative terms like "failed states," and with differing interests, the approach of these organizations nevertheless seemed to dovetail with the agenda of some governments and defence departments, including Canada's. The latter had become interested in "coherent" approaches as a national security strategy to fight irregular wars of the Post-Cold War period, which were soon to have names like "Whole-of-Government" (WGA) and 3D (Defence, Diplomacy, Development). The US Defense Department, for instance, called for a "unified statecraft" that would seamlessly integrate allies and non-governmental organizations.

Any potential theoretical benefits of "maximalist" aid approaches looked less likely to be fulfilled in practice, under the terms of co-operation. The chips were never even when the US Department of Defense sat across the table from USAID. Meanwhile, the majority world categorically rejected rights to humanitarian interventions at their world summits in 2000, and again in 2003. Kofi Annan of the UN tried to "forge unity" in the face of these divisions, assembling a blue-chip panel to write the International Commission on Intervention and State Sovereignty (ICSS) report to establish guidelines for military interventions. The report invoked the notion of "responsibility to protect," which Canada then played an instrumental role in formalizing and bringing to the UN for adoption as the Responsibility to Protect doctrine (R2P).

But much of this debate was rendered moot by 9/11 and the US response. The Security Council became the arbiter of interventions, rather than the intended General Assembly, and the "failed states" doctrine became openly driven by national security agendas. Humanitarian motives became attractive dressing for pre-emptive and belligerent wars. In 2001, US Secretary of State Colin Powell went so far as to hail humanitarian NGOs as "a force multiplier for us, such an important part of our combat team."

Against this background, Stephen Cornish, author of the article below, and staff member of CARE Canada, details the consequences of integrated approaches for humanitarian work. Though humanitarian organizations entered such collaboration with good faith, the Whole-of-Government and 3D approaches may indeed have co-opted humanitarian assistance for their own ends. The consequences have been dismal: the recipients of such "aid" have been left with less humanitarian assistance and more insecurity than ever.

Some humanitarian groups have resisted this agenda, realizing that it may very well undermine their basic motivations and purpose. Cornish concludes by posing some fundamental questions. What should be the limits to such integration? Are there grounds for clarifying and implementing civil-military communication protocols that can truly promote humanitarian work? Or is there simply no room for humanitarianism in the military interventions of our age?

* * *

The above Introduction, written by the editors, summarizes the ideas put forth in the first half of the larger article by Stephen Cornish which first appeared in the *Journal of Military and Strategic Studies*, Fall, 2007, Vol. 10 #1. The second half of the article, specifically on Afghanistan, is presented below.

TRANSFORMING AFGHANISTAN

Following the initial success of the US-led invasion of Afghanistan, a two year opportunity for reconstruction and development existed and was essentially wasted by the interveners:

A window of opportunity existed between 2002–2004 even in the Pashtun tribal areas for the UK and US to have made marked impact on development and reconstruction. $1 billion was delivered, much of it usurped by contractors, and warlords. The population's frustration began to grow and boiled over with the winter of 2004 (the coldest in 20 years) in which thousands of Afghans, many of them children, perished while the West continued security payments to the warlords and attention turned to other adventures.[1]

Much like the earlier US-led operation in Northern Iraq, the invasion of Afghanistan has gone from being seen as a combat operation called "Operation Enduring Freedom" to being seen as a UN-sanctioned, NATO-led, Whole of Government, forcible, military intervention aimed at stabilizing a failed state, reconstructing a war-ravaged country and giving economic opportunity, good governance and the rule of law to the long suffering Afghan population.

For NGOs – and arguably for most peacebuilding practitioners – peacebuilding is seen as a transversal process with an emphasis on grassroots or bottom-up (track III) inclusive, common ground activities which complement Track I activities like peacekeeping, governmental negotiations and planning, and Track II mediation and facilitation work conducted by NGOs, religious leaders and academics.[2]

An argument can even be made that while all levels of peacemaking and peacebuilding are important, most recent transitions towards peace have resulted from pressure that was "bubbling up from the grassroots."[3] In Afghanistan, however, we are witnessing an attempt at predominantly top-down societal transformation, imposed largely from the outside, coupled with the supporting role of the newly elected Afghan government.

The peace-enforcement and peacebuilding talked about is a bit of a misnomer, as large parts of the country remain embroiled in full-scale conflict. It remains to be seen whether or not a negative peace (the absence of war) can be achieved militarily, and positive peace (overcoming the issues which lead to or could lead to renewed hostilities) secured through economic benefits of assistance remains to be seen. And while there is a belief among some practitioners that one can encourage conflicts to subside, the majority believe that a conflict must play itself out before a situation can be ripe for peacebuilding.

In the past, both peacekeepers and NGOs have come under scrutiny for reinforcing the status quo that created the conflict in the first place, leading to serious questioning of UN-sanctioned peacebuilding and forcible interventions.[4] The latter are now more contentious, as they are seen as reinforcing the culture of violence, in which the lessons retained are that the biggest guns win. As a result, some NGOs question the international efforts' ability to succeed in Afghanistan under these assumptions.

THE DILEMMAS FOR MULTI-MANDATE ORGANIZATIONS

Multi-mandate organisations, that is, those that work on both relief and development, are further affected as they attempt to promote peacebuilding and implement government sponsored programming in more secure areas of the country. This dual role – not unlike the duality inside the UN agencies themselves – means such organisations are attempting to "work in conflict" by delivering humanitarian aid and to simultaneously "work on the conflict" itself through participating in, for example, the reintegration phase of the Disarmament, Demobilisation, and Reintegration (DDR) process.

Furthermore, with conflict resolution and peacebuilding activities, agencies are looking to "work on the conflict" itself and, as such, take on an additional set of risks as Lederach points out:

To be directly involved in peacebuilding activities in settings of violent conflict supposes a certain level of precariousness and risk (as in danger), and involves balancing very complex relationships. Peacebuilding represents sensitive, delicate and at times, very confidential work where lives are on the line and affected by the actions taken.[5]

Difficulties abound. Local actors may misinterpret benign and common activities like "conflict mapping," which conflict-sensitive aid agencies undertake to better understand how aid may interact with the conflict. They may not understand why international NGOs are looking into what appear to be strategic and military matters. The difficulties in responding to these challenges adequately are heightened under the integrated or strategic approach in Afghanistan where the line between politics, the military intervention and humanitarian assistance becomes deliberately blurred as assistance is used as a tool to support the desired peace:[6]

The distinction between humanitarian, political and military action becomes blurred when armed forces are perceived as being humanitarian actors, when civilians are embedded into military structures, and when the impression is created that humanitarian organizations and their personnel are merely tools within integrated approaches to conflict management.[7]

Multi-mandate organisations involved in peacebuilding in Afghanistan, must thus take increased care to ensure they do not further blur the lines by creating the impression that they are one with the political military project that is underway.

THE CHALLENGES TO AID: HUMANITARIAN & DEVELOPMENT WORK IN THE "WAR ON TERROR"

Unfortunately the difficulties for humanitarians (to say nothing of those for the general population) in Afghanistan have largely outweighed the benefits brought by the 3D approach to the conflict. The challenges that have arisen include the co-optation of aid for security ends, doing peacebuilding and development within the War on Terror framework, safeguarding humanitarian principles and ethics, and protecting civilians in a military setting.

The *Reality of Aid* report, which comments on the state of global development by combining the views of some 30 countries, dedicated its 2006 issue to examining the impact of security and conflict on aid. Its authors concluded that donor-led Whole of Government Approaches (WGAs) to interventions have "largely subsumed diplomacy and development interests and favoured defence or military responses" for managing conflict and for meeting the strategic goals defined by the donor governments involved.[8] This, they point out, is not only true in Haiti, Sudan and Iraq but in Afghanistan as well. This is something that aid agencies on the ground know all too well.

CO-OPTING AID FOR SECURITY ENDS

"The incentives to dress hard military objectives in soft humanitarian clothing have been present from the start, regardless of the party in charge."[9]

From the outset in Afghanistan, the US-led effort paid little heed to the laws of war, be it to the Geneva Conventions or to international humanitarian law.[10] It is thus not surprising that there should be a lack of respect for the existing civil/military cooperation guidelines or experience worked out in earlier UN forcible military interventions and integrated missions. Aid, it seems, was to be conceived as nothing more than a weapon in the war against terror.

Non-uniformed special services officers – intentionally or not – camouflaged themselves by adopting the white land-cruisers associated with aid agencies and by addressing local leaders and elders with promises of aid and assistance. These officers were also the eyes and ears of the military and utilised this access to collect information. In some areas pamphlets were also dropped promising aid in exchange for information about the Taliban. "The confusion over the role of humanitarian workers that resulted from these and similar incidents severely jeopardized their security."[11]

The resulting confusion caused by this blurring of the lines between humanitarian and military action was seen as a primary factor in the assassination of five Médecins sans Frontières aid workers in 2004. Following their deaths, a Taliban spokesperson stated that aid organisations were working for American interests and had thus become legitimate targets, which led MSF to quit Afghanistan after 24 years of presence.[12]

The above mentioned semi-clandestine operations have now largely been replaced with provincial reconstruction teams (PRTs), a more formalized form of aid co-optation for essentially political and military purposes. These US-designed units adopted by the militaries comprising the International Security Assistance Force (ISAF) were originally tasked with coordinating humanitarian aid and aid actors. They often operated outside of pre-existing UN coordination mechanisms, and they soon began functioning as "military-relief hybrids" even though their initial job descriptions did not mention carrying out aid projects themselves:[13]

The (Coalition Force) CF is both a fighting force actively engaged in an anti-insurgency shooting war and a "hearts and minds" operation that provides relief and services to the local population in a manner that is functional to its military objectives.[14]

After their launch by the US in 2002, both the British and American forces openly conceived of their PRTs' so-called humanitarian aid as an instrument in the war against terror.[15] In their classic form, the PRTs reflect the theoretical construct of the Three Block War (3BW) that US General Charles Krulack posited in the late 1990s, in which the military would effectively be conducting combat operations on one block, separating belligerents (or peacekeeping) on another, and distributing humanitarian aid on a third – all in the same theatre and all within a few hours.[16]

Both the US and Canadian forces adopted this untested construct believing that the "Third Block" of visibly placed development would buy consent and force security. Unfortunately they failed to realize that proper development demands both skills and know-how that their members may not necessarily possess, and broad-based community consent from the outset. They have learnt the lessons in a hard way, rebuilding the Parwan school three times, first by the US following the invasion – and then twice by the Canadian PRT, once after it was burned by the Taliban and a second time after Canadian forces destroyed it during renewed fighting.[17] Rebuilding a school it had bombed might appear to some like a good-will gesture – but the wisdom of such an action must surely be questioned in the wake of a Human Rights Watch's report recommending not to build schools after 200 had been subject to attacks (including threats, beatings, executions, and buildings being burned) by those opposed to the politico/military project underway.[18] Militaries engaging in hearts and minds type projects are in essence struggling for control of the civilian population, which can end up making civilians the targets of ongoing hostilities. Such efforts should be avoided.[19]

It must also be said that other states such as the Netherlands and Norway have attempted to separate military roles from humanitarian tasks and to have their PRTs give priority to building, not buying, consent for their mission, by strengthening relations with local officials and promoting pro-peace initiatives. The British forces, while maintaining the right to carry out quasi-development projects under their civilian-military coordination (CIMIC) activities, have civilianised their PRTs in order to guarantee better quality programming and to ensure that their activities are coordinated, and do not occur in areas already served by aid agencies.[20]

While some measured improvements have come about at the same time as dialogue between NGOs and military actors in Kabul is improving, many militaries have refused efforts to be bound by constraints on their PRTs' quasi-development efforts. Thus despite efforts to limit the blurring of the lines between military and humanitarian assistance by some militaries involved in NATO's peacebuilding mission, other member states and the ongoing Operation Enduring Freedom continue to transgress the line for tactical and strategic benefits.

In an effort to maintain their independence and in order to protect themselves from the perception of assisting the military projects in southern Afghanistan, some agencies have refused to consider using funds to extend project activities there until the Canadian military agrees to conduct only security and policing activities.[21] Meanwhile, in addition to the recent spate of largely politically-motivated killings and kidnappings of aid workers in Afghanistan, a new trend has been reported to us by the Afghanistan NGO Security Office (ANSO). Aid workers are being stopped and searched at unofficial checkpoints managed by the insurgency (including through their computers and mobile phones) for any signs of cooperation with the Afghan government or NATO coalition militaries.

The damage done is perhaps already irreparable; the perceptions that aid actors are merely emissaries of their countries' intervening military forces will not soon fade. Tragically, dozens more humanitarian workers have been killed and the consent-based, impartial NGO assistance model worked out over decades has been erased, further reducing assistance and development prospects for the population.[22] One commentator suggests that:

Any political-military intervention that has a humanitarian component instantly stigmatises humanitarians and puts them in danger. The stigma remains long after the military has departed, affecting trust and confidence with which humanitarians are perceived, literally adding years to the process of reconstruction, reconciliation and prosperity.[23]

Despite such grim prospects, the increased risk to aid workers, and the reduction in areas where they can safely and effectively work, a number of NGOs have stayed on and attempted to carry out their assistance missions under the less-than-favourable conditions afforded by the 3D approach in Afghanistan.

CARRYING OUT PEACEBUILDING AND DEVELOPMENT EFFORTS
– IN THE WAR ON TERROR

"Humanitarians would never deny that the creation of a stable peace is in everyone's best interest. However, they would also assert the need for human-itarian action to exist alongside peacebuilding efforts in order to uphold the principle of humanity and the protection of civilian life as the conflict rages."[24]

Inside Afghanistan there are largely two realities. The first reality ex-ists in the central, north and western regions where humanitarian agencies and multi-mandate organisations are, despite the relative insecurity, still able to carry out humanitarian assistance, develop-ment initiatives and peacebuilding ventures.

In these areas, the world's focused attention on Afghanistan has, despite the difficulties, resulted in a number of successes that are often over-shadowed by the obstacles that remain. Government-led, donor-sponsored and often NGO-implemented programmes have helped 350,000 families access micro-finance and micro-credit initia-tives, and 12,000 of Afghanistan's 24,000 municipalities have bene-fited from the establishment of community development counsels and the implementation of locally-managed development initiatives made possible by the Afghan Government's National Solidarity Pro-gram.

The second reality concerns eastern, southern and other areas of the country where aid agencies have largely had to withdraw or re-duce their programming to inadequate remote-controlled efforts be-cause of security constraints related to the ongoing War on Terror:

Reconstruction has been very slow in the South. The food aid system has failed, causing a severe famine. Much of the population of Southern Afghan-istan is alienated from ISAF. Unless these circumstance change, the Canadian mission in Kandahar will become less and less acceptable to the local popu-lation. Time is not on NATO and Canada's side.[25]

Perhaps as a result of such portrayals, the general understanding emerging is that the 3D approach is not working in Afghanistan and, furthermore, that its failings can largely be attributed to the ineffec-tual and uncooperative aspect of the "D": Development.

Ultimately NGOs receive and implement between 10 and 15% of donor aid arriving in the country. Yet they are increasingly being held responsible for all the development failures in the Afghan context. A "blame game" has arisen in which each actor points to the other as being responsible for the apparent failures of the Whole of Government approach in Afghanistan.

Development projects that have been funded through external support and often directed through private contractors and/or PRTs have been singled out as being particularly costly, wasteful, lacking in quality and often not taking into account community needs.[26] As well, Afghan government-led efforts have been stalled by a nascent and corrupt bureaucracy that has been overloaded by donor funding, despite its inability to manage and support such a heavy programming burden.[27]

THE MILITARY'S POSITION

ISAF and NATO have felt let down by all the above as they decry the lack of visible development benefits, which they believe would shore up the population's support following their hard won victories on the battlefields. According to Jack Granatstein, "The enemy has been strong enough that the government's and the Canadian Forces' commitment to the 3D approach has not been able to receive a fair trial." He places blame on the fact that the open war fighting has constrained the PRTs, which have spent more time protecting themselves than assisting the Afghan people, on CIDA for being ineffectual, and on Canadian NGOs for refusing to cooperate with the military.[28] For Granatstein, the pushing of the other non consequential "D's" to the background during times of strategic necessity – or when the battles rage - is simply a logical state of affairs and to be expected. For him, like many integrationists, the benefits of peace-enforcement will arrive once the battles have been won.

THE NGOS' POSITION

For many NGOs and peacebuilders alike it is precisely this type of security-first logic that is at the heart of the problem and ultimately leads to what some term a state-building paradox.[29] This refers to the fact that short-term gains on counter insurgency, counter-narcotics, and war on terror fronts continually undermine community-based peacebuilding efforts and development initiatives that are ultimately required for a more peaceable future and for the coalitions' eventual success. This paradox is especially acute when coalition operations have led to large-scale loss of civilian life and property, fostered anti-government and anti-NATO sentiment, and have ultimately either ignored or been complicit in the reduction of humanitarian space.

SAFEGUARDING HUMANITARIAN PRINCIPLES OF INDEPENDENCE/NEUTRALITY/IMPARTIALITY

"Reconciling military, diplomatic and humanitarian objectives may be a more effective way of stabilizing failed and fragile states, but it also creates inevitable trade-offs and requires a high degree of collaboration."[30]

The question is what trade-offs to make and how much can one agree to suspend one's own morality and principles in order to arrive at the greater good? Another lesson of the Afghan experience is that the degree of collaboration demanded is sometimes higher than agencies can afford without becoming complicit in the military's agenda. The same difficulties can also arise when collaborating with governments in development and peacebuilding efforts.

To remain independent, agencies must remain in charge of where, and with whom, they work. Yet in government or military-led peacebuilding efforts, agencies sometimes have little control over the types of projects or the locations where they are to be implemented.

What is often not understood is that many multi-mandate agencies have already sacrificed a portion of their neutrality, impartiality and independence by acting as implementing agencies for various Afghan ministries. Agencies have done this to ensure their ability to assist and to participate in the peacebuilding activities funded by the donors under the Whole Government Approach logic.

In fact more than 80% of NGO activities in the recipient country are already tied to government programmes. While good donorship principles oblige that a majority of collected funds be directed through multilateral organisations or into direct budgetary support to the host government, this shift has further disenfranchised many beneficiaries and shut down "key services not covered under the remit of the current government programmes."[31]

In the south of Afghanistan, the few NGOs still able to function have clearly been unable to meet the urgent needs of the civilian population. Defence actors have both offered to extend protection to aid agencies and have tried setting up "Priority Development Zones" (PDZs) in which security would be maintained by the NATO coalition members.[32] From the humanitarian side there is little belief in the solutions offered, something that perplexes the military and further fixes the stereotype that humanitarian workers are somehow antiquated and that they selectively use neutrality as an excuse to avoid working with the military.

Yet in southern Afghanistan, CARE's local partners have been approached and told that CARE's "aid is good for the local community and may continue. However if you or the programmes you implement become associated with NATO forces, then you will make yourself a target." This is not an idle threat. During my recent visit, four Afghan de-miners protected by ISAF and four armed UN security guards protecting a reconstruction engineer were killed during the same week.

CARE is responsible for the lives of some 800 national staff and their families, and is helping hundreds of thousand of Afghans in 12 provinces. We do this successfully under the traditional model of arranging safety through community acceptance and local integration. In this scenario, we must weigh very carefully the expansion of our activities into areas where the conditions for safe and successful delivery of assistance programming no longer exist.

The reality is that aid agencies make themselves targets by working in PDZs as they are seen to have taken sides, thus evaporating the consent-based security and community acceptance model on which they rely to carry out their programming. It is therefore no wonder that "aid agencies are very nervous about working side by side with the military. When that happens, their impartiality in the eyes of the community has been lost" and with it, their ability to safely and effectively carry out bottom-up, inclusive programming for the benefit of all.[33]

Compromises on impartiality lead to the conditionality of assistance and discrimination towards victims. This has become a hallmark of the way the WGA and the Afghan government distributes and relates to development issues and assistance.

As with many aid efforts, however, help for the displaced has been hampered by the Afghan government itself. Last March, the government declared that support for the camp dwellers should stop, so the people would be encouraged to return home. The [World Food Programme] now plans to use its

CIDA money to help get people out of the camps and back into their homes, with food-for-work-incentives.[34]

Using food aid as a weapon to force civilians back into unsafe areas should clearly not be supported by any aid agency, yet contravening the ban risks raising the ire of the Afghan authorities. That the WFP would be complicit in this, points to the abrogation of its humanitarian mandate in favour of short-term political priorities.

A case in point is the experience the author had dealing with a particular Afghan ministry. When the author wanted to begin programming in the volatile southern region, he was informed that the Ministry intended to guarantee CARE's safety through the use of armed emissaries provided by the communities themselves. In cases where security could not be guaranteed as a result of Taliban presence, information would be transmitted back to ISAF and the Afghan National Army so that they could "clean up the area," after which CARE would be encouraged to commence its activities. Extending the writ of the government's programming, and helping to rout out the Taliban, thus went hand in hand, in the opinion of the high-level Ministry official in question.

These kinds of practices – cooperating in such a government program, using food aid as a weapon, or carrying out programs together with the PRTs – would put CARE in direct contravention of the Red Cross Code of Conduct that humanitarian and development agencies signed back in 1995, precisely to guard against the politicisation and instrumentalisation of aid. That our organisation could not follow through with such an unethical bargain was never in question. It did, however, show the limits of deep integration and reconfirmed the wisdom of abiding by the core humanitarian principle of independence of action.

CIVILIAN PROTECTION/ USE OF FORCE ISSUES (JUST WAR AND HUMANITARIAN INTERVENTIONS)

In the long history of legal debates about humanitarian intervention there has been a consistent failure to address directly the question of the methods used in such interventions. It is almost as if the labelling of an intervention as humanitarian provides sufficient justification in itself, and there is no need to think further about the aims of the operation or the means employed.[35]

UN mandated and/or sanctioned forces, (other articles in this book deny that NATO's military intervention is UN sanctioned.) such as NATO's ISAF, become party to the war by engaging in forcible humanitarian interventions and peace-making efforts. As such, they must respect the rules of international humanitarian law (IHL). Besides the duty to promote indepenedent humanitarian assistance, the UN and its allies must abide by *just means*, respond propotionally to threats, and avoid civilian targets and institutions when possible, otherwise they will be in contravention of IHL and will forfeit the legitimacy of these HIs themselves.[36]

Following a spate of well publicized incidents in which US and coalition bombardments have led to high numbers of civilian casualties, the UN released a report stating that in the first part of 2007 allied and Afghan forces caused more civilians deaths than the insurgents.[37] The vast majority of recent civilian deaths in Afghanistan, however, are not related to individual soldiers on the ground in the fog of war. Civilian deaths are largely due to the coalition's increasing reliance on aerial bombardments[38] and long-range artillery support (as was done in Kosovo) to compensate for limited troop numbers[39] and in order to minimize coalition casualties:

Scores of civilian deaths over the past months from the heavy US and allied reliance on air strikes to battle Taliban insurgents are threatening popular support for the Afghan government and creating severe strains within the NATO alliance.[40]

In addition to the loss of life, increased coalition activity in the south has led to an increase in internally displaced persons (IDPs) and has caused wide-scale damage to civilian houses, wells and other infrastructure, exacerbating the humanitarian situation on the ground. One such attack near Herat in the summer of 2007 led to dozens of deaths, including civilians, created over 2000 IDPs, and left 170 houses wholly or partially destroyed.

The US and NATO have now both acknowledged the problem – although arguably they see it more in terms of losing hearts and minds and potential ramifications for their own force security, than in abiding by IHL and guaranteeing civilian protection. There is also a steady stream of apologies issued from NATO and the US forces, which are generally followed by the justification that the insurgents are taking sanctuary or hiding among civilians. Such behaviour on the part of the insurgency is clearly a breach of IHL, as are other tactics like suicide bombings, which must be condemned unreservedly. However, even in such cases as shielding, the response must abide by proportionality. While this is indeed a high standard, humanitarian interventions must uphold these standards if they wish to maintain legitimacy.[41]

There is some cause for hope here in the so-called "European exception": the Netherlands, France and other continental nations see their presence in Afghanistan more in terms of keeping the peace and nation building and thus are said to be uncomfortable with the military posture and collateral damage. The sanctity of human life and the right to assistance and protection are fundamental constructs of the humanitarian endeavour. When these are transgressed, and humanitarian workers are present, they have a duty to give voice to the victims and to bear witness to the suffering.

Where there is contact with the victims of catastrophe that is instigated or made worse by the direct or structural oppression by some humans or others, the ethical mandate of bearing witness in favour of the victims arises spontaneously.[42]

The Afghanistan Coordination Body for Afghan Relief (ACBAR), which includes both Afghan NGOs and international NGOs, has now felt it necessary to explicitly underline breaches in IHL by the the coalition and the Operation Enduring Freedom, while also condemning the indiscriminate methods used by the insurgency.

We strongly condemn operations and force protection measures carried out by international military forces in which disproportionate or indiscriminate use of force has resulted in civilian casualties. Such operations have frequently been carried out by forces or agencies outside NATO command, often American forces in Operation Enduring Freedom, and sometimes in conjunction with Afghan forces.[43]

Ultimately agencies that remain despite the challenges have a duty to advocate or witness on the victim's behalf. They do so in hopes that the military and political leaders will put in place policies and practices that allow soldiers on the ground to conduct their activities in ways that will better protect the civilian population. This should ultimately enhance rather than detract from the mission's general objectives of restoring peace and security, and ultimately stabilizing the failed state.

CONCLUSION

The co-optation of aid for political and military purposes in Afghanistan has spawned a politically aggravated, acute humanitarian emergency, largely unreported and unattended, in an ever-expanding area of the country. Both humanitarian minimalists and multi-mandate maximalists (including Afghan NGOs and INGOs) have largely had to abandon the heaviest conflict areas, as their consent-based presence was eroded and their safety undermined by the coalition forces that used aid conditionality, as a tool, and unwisely took on the appearance of aid workers.

The numerous challenges faced by aid agencies under the 3D approach have been greater than in previous humanitarian interventions and have, at times, seriously strained relations amongst the various actors. This has led many aid agencies to conclude that the moral overlap of goals to which they subscribed in order to participate in shared conflict transformation agendas is unworkable in heavily militarised 3D approaches, and untenable in War on Terror settings.

Humanitarian and development agencies have thus had to distance themselves from the deeper coordination and command and control agendas of other actors in the integrated approach. They have had to reaffirm their adherence to humanitarian principles and the code of conduct in order to create ever shrinking pockets of humanitarian space where they can still function. In future, multi-mandate NGOs and others who have adopted the working on conflict agenda, must remain more vigilant of their independence and retain the lesson that such activity (unless conducted for both sides) can have consequences which can negatively affect both their own ability to carry out humanitarian relief activities, and the ability of traditional humanitarian agencies who never subscribed to these "maximalist" goals.

While maintaining independence, all actors involved in the 3D in Afghanistan must continue to forge a strong culture of communication. Sharing the same terrain as they do, development, defence and diplomatic actors will all be better served through improved understanding of respective mandates, positions and operational cultures. While some may be disappointed that deeper coordination, coherence, or control by one lead actor are not possible or desirable, it was in fact entirely predictable from the moment the security agenda overtook the protection agenda as the lead motive for intervention.

Predictably the 3D approach has been dominated by the Defence "D." Whether this is due to its advantage in size and funding or its "can do" mentality can still be debated. What is less in doubt is that PRTS based on the 3BW concept (which pre-dates the war on terror) were deployed early on in the conflict and were seen as essential components in the heavily militarised solution to Afghanistan's problems. They did not originate spontaneously as a result of the failings of the other Ds, as is sometimes maintained.

While research suggests that equal partnership among actors in the coherent approach is the key to success, it is increasingly difficult to see how such a level playing field could ever be created in Afghanistan. In setting out the failure of leading with a heavily militarised solution to dealing with failed states and transforming these states through forcible transformation, Axworthy writes. "If one wants recent proof of the problems with this approach, just look at what happened in Afghanistan, where the warlords reign supreme. The population is faced with constant threats to their security, development is stymied and the export of heroin is setting new records."[44] This pessimistic view of progress to date was not, as seems likely, penned in the past months, but almost five years ago.

Regrettably Canadian politicians continue to echo Colin Powell's view of NGOs as "force multipliers" by selling the war at home as a combined 3D/humanitarian mission.[45] Instead of promoting such dangerous and short-sighted rhetoric, our politicians should instruct the military commanders to devise policies and practices which promote civilian protection and which safeguard humanitarian space.

Use of force issues are actually intensifying the population's suffering, and undermining the coalition's efforts in Afghanistan. As a result, special care must be taken to reduce displacement, destruction and death caused by aerial bombardments in civilian areas. A serious review of rules governing use of force could ultimately reduce civilian casualties and would, at minimum, ensure the respect of the "just means" principle which is essential for maintaining the legitimacy of the NATO- and UN-sanctioned mission.

Consent, it seems, cannot be easily purchased through visible PRT-led reconstruction projects, even if they are well intentioned, as they are often shortsighted and can lead the insurgency to target civilians. Both these facts are increasingly being registered by the soldiers on the ground and by the command structures of progressive-minded militaries, which are beginning to alter their military and donor policies.

While the civilianisation of military PRTs is a step in the right direction, it would be preferable for the military to completely break with the militarisation of aid. Even if properly conducted, bringing aid in one hand, with a gun in the other, will continue to politicise assistance and lead to perceptions that will ultimately further reduce humanitarian space. This is where the limits to civil/military guidelines and cooperation lie, as militaries are unwilling to discuss or forego their ability to conduct such quasi-development activities in conflict settings. As a result, and until such a time as the theoretical 3D construct can make room for an independent and operational humanitarian "H," it may indeed be best to simply remove the Development "D" from the equation.[46]

While Afghanistan is the central issue today, much more is at stake. The very legitimacy of humanitarian interventions could be lost if the international community is not careful to safeguard the core principle of humanity. Morality matters; and both right intentions and just means are essential to upholding the legitimacy of humanitarian interventions. Hopefully Canada will heed the warning signs before it's too late, as it is one of the lead architects of the Responsibility to Protect doctrine, which has the potential to avoid conflict, alleviate suffering, and protect civilians from the abuses of their own governments. What is abundantly clear is that since the start of the War on Terror, there has yet to be an effective and justified intervention that can be called humanitarian; and this should give all 3D actors (Defence, Diplomacy and Development) cause to pause and reflect.

NOTES

1   Vani Cappelli, "Alienated Frontier," ORBIS (Fall 2005): 723–4, www.fpri.org/orbis [26 July 2007].

2   Hugh Miall, Oliver Ramsbotham, and Tom Woodhouse, Contemporary Conflict Resolution (Cambridge: Polity Press, 2004), 20.

3   Ibid., 58–9.

4   Ibid., 59.

5   John Paul Lederach, Building Peace: Sustainable Reconciliation in Divid-

ed Societies (Washington, DC: US Institute for Peace Press, 1997), 132.

6 Haneef Atmar, Sultan Barakat, and Arne Strand, eds., *From Rhetoric to Reality: The Role of Aid in Local Peacebuilding in Afghanistan* (New York: INTRAC, 1998), 36–8.

7 Raj Rana, "Contemporary Challenges in the Civil-Military Relationship: Complementarity or Incompatibility?" *International Review of the Red Cross* 86, no. 55 (2004): 586.

8 "Reality of Aid," 2006, 1, www.reality of aid.org [26 July 2007].

9 Taylor Owen and Patrick Travers, "3D Vision. Can Canada Reconcile Its Defence, Diplomacy and Development Objectives in Afghanistan?" *The Walrus* (July/August 2007): 49.

10 Wheeler and Harmer, "Resetting the Rules of Engagement," Overseas Development Institute, Report 21, (March 2006) www.relief.web.int

11 Owens and Travers, "3D Vision," op. cit., 44–9.

12 Ibid., 46

13 Isabelle Bercq, "La militarisation de l'action humanitaire en Afghanistan," Note D'analyse, 2 (Groupe de recherche et d'information sur la paix et la sécurité, 9 May 2005), www.grip.org/bdg/g4572.htlm [20 Aug. 2007].

14 Antonio Domini et al. "Mapping the Security Environment: Understanding the Perceptions of Local Communities, Peace Support Operations and Assistance Agencies," Report commissioned by the UK NGO–Military Contact Group (New York: Feinstein International Famine Center; Medford, MA: Tufts University, 2005), 12.

15 Bercq, "La militarisation de l'action humanitaire en Afghanistan," 1.

16 "The rubric of 3BW offers the military a logical framework for the variance of their work in a way which makes sense to a combat-centric. However, 3BW was never developed as an operational strategy, but was a framework to try to understand the complexity of contemporary armed conflicts and other insurgencies." Sarah Jane Meharg, "Three Block Wars and Humanitarianism – Theory, Policy, and Practice," Final Report (Ottawa: Pearson Peacekeeping Centre, 2006), 7.

17 Story collected by the author (under Chatam House rules), Calgary, 20 March 2007.

18 Human Rights Watch, "Lessons in Terror – Attacks on Education in Afghanistan," July 2006, http://www.hrw.org/reports/2006/afghanistan 0706/index.htm [August 2007].

19 It is my understanding that the Canadian, British, and American militaries continue to have school construction targets to meet at this time.

20 Domini, "Mapping the Security Environment," op. cit., 14.

21 Rick Westhead, "Relief Groups Reject Afghan Projects," *Toronto Star,* 19 October 2006.

22 "There has been a sharp rise in attacks against aid workers (28 NGO workers killed from January to August 2006, compared with 31 aid workers killed during the whole of 2005) and conversely, a reduction in areas where agencies are prepared to work ... This has triggered a vicious circle: the insecurity is preventing reconstruction and this in turn is fuelling the population's distrust of both the international community and the government." Holly Ritchie, "Aid Effectiveness in Afghanistan at a Crossroads," ACBAR Briefing Paper (November 2006): 5, www.reliefweb.int/library/document/2006.acbar-afg-oinov.pdf [26 July 2007].

23 Ted Itani, "Politicization of Aid," *On Track* 12, no. 1, (Spring 2007): 3, Conference of the Defence Associations Institute, http://www.cda-cdai.ca/seminars/2005/English%202005%20Agenda.pdf

24 Gordon Smith et al., "Canada in Afghanistan: Is It Working?" *Canadian Defence and Foreign Affairs Institute,* 2007, 14, www.cdfai.org [August 2007].

25 Hamish Nixon, "Aiding the State? International Assistance and the Statebuilding Paradox," Briefing Paper Series (Kabul: Afghanistan Research and Evaluation Unit [AREU], 2007), 9.

26 Ritchie, "Aid Effectiveness in Afghanistan," 6.

27 J.L. Granatstein, *Whose War Is It? How Canada Can Survive in the Post 9/11 World* (Toronto: Harper Collins, 2007), 214–15.

28 Nixon, "Aiding the State," 1.

29 Owen and Travers, "3D Vision," 46.

30 Ritchie, "Aid Effectiveness in Afghanistan," op. cit., footnote 22.

31 "At the other extreme, a few agencies and donor representatives chose to embed themselves with the PRTs or to travel alongside CF convoys for their protection. This approach was chastised as dangerous by most assistance agencies." Domini, "Mapping the Security Environment," op. cit., footnote 14.

32 Rick Westhead, "Relief Groups," op. cit.

33 Graeme Smith, "'We Have to Act Faster,' CIDA Says. Officials Concede Canadian Aid Flows Slowly in Afghanistan," *Globe and Mail,* 21 January 2007.

34 Roberts, "Humanitarian War," *The Journal of International Affairs,* Issue 69 (1993).

35 Francoise Saulnier-Bouchet, "Action Humanitaire entre droit de la

guerre et Maintien de la Paix," *Les cahiers de Mars*, No. 166 (3rd trimester 2000): 6–7, www.msf.fr [February 2005].

36 A recent UN report said 593 Afghan civilians have been killed by violence linked to insurgents this year. But more of those deaths, 314, were caused by ISAF or Afghan security forces than by insurgents." Kim Barker, "Afghan Civilians Caught in Crossfire," *Chicago Tribune*, 8 July 2007.

37 "This year in Afghanistan, American aircraft have dropped 987 bombs and fired more than 146,000 cannon rounds and bullets in strafing runs, more than was expended in both categories from the beginning of the American-led invasion in 2001 through 2004, the Air Force said." David S. Cloud, "US Airstrikes Climb Sharply in Afghanistan," *New York Times*, 17 November 2006.

38 *Economist*, "Western Forces in Afghanistan – Unfriendly Fire," Editorial, *Economist*, 51, 23 June 2007.

39 Michael N. Schmitt, "War Technology, and International Humanitarian Law," *HPCR Occasional Paper Series*, Harvard University, Program on Humanitarian Policy and Conflict Research, (Summer 2005), 37.

40 Xabier Etxeberria, "The Ethical Framework of Humanitarian Action," in *Reflections on Humanitarian Action–Principle, Ethics and Contradictions*, ed. Humanitarian Studies Unit, (London: Transnational Institute/Pluto Press with the Humanitarian Studies Unit and the European Commission Humanitarian Office [ECHO], 2001), 93.

41 Agency Coordinating Body for Afghan Relief, "Protecting Afghan Civilians: Statement on the Conduct of Military Operations," 19 June 2007, www.acbar.org [24 August 2007]

42 Axworthy, *Navigating a New World*, Toronto: Knoff Canada, 2004, 194.

43 Maxime Bernier, "Why We're in Afghanistan," Op-ed, *National Post*, 24 September 2007.

44 Itani, "Politicization of Aid," op. cit., 3.

BIBLIOGRAPHY

Agency Coordinating Body for Afghan Relief (ACBAR). *Protecting Afghan Civilians: Statement on the Conduct of Military Operations*. 19 June 2007. www.acbar.org [24 August 2007].

Anderson, Mary B. *Do No Harm, How Aid Can Support Peace – Or War*. London: Lynne Rienner, 1999.

Atmar, Haneef, Barakat Sultan, and Arne Strand, eds. *From Rhetoric to Reality: The Role of Aid in Local Peacebuilding in Afghanistan.* New York: INTRAC, 1998.

Axworthy, Lloyd. *Navigating a New World: Canada's Global Future.* Toronto: Knoff Canada, 2003.

Barker, Kim. "Afghan Civilians Caught in Crossfire." *Chicago Tribune,* 8 July 2007.

Bercq, Isabelle. "La militarisation de l'action humanitaire en Afghanistan." Groupe de recherche et d'information sur la paix et la sécurité. 9 May 2005. www.grip.org/bdg/g4572.htlm [20 Aug. 2007].

Bernier, Maxime. "Why We're in Afghanistan." Oped section, *National Post.* 24 September 2007.

Bhatia, Michael, Kevin Lanigan, and Philip Wilkinson. "Minimal Investments, Minimal Results: The Failure of Security Policy in Afghanistan." Kabul: Afghanistan Research and Evaluation Unit, 2004.

Cappelli, Vani. "Alienated Frontier." ORBIS (Fall 2005): 715–29. www.fpri.org/orbis [26 July 2007].

Charny, Joel. "Upholding Humanitarian Principles in an Effective Integrated Response." *Journal of Ethics and Humanitarian Affairs* 18, no. 2 (2004).

Chomsky, Noam. *Hegemony or Survival.* New York: Henry Holt and Company, 2003.

Cloud, David, S. "US Airstrikes Climb Sharply in Afghanistan." *New York Times,* 17 November 2006.

Department of National Defence. "DEFENCE: Role of Pride and Influence in the World." *Canada's International Policy Statement.* www.forces.gc.ca [26 August 2007].

de Torrente, Nicholas. "Humanitarianism Sacrificed: Integration's False Promise." *Journal of Ethics and International Affairs* 18, no. 2 (2004).

Domini, Antonio et al. "Mapping the Security Environment: Understanding the Perceptions of Local Communities, Peace Support Operations and Assistance Agencies." Report commissioned by the UK NGO – Military Contact Group. New York: Feinstein International Famine Center; Medford, MA: Tufts University, 2005.

Easterly, William. *The White Man's Burden – Why the West's Efforts to Aid the Rest Have Done So Much Ill and So Little Good.* Toronto: Penguin Books, 2007.

Economist. "Western Forces in Afghanistan – Unfriendly Fire." Editorial. *Economist,* 23 June 2007.

Etxeberria, Xavier. "The Ethical Framework of Humanitarian Action." *Reflections on Humanitarian Action – Principle, Ethics and Contradictions*, ed. Humanitarian Studies Unit. London: Transnational Institute/Pluto Press with the Humanitarian Studies Unit and the European Commission Humanitarian Office (ECHO), 2001.

Goodhand, Jonathan and Philippa Atkinson. "Conflict and Aid: Enhancing the Peacebuilding Impact of International Engagement." *International Alert* (2001).

Gall, Carlotta and David E. Sanger. "Afghan Civilian Deaths Damaging NATO." *International Herald Tribune*, 13 May 2007.

Granatstein, J.L. *Whose War Is It? How Canada Can Survive in the Post 9/11 World*. Toronto: Harper Collins, 2007.

ICRC. *Summary of the Geneva Conventions of August 1949 and Their Additional Protocols*. Geneva: ICRC, 1983.

IFRC. "The Code of Conduct for the International Red Cross and Red Crescent Movement and NGOs in Disaster Relief": 1–6. Annex VI to the resolutions of the 26th International Conference of the Red Cross and Red Crescent Societies held in Geneva in 1995. www.ifrc.org/Docs/idrl/I259EN.pdf [24 September 2007].

Itani, Ted. "Politicisation of Aid." *On Track* 12, no. 1 (Spring 2007): 21–27. Conference of Defence Associations Institute. www.cda-cdai.ca/pdf/ontrack12n1.pdf.

Kurth, James. "Humanitarian Intervention after Iraq: Legal Ideals vs Military Realities." ORBIS (Winter 2005): 87–101. Foreign Policy Research Institute. www.fpri.org/orbis/5001/kurth.humanitarianintervention afteriraq.pdf [26 July 2007].

Lederach, Jean Paul. *Building Peace: Sustainable Reconciliation in Divided Societies*. Washington, DC: US Institute for Peace Press, 1997.

Macrae, Joanna and Nicholas Leader. "The Politics of Coherence: Humanitarianism and Foreign Policy in the Post-Cold War Era." *Journal Humanitaire – enjeux, pratiques et debats* 1, no. 11 (2000).

Miall, Hugh, Oliver Ramsbotham, and Tom Woodhouse. *Contemporary Conflict Resolution*. Cambridge: Polity Press, 2004.

Mortimer, Edward. "Under What Circumstances Should the UN Intervene Militarily in a 'Domestic' Crisis? In *Peacemaking and Peacekeeping for the New Century*, ed. O. Otunnu and M. Doyle. Lanham, MD: Rowman and Littlefield, 1998.

Nixon, Hamish. "Aiding the State? International Assistance and the State-building Paradox in Afghanistan." *Afghanistan Research and Evaluation*

Unit – Briefing Paper Series. Kabul: Afghanistan Research and Evaluation Unit, 2007.

Owen, Taylor and Patrick Travers. "3D Vision – Can Canada Reconcile its Defence, Diplomacy, and Development Objectives in Afghanistan?" *The Walrus* (July/August 2007).

Padilla, Arnold and Brian Tomlinson. "Shifting Trends: ODA, Global Security and the MDG's." *Reality of Aid* – 2006. www.realityofaid.org [26 July 2007].

Patrick, Stewart and Kaysie Brown. "Greater than the Sum of Its Parts – Assessing 'Whole of Government' Approaches to Fragile States." New York: International Peace Academy Press, 2007.

Powell, Colin, L. "Remarks to the National Foreign Policy Conference for Leaders of Nongovernmental Organizations." Washington, DC. 26 October 2001.www.yale.edu/ [25 September 2007].

Pugh, Michael. "The Social-Civil Dimension." In *Regeneration of War-Torn Societies*. London: Macmillan Press, 2000.

Rana, Raj. "Contemporary Challenges in the Civil-Military Relationship: Complementarity or Incompatibility?" *International Review of the Red Cross*, No. 86 (September 2004): 855.

Rieff, David. *A Bed for the Night – Humanitarianism in Crisis*. Toronto: Simon and Schuster, 2002.

Ritchie, Holly. "Aid Effectiveness in Afghanistan at a Crossroads." ACBAR Briefing Paper. 2006. www.reliefweb.int/library/document/2006. acbar-afg-oinov.pdf [26 July 2007].

Roberts, Adam. "Humanitarian Principles in International Politics in the 1990s." In *Reflections on Humanitarian Action – Principle, Ethics and Contradictions*, ed. Humanitarian Studies Unit, 23–54. London: Transnational Institute/Pluto Press with the Humanitarian Studies Unit and the European Commission Humanitarian Office (ECHO), 2001.

Roberts, Adam. "Humanitarian War: Military Intervention and Human Rights." *Journal of International Affairs* 69, no. 3 (1993).

Ross, Steven. "Breaking Point: Measuring Progress in Afghanistan." Center for Strategic and International Studies. www.csis.org/media/csis/pubs/ 070223_break ingpoint.pdf [20 July 2007].

Salama, Peter et al. "Lessons Learned from Complex Emergencies over the Past Decade." *The Lancet*, No. 634 (2004).

Saulnier-Bouchet, Francoise. "Action Humanitaire entre droit de la guerre et Maintien de la Paix." *Les cahiers de Mars*, No. 166 (2000). www.msf.fr [February 2005].

Schmitt, Michael N. "War Technology and International Humanitarian
    Law." HPCR *Occasional Paper Series*. Harvard University, Program on
    Humanitarian Policy and Conflict Research. Summer 2005.
Simpson, Erin and Brian Tomlinson. "Canada: Is Anyone Listening?" *Real-
    ity of Aid*. 2006. www.realityofaid.org [26 July 2007].
Slim, Hugo. "With or Against? Humanitarian Agencies and Coalition
    Counter Insurgencies." *Refugee Survey Quarterly* 23, no. 4 (2004): 34–47.
Smith, Gordon et al. "Canada in Afghanistan: Is It Working?" Canadian
    Defence and Foreign Affairs Institute, Calgary: 2007.
    www.cdfai.org/PDF/Canada%20in%20Afghanistan%20Is%20it%
    20Working.pdf [August 2007].
Smith, Graeme. "We Have to Act Faster, CIDA says: Officials Concede
    Canadian Aid Flows Slowly in Afghanistan." *Globe and Mail*, 21 Janu-
    ary 2007.
Terry, Fiona. *The Paradox of Humanitarian Action – Condemned to
    Repeat?* Ithaca: Cornell University Press, 2002.
US Department of Defense. *Quadrennial Defense Review Report*. 6 Febru-
    ary 2006. www.defenselink.mil/gdr/report/Report20060203.pdf
    [25 July 2007].
War to Peace Transitions Conference. *A Conference Report of the 8th
    Peacebuilding and Human Security Consultations*, Ottawa, Canada,
    April 2005.
Weir, Erin, A. "Conflict or Compromise: UN Integrated Missions and the
    Humanitarian Imperative." KAIPTC *Monograph* 4.0.
    www.trainingforpeace.org [September 2007].
Westhead, Rick. "Relief Groups Reject Afghan Projects." *Toronto Star*,
    19 October 2006.
Wheeler, Victoria and Adele Harmer, eds. "Resetting the Rules of Engage-
    ment– Trends and Issues in Military-Humanitarian Relations." *Humani-
    tarian Policy Group Research Report*, Overseas Development Institute,
    Report 21, (March 2006) www.relief.web.int
Wilkinson, Philip. "Sharpening the Weapons of Peace." In *Peacekeeping
    and Conflict Resolution*, ed. T. Woodhouse and O. Ramsbotham.
    London: Frank Cass, 2000.

Our Political and Military Americanization: Afghan Torture Furor Shows How Canada Kowtows to the US

LINDA McQUAIG

It was almost enough to revive one's faith in Canada as a functioning democracy, not to mention a member of the civilized world.

After weeks of unrelenting pressure – led by the media and the opposition parties – the Harper government was forced to abandon a deal that made Canada complicit in torture in Afghanistan.

Before we go further, however, let's emphasize that the much-improved deal governing the treatment of our detainees in Afghanistan came about despite the sustained and determined efforts of the Harper government to thwart such monitoring of human rights.

For more than a year, the Conservatives had been content to hand over detainees to Afghan custody, despite ample evidence – including from Canadian officials – that Afghanistan routinely tortures those in its custody.

Even after controversy erupted over the situation, the Harper government was evasive and uncooperative, dismissing detailed reports of torture as mere "allegations of the Taliban." This dismissive approach was echoed by *Globe and Mail* columnist Margaret Wente, who made clear that her sympathies lay with Canadian military leaders, not with Afghans who reported being hung upside down and punched so hard their teeth were knocked out.

"I have deep sympathy for our military leaders," wrote Wente, explaining what she saw as the difficult bind our generals are in. "They can fight a war. Or they can babysit 'our detainees'…"

To Wente, ensuring that our detainees aren't tortured – a requirement of the Geneva Conventions, which Canada has signed – is the equivalent of "babysitting" them.

Then there was our top general, Rick Hillier, whose fingerprints are all over the original deal, and who made light of the furor by diligently trying to divert attention onto the flashy arrival of the Stanley Cup and a group of NHL old-timers in Kandahar.

First stop for the hockey celebrities was the local Tim Hortons that Hillier famously brought to Afghanistan. Sadly, it seems Hillier's taste for Canadian traditions doesn't necessarily extend beyond hockey and doughnuts to include respect for human rights and the rule of law.

Surely it doesn't need to be noted that torture is among the lowest forms of human depravity. But, while it has lost acceptability in civilized circles in recent centuries, it has made a disturbing revival under US President George W. Bush.

Invoking the attacks of 9/11 as justification – as if there were no atrocities on this scale in history – the Bush administration has demonstrated a comfort level with torture that would befit the most brutal medieval king.

If we needed any evidence that Canada was being sucked into this maw of depravity by our involvement in Bush's "war on terror," we've now got it. Indeed, the detainee transfer agreement that Hillier signed with the Afghan government in December 2005 had overtones of Bush's "extraordinary rendition" program, under which terror suspects are handed over to a brutal country for detention and interrogation.

In both cases, there was clear knowledge that torture would occur, and no steps taken to prevent it.

That 2005 deal, put in place during Paul Martin's Liberal government reign, also illustrates how far we've drifted from our European allies in NATO, who insisted on considerably more stringent monitoring of the detainees they handed over to Afghanistan.

All this suggests a chasm between the values traditionally espoused by Canada – fairness, decency, and the rule of law – and the nefarious post-9/11 set of notions in which the leader of the "free world" is given a free hand to do as he wants with "evil-doers."

Globe and Mail columnist Lawrence Martin observed that "the new Canada has abandoned the independent strain we had," and that, in our growing closeness to Bush's America, "we are now consorts."

That sort of subordinate role is clearly what the Harper government, as well as some of our élite military and media types, have in mind for us. But it doesn't seem to be what the Canadian public is willing to accept.

This Afghan saga reminds me of the case of Maher Arar, the Canadian engineer tortured in Syria. In both cases, Ottawa tried to downplay a growing scandal about Canadian complicity in torture. But Canadians demanded accountability and eventually forced Ottawa to abide by the rule of law, not the lawless ways of the Bush administration.

It seems that, while our political leaders may be comfortable accommodating Bush, most Canadians have yet to develop a taste for toadying.

No Life Like It: The PR Battles of the Canadian Military

IRA BASEN

It must have been a good day to be Rick Hillier. His announcement that he will be stepping down in July as Canada's top soldier provoked a flood of gushing tributes in the normally reserved Canadian press.

A *Globe and Mail* editorial called him "the right man at the right time" who "put the bite back into the Canadian Forces." The editors also praised him for "refashioning the spin from Ottawa that had long sought to portray Canada's military as an NGO," a reference to an aid-giving non-governmental organization.

The paper's lead columnist, Christie Blatchford, one of the general's biggest fans in the Canadian media, wrote that Hillier "made it respectable again to be in the Canadian Forces," and "gave the Canadian soldier his mojo back."

These comments reflected the conventional wisdom surrounding Rick Hillier. As the story goes, it has been Hillier who, through his single-minded devotion to his troops and his considerable political and public relations skills, succeeded in pulling the Canadian Forces out of its deep funk.

This was a funk brought on by years of neglect by hostile or indifferent federal governments and a succession of feckless ministers of defence, a period the departing general himself once referred to as a "decade of darkness," setting up a conveniently flattering contrast to the current period of military enlightenment.

As with most conventional wisdom, this one is not without merit. There is no question that Hillier is extraordinarily media savvy and has managed to beguile the Canadian press in a way that is the envy of politicians, government officials and business leaders.

But the story of how the public face of the Canadian military has been so dramatically transformed over the past few years is more complex than one can usually find even on an editorial page.

In the end, this was a process that had begun well before the loquacious Newfoundlander took up his position early in 2005.

OVER-PRUNING?

Conveying a positive public image has been a preoccupation of the Canadian military for much of its long history, though its record of success has been spotty at best.

In 1962, the Glassco Commission, established by then Prime Minister John Diefenbaker, reported with some alarm that the information services branch of the armed forces totaled 190 people. This compared to just five communications staff in the entire federal Department of Transport.

The commissioners also noted that in a typical 14-day period in 1961, the military issued 68 press releases, distributed 2,500 photos and more than 100 radio and television spots.

They pronounced this output to be "disturbing," both for "its volume and intensity, and also for the high proportion of material offered not as source material, but as a finished product to be carried by the media," and urged Ottawa to reduce the force's reliance on public relations techniques.

After the forces were amalgamated in the early 1970s, the public information office was centralized and dramatically reduced, from nearly 300 people, to just a few dozen. Their job description was basically confined to answering specific questions posed by the media.

This was the case throughout the 1970s and 1980s, with little money or attention directed toward improving the public image of the Canadian military. By the dawn of the 1990s, there were only about 70 communications officers in the public affairs branch and most of them were inadequately trained to deal with the demands of the modern media. Then along came Somalia.

PR LANDMINE

The forces were certainly unprepared to deal with the fallout from the military's ultimate PR nightmare – the torture and murder of a Somali teenager by members of the Canadian Airborne regiment in 1993, which was quickly followed by the release of videos depicting some of the Airborne's more sadistic hazing rituals.

The Liberal government of the day quickly disbanded the Airborne, but the PR damage was done.

After Somalia, the public image of the Canadian military was one of inebriated, tattooed soldiers spouting racist rhetoric and smearing feces on one another.

The Cold War was over and Canadians were already having difficulty understanding what exactly its military was supposed to be doing. Add to that a government trying to reduce billions of dollars from a budgetary deficit and you can see where the "decade of darkness" had its beginnings.

But the military learned several lessons from Somalia. Among them was the need for a significantly larger and, more importantly, better trained public affairs department.

No longer could communications be the place to put officers with nowhere else to go in their careers. At around this time, the Canadian Forces began to recruit trained PR people, elevated the rank and pay scale of public affairs officers and hired civilians to do PR work as well.

By the time Hillier was appointed chief of the defence staff in 2005, the department had grown to more than 150 people. Collectively, they saw their mission as lifting the darkness that had fallen on the Canadian Armed Forces.

NO LIFE LIKE IT

One of their weapons was to gain a better understanding of how to get their message out through the press. In this vein, courses in media relations were established at military colleges. Articles on how to deal with the media started to appear in military journals.

Their efforts were aided by a series of domestic natural disasters in the late 1990s that proved highly beneficial in changing the public image of the Canadian military.

The sight of soldiers filling sand bags during the Red River flood, restoring power during the great ice storm of 1998 (under the command of Rick Hillier), even shoveling the snowy streets of Toronto, all helped give Canadians a warm and fuzzy feeling towards their own military.

To be sure, Canadian soldiers had done these worthy domestic duties before – during the October Crisis in 1970 and in Oka, in a tight standoff with natives, in 1990.

But then along came Sept. 11, 2001 and suddenly the Canadian Forces once again had a real enemy to fight and a new purpose in life.

In the so-called war on terror, the now media savvy military would reverse decades of hostility towards the press and turn it into its staunchest ally. The "embedded" reporter program, which Gen. Hillier endorsed, copying the Americans, was a PR bonanza for the military.

Reporters, most of whom were blissfully ignorant of military life and operations, were allowed unprecedented access to soldiers in the field.

What emerged from their reportage – and from a new openness that allowed soldiers to talk directly to the media and even write on internet blogs – was a portrait of Canadian fighting men and women that managed to completely reverse those horrifying images of a decade earlier.

Now the public face of the Canadian military were clean-cut, hockey-loving, Tim Horton's coffee-drinking kids who loved their moms and their country and were proud to help the people of Afghanistan get back on their feet. Public Affairs couldn't have scripted it any better. The "mojo" was back.

In reality, neither stereotype reflects the true diversity of the people who make up the Canadian forces, but this new improved image didn't happen by accident and likely would have happened even without someone with the media smarts of a Rick Hillier in command.

What the general did was put a human face on a new military brand that was already largely created by the time he arrived at the top job.

Marketers will tell you that attaching a face to a brand is important. What would President's Choice have been without Dave Nichol?

In an April 2008 interview with the *National Post*, Hillier boasted that "we've achieved the irreversible momentum that I wanted to have." But marketers will also tell you that there is no such thing as irreversible momentum, that even the best brands stumble as President's Choice did badly after Nichol's departure.

The challenge for the next chief of defence staff will be how to maintain the brand, now that its public face has gone and, at the same time, been lionized as the one who made all the good things happen.

Is the War in Afghanistan Legal?

LIGUE DES DOITS ET LIBERTÉS

I would like to take this opportunity to draw attention to an issue raised by Canada's military intervention in Afghanistan that is of great concern to the Ligue des droits et libertés, namely Canada's disregard for international law and its failure to abide by its commitments under the international pacts and conventions that it has ratified, in particular *the Convention Against Torture and Other Cruel, Inhuman or Degrading Treatment or Punishment* and the *Geneva Convention relative to the Treatment of Prisoners of War.*

AFGHAN PRISONERS AND THE ISSUE OF TORTURE

On December 18, 2005, General R.J. Hillier, Chief of the Defence Staff of Canada, and the Minister of Defence of Afghanistan signed an *Arrangement for the transfer of detainees between the government of Canada and the Islamic Republic of Afghanistan.*

Like the United States, Canada does not recognize combatants captured by Canadian Forces in Afghanistan as prisoners of war. According to Lieutenant-General Michel Gauthier, in charge of all

Canadian Forces deployed abroad, "The regulations [concerning prisoners of war] apply in an armed conflict between states, and what's happening in Afghanistan is not an armed conflict between states. And therefore there is no basis for making a determination of individuals being prisoners of war."[1]

Prisoners captured by Canada are nonetheless subject to Article 3 of the four 1949 Geneva Conventions, which applies precisely to "internal" conflicts, stating:

"In the case of armed conflict not of an international character occurring in the territory of one of the High Contracting Parties, each party to the conflict shall be bound to apply, as a minimum, the following provisions:

1. Persons taking no active part in the hostilities, including members of armed forces who have laid down their arms and those placed outside of combat by sickness, wounds, detention, or any other cause, shall in all circumstances be treated humanely, without any adverse distinction founded on race, colour, religion or faith, sex, birth or wealth, or any other similar criteria.

To this end the following acts are and shall remain prohibited at any time and in any place whatsoever with respect to the above-mentioned persons:

- Violence to life and person, in particular murder of all kinds, mutilation, cruel treatment and torture;
- Taking of hostages;
- Outrages upon personal dignity, in particular, humiliating and degrading treatment;
- The passing of sentences and the carrying out of executions without previous judgment pronounced by a regularly constituted court affording all the judicial guarantees which are recognized as indispensable by civilized peoples.

Canada must also abide by Article 3 of the *Convention Against Torture and Other Cruel, Inhuman or Degrading Treatment or Punishment*, which stipulates:

1. No State Party shall expel, return or extradite a person to another State where there are substantial grounds for believing that he would be in danger of being subjected to torture.

2. For the purpose of determining whether there are such grounds, the com-

petent authorities shall take into account all relevant considerations including, where applicable, the existence in the State concerned of a consistent pattern of gross, flagrant or mass violations of human rights.

According to the Arrangement, Canada bears no responsibility once detainees are transferred.[2] As a Canadian government representative said in response to criticism of the Arrangement, "The Afghan government clearly stated their intention to follow the Geneva Conventions. For us, this is acceptable."[3]

Yet the Afghanistan Independent Human Rights Commission,[4] United Nations High Commissioner for Human Rights, Louise Arbour[5], and the US Department of State[6] have all reported that torture of detainees by Afghan security forces is common practice.

As well, documents from the Department of Foreign Affairs, released on November 13, 2007 under the Access to Information Act, show that the Canadian government knew about the allegations of torture.

Canada's failure to honour its obligations with regard to torture goes beyond the issue of the fate of Afghan prisoners. Despite censure from UN committees, the Canadian government, in the framework of removal procedures set out in the *Immigration and Refugee Protection Act,* has not ruled out sending people to countries where they could be tortured or subjected to cruel or inhuman treatment.

Such conduct is contrary to the requirements of relevant international law, including the *Convention Against Torture and Other Cruel, Inhuman or Degrading Treatment or Punishment,* which clearly impose absolute obligations as to results. In handing individuals over to States that torture them and washing its hands of what happens, Canada defies the United Nations Human Rights Committee and Committee against Torture by disregarding the censure and recommendations from these two UN bodies in 2005.

Canada should recognize the absolute nature of the prohibition of torture, cruel, inhuman or degrading treatment, which in no circumstances can be derogated from. Such treatments can never be justified on the basis of a balance to be found between society's interest and the individual's rights ... No person, without any exception, even those suspected of presenting a danger to national security or the safety of any person, and even during a state of emergency, may be deported to a country where he/she runs the risk of being subjected to torture or cruel, inhuman or degrading treatment. (Canada) should clearly enact this principle into its law. (Report of the Human Rights Committee, November 2005)

ILLEGAL INTERVENTION

The war Canada is waging in Afghanistan is illegal, because it violates the *Charter of the United Nations* and international law on the use of force.

One of these exceptions [unilateral use of force] is precisely the 'inherent' right to self-defence, allowing any State to repel an armed attack against it. The use of this right, now governed by Article 51 of the UN Charter, has from the outset been subject to two conditions of customary origin: necessity (use of force as a last resort, to avoid imminent and actual jeopardy) and proportionality (use of force congruent with that deployed by the adversary). Furthermore, pursuant to Article 51, the jeopardy contemplated can only be an armed attack in progress,[7] and the counterattack must be limited in time and space and aimed at repelling the attack. Thus international law does not recognize "preventive self-defence" to avert a threat that is feared, or unilateral intervention to defend individuals or groups deemed to be vulnerable, targeted assassinations or armed punitive reprisals.[8]

Contrary to the widely held opinion that military intervention is legal if it is backed by a UN Security Council resolution, the test of legality is compliance with the *Charter of the United Nations* and international legal instruments. Security Council resolutions are the fruit of political negotiation, and resolutions can certainly be passed that violate international law. The sanctions imposed on Iraq after the First Gulf War are a good example. Those sanctions, which have resulted in the deaths of thousands of children, constitute collective punishment of an entire population and were contrary to international humanitarian law.

Putting the intervention under the aegis of the United Nations would not make the military occupation of Afghanistan any more acceptable.

THE LIGUE DES DROITS ET LIBERTÉS SUPPORTS THE CALL TO WITHDRAW CANADIAN TROOPS FROM AFGHANISTAN

Contrary to the claims of the Canadian government's propaganda aimed at convincing public opinion that military intervention in Afghanistan is justified, the purpose of the intervention is not freedom, prosperity and security for the Afghan people. It is a war of occupation waged for strategic and economic objectives. The first freedom of any people is self-determination.[9] As an organization dedicated to defending human rights, we condemn the attempt to disguise this war of conquest and domination as a humanitarian operation, and we demand that Canadian troops be withdrawn from Afghanistan.

Furthermore, we demand that Canada abide by the Convention Against Torture and never again send anyone to a destination where he or she risks being tortured or subjected to cruel, inhuman or degrading treatment.

NOTES

1 Paul Koring: "Troops told Geneva rules don't apply to Taliban," *Globe and Mail*, May 31, 2006.
2 Ligue des droits et libertés, "En Afghanistan : quel sort le Canada réserve-t-il à ses prisonniers?" *Bulletin de la Ligue des droits et libertés*, Fall 2006.
3 Michael Den Tandt, "Ottawa stands behind handover deal with Afghanistan," *Globe and Mail*, April 3, 2006.
4 Afghanistan Independent Human Rights Commission, Annual Report 2003–04.
5 "Complaints of serious human rights violations committed by representatives of these institutions, including arbitrary arrest, illegal detention and torture, are common. Thorough, transparent and public investigations are absent and trials regularly occur without adhering to the due process rights enshrined in the Constitution." Commission on Human Rights, 62nd session, Report of the High Commissioner for Human Rights on the situation of human rights in Afghanistan and on the achievements of the technical assistance in the field of human rights, document E/CN.4/2006/108.

6 "Credible observers reported that local authorities in Herat, Helmand, and other locations routinely tortured and abused detainees. Torture and abuse consisted of pulling out fingernails and toenails, burning with hot oil, sexual humiliation and sodomy ..." US Department of State Country Report on Human Rights Practices 2005, Afghanistan, March 2006.

7 The term was defined more precisely in 1974 by Resolution 3314 (XXIX) of the General Assembly.

8 Me Jean-François Gareau, "Mesures outre mesure : Le Canada et l'opération Juste rétribution," *Bulletin de la Ligue des droits et liberté,* Fall 2006.

10 *International Covenant on Civil and Political Rights,* Article 1: All peoples have the right of self-determination. By virtue of that right they freely determine their political status and freely pursue their economic, social and cultural development.

The Answer To Why Canada Is
War-fighting in Kandahar

RICHARD J. PRESTON

The Manley Report evaded the issue of how the decision was made
to send Canadian combat troops to Kandahar, and when asked on
CBC-TV Mr. Manley laughed but did not explain his startling phrase
"for whatever reason." Eugene Lang was chief of staff to John Mc-
Callum and then to Bill Graham, the two Ministers of National Defence during 2002–06, and so he was in an ideal position to know
what the reason was.

In a very important and authoritative book, *The Unexpected War*
that he co-authored in 2007 with Janice Stein, Lang tells us in clear
detail the reason why we are now fighting in Kandahar. He says that
most of the foreign policy establishment (including the civilian and
the military side of the Department of National Defence, and the Department of Foreign Affairs) was certain that Canada had made two
major political blunders: the refusal by Jean Chretien to join the US
invasion of Iraq, and then the refusal by Paul Martin to join the US
Ballistic Missile Defence program. Although Donald Rumsfeld reas-
sured Minister Bill Graham that there were no hard feelings, the prevailing feeling in the foreign policy establishment was that the truth
was otherwise. They wanted to make amends with the US administration, and to show America, and Canadians too, that the Canadian army was a "cutting edge" force to be reckoned with.

In 2005, Charismatic General Rick Hillier proposed a five-part military configuration for a Canadian presence in Kandahar. Hillier's military initiative persuaded Minister Graham and others in DND, and so it became a political initiative that reached and persuaded Prime Minister Paul Martin. Martin had not been much interested in war-fighting in Afghanistan, but was very concerned about protection of civilians in Darfur, and possibly Haiti. Hillier very firmly guaranteed Martin that there would be sufficient Canadian military to manage a "Responsibility to Protect" intervention in Darfur, or even in Haiti, too. But General Hillier's own goal was to make up for what he perceived as Canadian weakness by offering the Bush administration a Canadian combat deployment in Kandahar, while other NATO countries preferred the less dangerous areas of the country. He did not accept Dutch intelligence cautions on the extent of danger in southern Afghanistan, including Kandahar.

General Hillier and the rest of Canada got a major surprise that we were not prepared for, and we are now caught in a very uncertain situation. Canada has now advanced its commitment from 2009 to 2011. But who knows what 2011 may bring? Fighting an insurgency of this sort may take a generation, by Hillier's (and others') estimation. The spring 2008 "Taliban – al Qaeda" offensive now looms, Canada and the rest of NATO are not in a winning position because of the localized and fleeting attacks that the insurgency uses. Most NATO partners are averse to combat tactics, and the future of NATO is in doubt. I suspect that Osama bin Laden is pleased to have succeeded in drawing the US and NATO in general and Canada in particular into a larger Afghan war.

At home, Stephen Harper has apparently used the Manley Report mainly to score a parliamentary win over Stephane Dion. The PM continues to keep his own counsel, and therefore shows Canadians little leadership or even willingness to give the Afghan situation the deep understanding it deserves, although he has taken one of the steps recommended in the Manley Report, setting up a cabinet level committee on Afghanistan.

It is also possible that General Hillier overestimated his military potency. The world view of generals, including the remarkably competent and up-to-date General Hillier, is very different from the world view of diplomats. We need a balance of perspectives. When Eugene Lang started his job as chief of staff to the Minister of National Defence, he was warned of this opposition between the perspectives of DND and DFAIT. The Conservative ministers face the major task of restructuring or revitalization within DND and DFAIT, and this may or may not be effected. Canada needs these governmental checks and balances.

What, then, is Canada to do? We lack an adequate government structure to present and sustain an alternative to the focus on warfighting that we are now caught up in. President Karzai and many other Afghan leaders have asked for aid in the peaceful means of education and health. We need a minister and department with a mandate of conflict transformation by peaceful means; a Department of Peace.

Afghanistan and Canada

Women's Question

The Role of Women in Building Afghan Society

CHESHMAK FARHOUMAND-SIMS

It has been suggested that in Afghanistan most girls will experience what we would identify as discrimination from birth. Afghan author Hafizullah Emadi contends that, families celebrate the birth of a son, who is seen "as the preserver of the family's name and inherits the property," while a girl's birth often goes unnoticed, as "she is considered to be disposable property destined to enter another's home upon marriage" (Emadi 2002, p. 31).[1] Decades of war, violence and insecurity have compounded social factors such as cultural norms, traditional practices, conservative interpretations of Islam and poverty which impact girls' and women's human rights, as defined by national laws and international norms. Although there have been episodes of attempts to improve the lives of Afghan girls and women throughout the 20th century, historically, Afghan girls and women – particularly those in the rural areas – have been routinely deprived access to education and forced – or sold – in early marriages as a means to resolve interpersonal conflicts, and to provide poor families much needed funds through the bride price that is traditionally given in marriage (Oates 2006; Bahgam & Mukhatari 2004), and subjected to high levels of violence and abuse within their families and their communities (Oates & Nijhowne 2008).

Despite their daily struggles throughout almost 30 years of war, the plight of Afghan women did not come to the forefront of international consciousness until the tragic events of September 11, 2001. Within days of the tragedy, news coverage shifted to the Taliban's 'gender apartheid,' and images of burqa-clad women, and accounts of human rights violations against Afghanistan's women began to dominate Western media. It became immediately apparent also that the American administration and its allies were suddenly obsessively concerned with the 'liberation' of Afghan women and began to inject the rhetoric of this 'liberation' in their justifications for launching a military campaign on the Taliban and their al Qaeda guests. George Bush and Tony Blair were joined by first ladies Laura Bush and Cherie Blair in their condemnation of Taliban policies and speeches linking the success of the 'war on terror' to the 'liberation' of Afghan women and girls. They were joined in their efforts by prominent feminists and feminist organizations in the United States. However, the rhetoric failed to appreciate that the suffering of Afghanistan's women did not begin with the Taliban regime, nor the oppressive edicts imposed during their regime. Moreover, the discourse strategically ignored the violations of women's rights engaged in by former Mujahedin warlords and US allies who terrorized the country and are recorded to have participated in gross violations of human rights against the Afghan population as a whole.

The cloaking of the 'war on terror' within a rhetoric of women's rights has had severe implications for women's rights activism and gender equality efforts both in Afghanistan and globally. This discourse of 'liberation' exposed orientalist attitudes that continue to dominate Western engagement with Muslims and the Muslim world. In Afghanistan, as in many Muslim countries, women's human rights issues have served as the battleground for the forces of modernization and traditionalism, and efforts to 'liberate' and 'save' Muslim women from the oppression of Muslim men has characterized relations between the West and the Muslim world from the early days of contact between the two cultures. These efforts expose cultural views and opinions in the West that are perceived and described by Muslim men and women as racist, and devoid of a deep understanding of Islam, local cultures and the historical developments in the region that have contributed to the ascription and construction of gender roles in the Muslim world. They also feed into counter-perceptions and attitudes that exist, and are used for political purpose, by conservative Muslim forces who argue that Western values, norms and codes of conduct are anti-Muslim and that their imposition through imperialism must be circumvented in order to protect Islam and Muslim ways of life. These counter narratives foster negative perceptions of the West and contribute to a deepening conflict, which serves as the basis for existing tensions.

Seven years later, the promise of gender equality in Afghanistan remains unfulfilled.[2] The 'war on terror' and the international community's engagement in Afghanistan has led to modest gains, but has not transformed the lives of Afghan women in any sustainable or meaningful way.[3] Familiarity with the a history of Afghanistan and acquaintance with the historic failure of efforts to advance women's rights provides insight into how and why current efforts have proven more challenging than anticipated by the architects of the 'war on terror' and the international organizations engaged in gender equality efforts. Knowledge of this history will facilitate a more productive and successful approach to promoting sustainable and deep-rooted transformation of gender relations in Afghanistan.

BRIEF HISTORY OF AFGHANISTAN AND ITS CONFLICTS

Contemporary Afghanistan is a beautiful and rugged land-locked nation situated in Central Asia, and bordered by Iran, Turkemnistan, Uzbekistan, Tajikistan, China and Pakistan. Its population of 32 million is characterized by ethnic diversity[4] including Pashtuns (44%) Tajiks (25%), Hazaras (10%), Uzbeks (8%); others such as the Aimaks, Turkmen, Nuristanis, and Baluchis make up the rest of the population.[5] Afghanistan's location in Central Asia has not only contributed to its diverse population but has also lent itself to a turbulent history of invasion, conquest, occupation and violent armed conflict. This history of conquest dates back to the times of the Persian empire to as recently as the Soviet occupation and beyond, and has contributed to a highly militaristic culture which persists today and is highly distrustful of foreign intentions.[6] Afghanistan has been a largely agriculture based economy, but it is rich in valuable natural resources such as copper, iron, manganese, gold, silver, sulphur, chromium, tin, salt, marble, plaster, and coal, as well as vast amounts of precious stones such as lapis azuli, rubies and turquoise (Emadi 2005).

Modern Afghanistan, and the Durani Dynasty which ruled it for over two centuries, was established in 1747 and gained independence in 1919 when Afghanistan defeated the British in the third Anglo-Afghan War. The Durani Monarchy lasted until 1973 when the King Zahir Shah's cousin Mohammed Daoud staged a coup and brought the Communist party of Afghanistan – the People's Democratic Party of Afghanistan (PDPA) – to power.[7] The Communist take over was highly unpopular: the party unleashed a campaign of terror against groups they perceived as rivals; began an aggressive and unpopular modernization program which involved social, economic and political reform, as well as efforts at promoting women's rights and gender equality; and undertook efforts to marginalize powerful religious and tribal leaders, programs they imposed with military force. The Communist government was perceived to be anti-religious, and their universal literacy and unprecedented gender equality initiatives were offensive to sensitivities of the mostly religiously conservative rural population, particularly religious and tribal leaders who saw these as a threat to their authority and traditional power structures. Before long, Afghan military forces began to refuse to use violence on the population; the military uprising spread throughout Afghan military garrisons, and state structures began to disintegrate, leading to the Soviet offer of assistance to prevent a complete disintegration of government structures. The Soviets feared such a disintegration would create a power vacuum that the US would fill, at a time when they had lost their most important ally in the region, the Shah of Iran. The PDPA accepted, but the arrival of the Soviet troops intensified the opposition and inspired a grassroots organized armed resistance movement known as the Mujahedin.[8]

As the Soviet Union increased its troop deployment to Afghanistan, the Mujahedin gained widespread support from the United States, who began providing them with money, arms and training to fight in yet another Cold War era proxy war. After 10 years of fighting with devastating results, the Soviet Union withdrew its forces following the Geneva Accord in February 1989. In all, 13,310 Soviet soldiers and over 1.24 million Afghan civilians had died in the war (Saikal & Maley, 1989, p. 13), and six million were displaced within Afghanistan or to other countries. This immense toll on Afghanistan and its population did not end with the departure of the Soviets in 1989. The end of Soviet occupation resulted in an abrupt loss of interest and commitment to Afghanistan by the United States. The increased political insecurity led to a new and even more violent struggle between the Mujahedin factions, among themselves and against the Communist government of the PDPA, which was finally defeated in 1992. The political vacuum that ensued resulted in an intensified military campaign among the Mujahedin. During this time, the country was divided between warlords, who along with their heavily armed militia, enjoyed complete control in the various regions of the country where they continued to fight for power and authority. These warlords have long histories of animosity and of switching loyalties, yet ironically have now come to dominate the new and 'democratically' elected Afghan parliament.[9] While the West highlights the suffering, oppression and atrocities of the Taliban period, Afghans argue that the pre-Taliban civil war period of 1992–95 constitutes the bloodiest and most destructive period in Afghan history. During that time, neighbourhoods became the frontlines of battles between competing warlords leading to the destruction of whole towns, to tens of thousands of civilian deaths, to the kidnapping and rapes of countless women, to a protracted refugee crisis, to the destruction of Afghanistan's political, economic and social infrastructures and most importantly to fostering further extremism within sectors of Afghan society and politics. In fact, the Taliban movement was born as a response to the growing violence, greed and corruption of the warlords (Gagnon 2005) and initially was welcomed by a war-weary population ready for an end to the violence and the return of some semblance of normalcy to their lives.[10]

By 1996, the Taliban had captured the capital and pushed the warlords into the northern part of the country, and began their construction of a theocratic state based on their strict interpretation of the Quran, which was enforced with brutal force, repressing human rights, civil liberties and most acutely women's rights and freedoms. Immediately upon taking control of Kabul, the Taliban imposed edicts which severely regulated people's lives, including strict limits on personal freedoms, with the severest restrictions imposed on women.[11] Under the Taliban regime, women were forbidden to leave the house unaccompanied by a male family member serving as chaperone, denied access to education and employment, and forced to wear the burqa at all times in public. While these edicts did not drastically change the lives of women in rural parts of the country, they significantly impacted urban-based women, who, although previously experiencing some restrictions due to security reasons, were now completely isolated and prevented from any role in the public sphere. Since women were no longer allowed to work, even when professionally qualified as doctors, this meant that Afghan women had no access to healthcare, resulting in one of the highest maternal and infant mortality rates in the world. Young men from the Ministry for the Prevention of Vice and the Promotion of Virtue regularly policed the street to ensure compliance, and would dole out punishment to those who defied the new rules.

The Taliban argued that their new rules were based on Islamic law. Muslim scholars and others disagreed, arguing that the new laws did not reflect Islam or its laws but were in fact rooted in tribal traditions. Those familiar with Afghan culture and the Kandahari context went further to argue that that Taliban edicts went beyond Pashtun cultural norms. Gagnon asserts that, "The repressiveness did not belong to Kandahar but to the Wahabi sect of Islam" (Gagnon, 2005, p. 34). My personal view is that the Taliban were a product of a combination of strict tribal cultural norms affected by the religious influences gained as students of Pakistani madrassas where religious teachers presented a very narrow and conservative interpretation of Islam in a context of patriarchy and male domination (Rashid, 2000, p. 32, and conversations with Afghans in 2003 and 2008). Consider that most of the young men who joined the Taliban were war orphans growing up in refugee camps whose education was limited to the very strict religious madrassas set up in Pakistan. There they learned narrow and extreme interpretations of Islam and the Quran by teachers who were largely illiterate, uneducated and therefore unable to read and assess religious texts and commentaries or to teach the Quran to their pupils in an effective and moderate manner.[12] Furthermore, many of the people I spoke to in Kabul in 2003 informed me that the early Taliban fighters – as orphans, or young boys who were sent to these schools from a young age – largely grew up with little or no contact with women in their lives. Those I spoke to suggested that the absence of female role models and the lack of socialization with mothers, sisters, aunts, grandmothers, cousins and other females in their lives inevitably helped to shape the very patriarchal and misogynistic views they hold about women, their roles, responsibilities and rights in the family, the community and society as a whole. Ahmad Rashid points to this in his book "Taliban" as well:

The mullahs who had taught them stressed that women were a temptation, an unnecessary distraction from being of service to Allah. So when the Taliban entered Kandahar and confined women to their home by barring them from working, going to school and even from shopping, the majority of these madrassa boys saw nothing unusual in such measures. They felt threatened by that half of the human race which they had never known and it was much easier to lock that half away, especially if it was ordained by the mullahs who invoked primitive Islamic injunction which had no basis in Islamic law (2000, p. 33).

The Taliban and the plight of Afghanistan's population fell off the international radar until the events of September 11th, 2001: the attacks on the World Trade Centre and the Pentagon. By then, Afghanistan was completely destroyed in every sense of the word. Its cities, towns and villages flattened by years of fighting, its infrastructure non-existent, and its population shattered physically, emotionally and psychologically. The years of conflict were worsened by drought and starvation along with the intensification of religious extremism and the systematic violations of human rights conducted with impunity. It was in this context of utter despair and destruction that the international community – including the United Nations, the EU, the US and its allies – re-engaged with Afghanistan. Within a month of the fall of the Taliban, an internationally-brokered conference was convened in Bonn, Germany in December 2001 under the auspices of the United Nations. The Bonn Meeting brought representatives from the four major Afghan factions[13] who were given the task of consulting and beginning the difficult task of rebuilding Afghanistan. The parties at the table represented military commanders, representatives from various ethnic groups, expatriate Afghans as well as representatives of the exiled Monarch. The meeting was highly political: dominated by the Northern Alliance, it excluded the Taliban and was heavily influenced by the United States, who along with representatives from 18 other countries participated in the meetings as 'foreign observers.'[14] The resulting document, known as the Bonn Agreement "set out a schematic roadmap and timetable for establishing peace and security, reconstructing the country, reestablishing some key institutions, and protecting human rights."[15]

Having highlighted the 'liberation' of Afghan women as a justification for the attack and intervention into Afghanistan, there was intense pressure from the international actors at Bonn (the UN, the US, and the EU) to commit to and incorporate gender equality in the Bonn agreement and thus be among the priorities of the transitional government. The Bonn Agreement called for "the establishment of a broad-based, multi-ethnic, fully representative, gender sensitive government and drew attention to Security Council Resolution on Women, Peace and Security (1325), reminding all factions that the participation of women and attention to their rights and status are critical to national peace and reconstruction processes."[16] Responding to these pressures, the Afghan parties gathered at Bonn committed themselves to gender equality principles. For women's rights activists, the highlight of the Agreement was the establishment of a Women's Ministry which would be committed to advancing the status of women in Afghanistan through the promotion of literacy programs, social-economic development projects and other initiatives aimed at increasing women's participation in the social, political and economic life of the country.[17] They were also cautiously optimistic about the promise of equality provisions in the new Constitution and the opportunity for women to participate in the political process of the country by standing for election and exercising a right to vote. They were rightfully skeptical that the end of the Taliban would usher in an era of peace, prosperity and equal rights and opportunities for women. Their skepticism was well-placed.

The 'war on terror' and the ensuing international engagement in Afghanistan have not addressed the cultural, historical and traditional foundations for gender discrimination and violence in Afghanistan. Hence, despite seven years of international presence on the ground, Afghan women continue to face strict cultural, religious and traditional barriers that prevent them from enjoying equal rights in practice. This was clear and evident when women participants experienced intimidation and threat from powerful warlords at the Presidential and Constitutional *loya jirgas* (the traditional decision-making council meetings of Elders). Another example is the linking of the equality clause in the new Constitution to an unclear framework of Islamic Sharia law, leaving it open to interpretation by Afghanistan's appointed Grand Imam. This stipulation is of great concern to women's groups in Afghanistan and their supporters who fear that conservative interpretations of Sharia will threaten women's autonomy, human rights and legal standing. As for the much anticipated Ministry of Women's Affairs, lack of capacity and funding has ghettoized women's rights and relegated this Ministry to the margins with little or no influence or impact.

While the establishment of the Ministry for Women's Affairs, the inclusion of an equality clause in the Constitution, the participation of women in elections, and their standing and winning seats in the new Parliament and so on were important first steps, they have not translated into immediate or sustained improvement in the lives of women. As of May 2008, seven years after the departure of the Taliban, women's lives in Afghanistan have changed very little. Afghanistan still has one of the highest maternal mortality rates in the world; domestic violence, often brutal, still plagues the lives of a large number of Afghan women; Afghan girls are subjected to forced and early marriage, sold to pay for food and medicine, or otherwise repay drug debts.[18] The reality is that addressing women's equality issues, undoing decades – indeed centuries – of inequality and translating rights from paper to practice goes beyond these initiatives and will require patience and careful attention. These efforts must take a multifaceted approach which is culturally and religiously sensitive, grassroots based, and supported by domestic, regional and international networks and forces as well as the international community. Failure to do so will threaten gains that have already been made and provoke resistance, violence and further destabilization. Acquaintance with Afghan history and women's role in it would be instructive in these efforts.

WOMEN IN AFGHANISTAN: A HISTORICAL OVERVIEW

Women's rights have long been the subject of debate and controversy in Afghanistan. There has been a long history of women's subordination in Afghanistan, which did not begin or end with the Taliban regime. Hence, women's rights issues cannot be neatly categorized into pre- and post-Taliban eras (Ahmed-Ghosh, 2003) and are more directly a function of a deeply complex social, economic, historical and political context impacted by the rise of religious fundamentalism and decades of militarism and insecurity. Underdevelopment, patriarchy, conflict and the absence of strong state institutions and structures have allowed traditional attitudes based on culture, custom and to some extent religion flourish and prevented meaningful transformation of gender relations in Afghanistan. It has been very difficult and in some contexts impossible to improve women's access to rights and opportunities, especially in the rural areas where tribal culture and custom along with narrow interpretations of religious law take precedence over legal and constitutional laws designed to improve the lives and conditions of the population, including women.

Ironically, the various reports describing the situation of women in Afghanistan over the last thirty years belie research on people's attitudes about women's rights issues. For example, a *Physicians for Human Rights* study released in January 2001 found that 90% of the one thousand Afghan men and women sampled "claimed to strongly support the rights of women to have equal access to education and work opportunities, freedom of expression, legal protection for women's human rights and participation in government" (PHR 2001, p. 2). A further 80% of those surveyed agreed that "women should be able to move about freely and that the teachings of Islam do not restrict women's human rights," and 75% felt that "women should be able to associate with people of their own choosing" (PHR 2001, p. 2). The question, then, is why these prevailing attitudes are not translating into noticeable change in families, communities and the country, nor in government policies.[19] Thirty years of intense militarism and its consequent religious fundamentalism can perhaps partially explain the discrepancy between attitudes of the general population and the policies enacted by rulers that largely do not represent their constituents.[20]

Afghan women do not constitute a homogenous or a monolithic entity, and have enjoyed varying degrees of access to rights, opportunities and freedoms throughout the 20th century. This access has depended on a variety of factors: family and tribal affiliation, ethnicity, religion, degree of conservatism in the family, their community and tribe, their (and their family's) level of education, urban versus rural habitation. In the rural areas for example, where communities are made up of extended family units, and women's handicraft skills are needed to supplement the family income, women enjoy a certain level of freedom of movement compared to larger villages and or the city, where it is generally expected that male family members would accompany women on excursions where they might come into contact with non-mahram men.[21] In fact, not much has changed in the rural areas of Afghanistan; for example, a British observer in 1810 notes that in the rural area, women were unveiled and enjoyed freedom of movement without restraint within their camp or village, while women in the urban areas were "wrapped in large white sheets" even though they could attend public gatherings and events" (cited in ICG 2003, p. 8).[22] Dupree notes that even under the Taliban, it was largely city based women who were impacted by the harsh edicts, and nomadic and rural women were not affected by the controversies and regulations:

Rural women mostly live in secure kin-related settings where they move about with considerable freedom. When they venture beyond these protected areas, they travel swathed in *chaders* escorted by male relatives. Handicrafts are made at home; when they work outside, women work in family groups. Above all, their primary ambition in life is to become a mother, preferably of many sons. Through motherhood, the creativity of handiwork and efficient household management, rural women achieve status and a sense of personal fulfillment (ICG 2003, p. 163).

Throughout the last thirty years of conflict, Afghan women have been provided increased space for asserting their agency and participating in social, economic and political realms. Women's participation in political opposition and resistance to the Soviet occupation did result in some limited and measured gains, or prompted "contrary changes in the life of Afghan women" (Ellis, 2000, p. 40). Some women were able to access greater opportunities for education, training and employment under the Communist plan to advance women's rights; many were imprisoned or tortured for their anti-government or anti-Mujahedin activities; others suffered physically and emotionally from the consequences of the armed conflict, including kidnappings, rape, force marriages, the loss of loved ones, property and livelihoods; and some joined the resistance, which gave them "enhanced standing in the community and the opportunity to learn new skills such as organizing rallies and the use of firearms" (Ellis 2000). In fact, much of the grassroots opposition to Soviet presence and occupation came from urban-based women who organized anti-government street protests, and demanded the release of political prisoners. Women protesters were routinely arrested, tortured and many of them killed during government responses to demonstrations or while in prison (Ellis 2000; Emadi 2002).

Other women supported the resistance by cooking and cleaning for the Mujahedin, carrying food to them, hiding them from Soviet troops, carrying arms – sometimes under their burqas – and killing

Soviet soldiers as they came through their towns and villages. Some would lure Soviet soldiers away from their platoon so they could be killed.[23] Some of these women were extremely organized in their underground activities. For example, one group had three sections. The first investigated people suspected of collaborating with the enemy; another followed suspects and discovered their connections, while a third carried out the assassinations (Ellis, 2000, p. 8). Despite their courageous efforts and demonstration of their ability to participate in national liberation, their efforts did not translate into immediate and tangible rights in the aftermath of Soviet occupation. In fact, immediately upon taking over the government, the Mujahedin regime imposed Taliban style edicts which severely limited women's rights and access to education, employment, and freedom of movement (Dupree 1998, Emadi 2003). The Mujahedin edicts set the foundation for the much harsher regulations imposed by the Taliban. While Afghan history does attest to varied degrees of 'freedom' over time and in different 'spaces,' on the whole, it can be argued that Afghan women, in general, do not and have not enjoyed rights, opportunities and freedoms accorded to them in the Quran, nor in international human rights instruments.[24]

Finally, gender dynamics has always been a highly contentious, complex and politicized issue in Afghanistan, and a function of the interplay between internal social dynamics and perceived or real external influences. Since the early days of nation building in the late 1800s, Afghan rulers have sought to implement nation-building projects that included modernization and development programs, including efforts to improve the status of women. Although their efforts were national in scope, they focused especially on the rural areas of the country where the majority of the population resides. Ahmed-Ghosh argues that "Women in Afghanistan are not an isolated institution; their fate is entwined with and determined by historical, social, economic and religious forces" as well as "a range of internal tensions, and outside political forces that have impacted Afghanistan in significant ways" (Ahmed-Ghosh, 2003, p. 2). This interplay of internal and external forces has intensified the political nature of gender relations and efforts at gender equality, and impeded efforts to try and transform them. According to Moghadam, revolutionary change, state building and women's rights operate hand in hand (1994, p. 97). In fact, every effort at modernization and state building since the early 1900s has included efforts to advance women's rights and has also resulted in intense opposition (Ahmed-Ghosh 2003, Emadi 2002). Readings of Afghan history show that "Afghanistan may be the only country in the world where during the last century kings and politicians have been made and undone by struggles relating to women's status" (Ahmed-Ghosh, 2003, p. 1). Effectively, all modernization efforts included aggressive literacy programs, as well as new laws pertaining to women's rights, and even new state constitutions which proved extremely controversial, particularly among religious and tribal power holders in rural Afghanistan. Their resistance and opposition led to riots, violence and ultimately to the assassination of one King, and forced departure of another, and arguably fueled anti-Soviet sentiments in the 1980s and a growing anti-Western sentiment in contemporary Afghanistan.

EFFORTS AT GENDER EQUALITY

Although the plight of women under the Taliban regime was a central theme in post September 11th discourse, the situation of women in Afghanistan has always been precarious. Despite some advances in the 1920s and late 1960s and 1970s, efforts to improve the status of women have met with opposition and resistance. This opposition was strengthened by perceptions that directives on modernization and women's equality were a result of foreign interference and imperialist objectives. This was seen in the 1920s, as well as the 1970s. I believe there are elements of this attitude developing in contemporary Afghanistan. In each case, when efforts at social-economic development have included advances in women's rights and opportunities, and were undertaken when foreign actors were present in Afghanistan, it supported the view that the policies were not Afghan-initiated, but rather imposed by external actors in order to meet their own objectives. And even if this were not wholly true, perceptions prevailed. My reading of the history of gender equality efforts in Afghanistan suggests that at the same time as outside actors (Britain, the EU, the Soviet Union, and now the US,) have encouraged gender equality, the initial desire to promote modernization, and to include the advancement of women within these efforts have been initiated and directed by Afghans. Unfortunately, the premature nature of the modernization programs, the manner in which they were imposed, and the lack of consultation and engagement of local actors to ensure program relevance has been an important factor characterizing failure in every case.[25] Even though many of these modernization and gender equality policies were inspired by elite experiences in the West, actively encouraged and supported by Western actors, and imposed with their assistance, the connection between perceived and real imperialist objectives and gender equality has been made in the minds of the largely rural, illiterate population who continue to resist a change in status quo relationships and power structures.

It is important to note that women in Afghanistan had varying experiences in terms of rights and opportunities, and that far from being ignored, have been the subject of national policy debates over many decades. The destruction of Afghanistan and the plight of its women were a shocking contrast to the possibilities demonstrated in the years preceding the Russian occupation. Those who lived and traveled in Afghanistan in the 1960s and 70s describe a very different picture of life from the one we have seen in more recent years. They describe an Afghanistan under Zahir Shah's rule where things were improving economically, politically and socially, despite the urban /rural divide. Kabul was like many other major cities in the world bustling with activity, a night life and high fashion. An estimated 90,000 tourists traveled through Afghanistan during the 1970s.[26] Nancy Dupree, who lived in Afghanistan with her anthropologist husband Louis Dupree, describes that time as follows:

In the 1960s, the country made a strong movement toward development, meaning road building, communications and education. This was very successful. People were going around the world to learn the professions. There were thousands of engineers, many intellectuals. Millions of dollars were coming in through foreign investment from the Germans, the Russians, the Indians and others. There were jazz clubs, nightclubs, great restaurants of all kinds. Women had come out of the home and could move about in the public sphere. They wore the veil, but on a voluntary basis.[27]

In 1959, Kabul University was declared co-educational, and increasing numbers of girls attended schools while large numbers of women entered the work force as public servants, teachers, doctors and lawyers. There was also some measure of political gain for the women of Afghanistan. In 1958 the country sent its first female delegate to the United Nations; the year following the 1964 Constitution universal suffrage was established. The first woman Minister of Public Health served in the Afghan cabinet from 1965–69, while two women were appointed to the Senate and another was made a political advisor to the Prime Minister. On the social front, voluntary observance of the *purdah* (seclusion) was reintroduced (ICG 2003).

However, these reforms mostly benefited upper and middle class women in the urban areas and did not necessarily affect the lives of the majority of Afghans who lived in the rural areas. For the rural based population little has changed over the twentieth century, given the lack of connection with the central institutions of the state and the strong rural based power structures of tribal and religious elders. Nevertheless, it is important to note the potential for progress and life improvement that preceded the contemporary conflicts.

Efforts to promote women's rights and to increase their opportunities pre-dated the 1950s. The earliest recorded efforts to improve the situation of women in Afghanistan can be traced back to the first monarch Amir Abdur Rahman, who ruled Afghanistan from 1880 to 1901, and was the first Afghan ruler who attempted to unite the nation into a centralized state. Abdur Rahman initiated the first radical reform agenda as part of his efforts to consolidate and modernize the Afghan nation, which included efforts to improve the status of women. In these efforts, Abdur Rahman seems to have been greatly influenced by his wife, who was "the first Afghan queen to appear in public in European dress without a veil. She rode horses and trained her maidservants in military exercises and had a keen interest in politics and went on numerous delicate missions to discuss politics between contending parties" (Dupree, 1986, p. 12). As part of his efforts to improve women's status, Abdur Rahman introduced a drastic reformation of customary laws that he felt were harmful to women: enforcing women's rights to inheritance under sharia; the abolition of customs requiring women to marry their dead husband's next of kin; raising the age of marriage and giving child brides the right to refuse the spouse chosen for them; and giving women the right to request a divorce under certain circumstances as well as the right to sue their husbands for alimony (Ahmed-Ghosh, 2003, p. 3, ICG 2003).[28]

Upon Abdur Rahman's passing, his son Habibullah (1901–19) became ruler and strove to continue his father's legacy and build on it. He was particularly committed to modernizing Afghanistan with an emphasis on education and technology. He opened the country to modern education systems which "created a class of intellectuals separate from the clergy for the first time" who were thus educated for public service (Rubin, 2002, p. 53). He also established the first college in Afghanistan in 1903, and royal military college in 1904, as well as the first hospital, hydro-electrical plant, factories and increased trade with central Asian neighbours including Russia and India (cited in Ahmed-Ghosh 2003, p. 3, Rubin 2002, p. 53). Habibullah also permitted the return of families exiled by his father: Mahmud Beg Tarzi, who later became Habibullah's son's father-in-law, being one of the most important returnees. Having studied and been exposed to liberal modernization ideologies in their time abroad, those previously exiled returned to Afghanistan and became the core of the new Afghan elite (Rubin 2002, p. 54). From these positions they were able to influence policies of reform. Ahmed-Ghosh suggests that Mahmud Beg was probably the most influential reformist in Afghan history, who among other things established the first modernist-nationalist newspaper in the country and advocated for modern education" (Ahmed-Ghosh 2003, p. 3).[29] Tarzi was also an advocate for women's advancement, arguing that "women as people deserved full citizenship" and were "an asset to future generations" whose rights were not denied in Islam (Ahmed-Ghosh, 2003, p. 3). He promoted his views in his newspaper with regular commentary in a women's section called 'Celebrating Women of the World,' which was edited by his wife Asma Tarzi (Ahmed-Ghosh, 2003, p. 3). Schinasi argues that, "no one before Tarzi had pronounced such words as 'liberty,' 'respect for the homeland and religion,' 'union,' 'progress,' or 'school' (1979, p. 36). It can be assumed that his liberal views, shared by Habibullah influenced gender policy as well. On the gender front, Habibullah set limits to bride price and other marriage expenses, and tried to enforce the Islamic law of men not taking more than four wives by banning the keeping of concubines and female slaves, which had become a dominant practice. It was also at his encouragement that Habibullah opened English schools for girls, which "tribal leaders and mullahs saw as going against the grain of tradition" (Ahmed-Ghosh, 2003, p. 4).

Following Habibullah's assassination, his son Amanullah, who married Tarzi's daughter Soraya, claimed the throne (1919–29) and built on his father's policies with an aggressive modernization program (Emadi 2002, Ahmed-Ghosh 2003, Rubin 2002). His first objective was to liberate Afghanistan from the British, which he did in 1919. According to Barnett Rubin, "Amanullah's reforms resembled those that had transformed other absolutist states to nation states. They included radical new measures in all three areas identified by Migdal as necessary to the reconstitution of social control: taxes, land tenure, and transportation" (Rubin, 2002, p. 55). He also took steps to strengthen the legality and accountability of the state by "establishing a complete legal basis for state power, and drafting Afghanistan's first constitution." The new constitution (1923) "provided a blueprint for building a modern civil society" and "stressed local economic development (Emadi, 2003, p. 60). It also introduced the concept of universal citizenship with universal rights (Rubin, 2002, p. 55) and abolished slavery which was still in practice at the time (Emadi, 2003, p. 60).

Central to his modernization policies were a campaign to eradicate illiteracy, and efforts to advance gender equality and transform the highly unequal status of women in Afghanistan, particularly in the rural areas. In 1922, he created the country's first modern education system, established adult literacy classes in order to "train a new generation of state and civil service personnel," and began sending students to France, Germany, Turkey, Iran, Switzerland and England for higher education (Emadi, 2003, p. 61). Cognizant of the importance of religious education to the population, his intention was not to replace or dismiss religious instruction, but rather to "broaden the horizon of religious teachers and clerics" (Emadi, 2003, p. 61). He also recognized the importance of making changes slowly and patiently, so as to not inspire fear or resistance on the part of the clerical class. He stated: "We are keenly alive to the value of education. But to bring learning to my people must be a slow process ... We hope to lay our plans well and truly, but not too fast. Religion must march hand in hand with learning, else both fall into the ditch" (Emadi, 2003, p. 61).

Amanullah's efforts to advance women's rights were unprecedented. The 1923 constitution included a family code section which significantly improved the legal standing of women. He banned child marriage, mandated judicial permission to marry additional wives, removed some family law matters from clergy jurisdiction, and reiterated his father's rule concerning a widow's right to choose her next spouse (ICG 2003). He also made education compulsory for all citizens, and opened the first high school for girls, expanded the education system and opened it to foreign influence. He sent elite students, including girls, for overseas education (Emadi, 2003, p. 56). He even established the Association for the Protection of Women in 1928, and appointed his sister Kubra as head of the organization "to coordinate, supervise, and guide its work concerning women's liberation. The association worked to promote women's welfare and encouraged women to protest to the society if their husbands, brothers and fathers mistreated them" (Emadi, 2003, p. 64).

Amanullah was a visionary. He and his wife Soraya traveled extensively to Turkey, Iran and Europe; they keenly observed Western developments and tried to implement them in Afghanistan (Emadi, 2003, p. 63). He was convinced that universal education was the key to Afghanistan's prosperity. But the country was not ready for such reforms and so quickly. His policies challenged sensitivities and undermined the power of the religious authorities, leading to his ultimate demise. Conservatives did not approve of his education policies nor his other radical social, economic and political reforms (Emadi, 2003, p. 63). The conservatives' sensibilities were further agitated by the British, who were displeased with Amanullah's independence and sought to replace him with a more compliant leader. To do this, they produced photo-shoped pictures of Queen Soraya's head on immodestly dressed bodies and spread them among the religious and tribal elite creating the appearance that the Queen had acted inappropriately and thus compromised Afghan cultural and religious norms while traveling overseas. The protests against Amanullah and the Queen intensified and weakened the leader's waning legitimacy, encouraging the disenchanted tribal leaders to revolt. Aided by the British, who wanted to weaken the Afghan ruler for their own political purposes, the tribal leaders' revolt forced Amanullah into exile in Italy in 1929. He later died in Switzerland in 1960 (ICG 2003, Rubin, 2002, p. 58)

Amanullah's downfall led to a brief rule under Habibullah, and then the rise of Nadir Shah in 1929. In an effort to consolidate his weak power, Nadir Shah abolished most of Amanullah's reforms and based all legal codes on narrow interpretations of Islam (ICG 2003). His contributions included improvements in road construction and communication technology, as well as a banking system (Rubin, 2002, p. 60–2). He also introduced a new constitution in 1931 strengthening the role of the religious clergy and giving them an institutional role in legislature and representation (Rubin, 2002 p. 62). His contributions to women's rights were unremarkable and in fact retracted many of the previous reforms in order to appease the clergy and tribal leaders. His son Zahir Shah succeeded him in 1933 upon his father's death. Over the next four decades of his intermittent rule, he produced a better record both on modernization and on gender equality policies, especially under Daoud's Prime Ministership. He adopted a more cautious approach to women's education and established several segregated girls' schools, and he encouraged the employment of women in professions that were considered appropriate, such as teaching and healthcare (Emadi, 2002, p. 69). The intellectual and political elite who had slowly gained prominence began to push for the advancement of these modernization policies. They "did not regard women's oppression as part of the social, political and economic structures but rather attributed it to people's ignorance and prevailing cultural tradition" (Emadi, 2002, p. 70). And even though the mostly male elite did not believe in equality of sexes, they did support women's education and emancipation.

Prime Minister Daoud's administration (1953–63) represents the landmark of modernization and emancipation in recent Afghan history and by the late 1950s, included some impressive strides in women's human rights, particularly in the urban areas, and especially Kabul. For example, in 1959, Kabul University was declared co-educational, and increasing numbers of girls attended schools while large numbers of women entered the work force as public servants, teachers, doctors and lawyers. There was also some measure of political gain for the women of Afghanistan. A delegation of Afghan women attended a conference in Ceylon, and in 1958 the country sent its first female delegate to the United Nations. Women were also hired in government offices, the telecommunications agency and even as hostesses on the nation's airline (Emadi, 2002, p. 71). When these moves did not lead to the anticipated outrage or opposition, Daoud and his colleagues decided to push the boundaries by instituting a more aggressive modernization program, including the legal unveiling of women and harsh penalties for noncompliance. This proved to have gone too far and before long tribal chiefs and religious elders in several Southern provinces rebelled staging massive protests, attacking state owned institutions (Emadi, 2002, p. 71). Unfortunately, Daoud used the military to crush the opposition, imprisoned hundreds of people, and executed several organizers before moving forward with his programs which included providing more women with opportunities in the public service and representing Afghanistan in the international arena.

Emadi argues that while many advances can be attributed to Daoud, that capitalist development also contributed to women's emancipation. Consumer capacity flooded the city's markets with products aimed at women, leading "local entrepreneurs and merchants to join with the government to press for women's liberation" (Emadi, 2002, p. 72). Furthermore, the reforms, despite their immediate impact, and because of Afghanistan's pervasive urban/rural divide, mostly benefited upper and middle class women in the urban areas and did not necessarily impact the lives of the majority of rural Afghans. The same urban/rural divide continues to hamper development and gender equality policies in the years following the fall of the Taliban.

Things changed again in 1973 when the King's cousin organized a coup resulting in the King's exile and Daoud's establishment of Afghanistan as a republic. In an effort to consolidate his regime, Daoud quickly called for the drafting of a new Constitution (1974) which among other things granted women equal rights and obligations under the law, and provided them with rights to education and development. While these efforts had some impact on the elite class, once again the benefits did not trickle down to rural society. When Karmal took over leadership of Afghanistan in 1978, he built on these initiatives by prohibiting forced marriage of girls and widows; banned arranged marriages; introduced a minimum age of marriage for women and men; abolished the bride price; made female education compulsory; encouraged women to unveil and become more active members of society; and enforced literacy classes in the rural areas. The weakness of these measures lay in the methods used to enforce them, and Karmal's forced reforms, without sensitivity to culture and religion, "almost guaranteed failure"[30] and gave rise to fanaticism and violence throughout Afghanistan.

The situation of women during the Civil War (1992–95) and under Taliban rule deteriorated significantly. Most people are well aware of the violations of women's human rights under the Taliban regime, but it is important to note that systematic violations of women's human rights did not begin with the Taliban regime and were evident and of grave concern during the civil war years and Mujahedin rule. Northern Alliance forces (also known as the United Front), which represented a coalition of Tajik, Uzbek and Hazara parties, were also complicit in violations of international human rights and humanitarian law, with women bearing the brunt of the violence and discrimination. According to human rights organizations, "in the civil war, women suffered massive, systematic and unrelenting human rights abuses that permeated every aspect of their lives."[31] Both groups, Mujahedin and Taliban, have been known to kidnap, rape, forcibly marry and otherwise impose misogynistic edicts based on extreme interpretations of Islam against women. Under both regimes, women lost their freedom of movement, liberty, and previously enjoyed rights to education, employment, heathcare and other basic human rights. The Taliban went further in their maltreatment of women by banning women from public live. They completely forbade girls' education, prohibited the movement of women in public without the permission and accompaniment of a male relative and enforced the wearing of the burqa outside of the home. Their extremism went so far as to require windows to be painted black to prevent anyone from seeing a woman in her home. Their oppressive rules were enforced by 'religious police' from the Ministry for the Promotion of Virtue and the Prevention of Vice who patrolled the streets and indiscriminately beat women publicly for such offences as wearing socks that were not sufficiently opaque, showing wrists, hands, or ankles, for working, begging or being in public without a male relative.[32]

BARRIERS TO WOMEN'S RIGHTS

Decentralization

One of the pervasive barriers to gender policies taking hold in Afghanistan has been the de-centralized nature of the state along with the weak structures that support it. Since its formation in the eighteenth century and its independence in 1919, Afghanistan has been a largely fragmented state (Rubin 2002), its rulers unable to establish a 'state' in the traditional sense of the word, with a strong central government, capable of providing services for its largely rural population. There are several factors that have contributed to this 'fragmentation,' including terrain, ethnic diversity with its rivalries, and dominant tribalism and regionalism. According to several Afghan scholars, these factors, combined with "varied interpretations of Islam have created fractious cultures" while Afghanistan's rugged and spatial impenetrability "has prevented Afghanistan from ever forming a consensual and coherent sense of nationalism,"

which along with foreign interference "has contributed to the fragmentation of the Afghan polity" (Ahmed-Ghosh, 2003, p. 2) preventing it from ever having "experienced a strong centralized state
with a common legal system" (Moghadam 1997 in Ahmed-Ghosh,
2003, p. 2, Rubin 2002), and a sense of national identity. This fragmented nature of Afghanistan has resulted in tribal leaders politically dominating regions, essentially creating their own 'fiefdoms' ruled
by well-armed loyal militia. Ismail Khan in the western Afghanistan
city of Herat, and Abdul Rashid Dostum in the north are just two examples. Many of these warlords have a long standing relationship
with one another, which over the years has included tenuous alliances of convenience during the Soviet occupation and violent conflict among themselves since the departure of the Soviets.

This de-centralized structure, and the dominance of tribalism
have been especially detrimental for the wellbeing of Afghan women,
who are used as pawns for the social, economic and political advancement of their male kin. Ahmed-Ghosh suggests that "the political and powerful nature of tribal dictates in the Afghan countryside,
and the oppositional ruling parties and elite are instrumental in determining the scope of women's lives" (2003, p. 2). And, according
to Moghadam,

the issue of women's rights in Afghanistan has been historically constrained
by (a) the patriarchal nature of gender and social relations deeply embedded
in traditional communities and (b) the existence of a weak central state, that
has been unable to implement modernizing programs and goals in the face of
'tribal feudalism.' (1997, p. 76).

Patriarchy and Androcentrism

Furthermore, despite variations in customs and tradition among villages, tribes and regions, "women's subordination to men is a common feature in all the diverse segments of the country's population"
(Emadi 2002, p. 29).[33] The basis for gender inequality in Afghanistan, and the subordination of women is a result of a complex web
of internal social, cultural, religious, economic, political factors compounded by long term violent conflict and external interference,
which have contributed to religious extremism, to the detriment of
women. At the heart of gender inequality in Afghanistan lies patriarchy and androcentrism. Emadi, in his book about Afghan women,

Repression, Resistance and Women in Afghanistan, suggests that "The status of women is manifested in women's access to economic, political, educational, and organized resources outside of the home" (2002, p. 29). He argues that as Afghanistan developed economically, the division of labour between men and women relegated men to the public sphere where they "gained control of resources," while women were increasingly marginalized from the public sphere of influence and their role was "to increase production and reproduction." (Emadi, 2002, p. 29). This division of labour interacts with "women's roles and responsibilities in society being largely determined by a combination of cultural mores and religious precepts as understood by men" in a patriarchal culture dominated by the "universal intellectual paradigm of androcentrism which rests on the common belief that maleness is the natural order of things (Emadi, 2002, p. 29-30). Narrow religious interpretation and 'culture' continue to sustain patriarchy and androcentrism in Afghanistan, and to justify the subordinate position of women and the violation of their human rights.

External Interference

Although Afghanistan's internal issues are contentious and complex, they cannot be fully understood without consideration of external interference. Ahmed-Ghosh has written that "foreign interference by the British, Soviet Union and the United States of America, dating back to the 1880s critically impeded social development in Afghanistan" (2003, p. 3). This is particularly important for my study because the external interference impacting social and economic development has had dire consequences on Afghan women and their efforts to improve their status. The external interference contributed to the creation of a deeply militaristic culture among Afghans, impeded development efforts, fueled religious fundamentalism, and incited backlash against anything perceived to be Western, including efforts to promote gender equality.

In addition to culture, religion plays an extremely important role in Afghanistan, deeply influencing culture, norms and every day practices. The country has followed the Hanafi[34] school of Islamic jurisprudence since the 1930s when Nadir Shah chose it to become "the basis of civil and criminal laws (Emadi, 2002, p. 68), and the vast majority of the population follows Sunni Islam, with a smaller

Shia population as well as religious minorities including Sikhs, Hindus, and very small Christian and Bahá'í communities. Although Islam plays a very important role in Afghan daily life, it is often superceded by tribal culture, custom and practices. Although many of these tribal and cultural practices contravene Islam, they dominate interpersonal and community relationships, and are often conflated with religion, giving the appearance that they are rooted in religious rather than tribe and culture. According to Ahmed-Ghosh, "Tribal laws and sanctions routinely take precedence over Islamic and constitutional laws in deciding gender roles, especially through kinship hierarchies in the rural regions" (2003, p. 2). Furthermore,

Tribal power plays, institutions of honour, and inter-tribal shows of patriarchal control have put women's position in jeopardy. Tribal laws view marriages as alliances between groups; women are pawned into marriages and not allowed to divorce, total obedience to the husband and his family is expected, and women are prevented from getting any education. Women are perceived as the receptacles of 'honour,' hence they stay in the domestic sphere, observe the veil and are voiceless. The honour of the family, the tribe, and ultimately the nation is invested in women. (Ahmed-Ghosh, 2003, p. 2–3).

Nira Yuval Davis has said that, "women are not just the biological reproducers of the nation, but also its cultural reproducers, often being given the task of guardians of 'culture' who are responsible for transmitting it to the children and constructing the 'home' in a specific cultural style." (1997, p. 116). This is an interesting quote in two ways. First, it points to one of the most pervasive reasons why women experience gender discrimination, and the subsequent lack of access to rights and opportunities. When her role in society is limited to that of wife and mother, and not expanded to include rights to public engagement and participation, she becomes a vessel for the biological production of the next generation and her role is limited to the training of that child so that cultural norms can be passed down. The second point is that as cultural reproducers, women are inadvertent participants in the continuation of patriarchy and their role within it. This is not to 'blame' women, but to recognize that they also become a part of this system by not having the means, power or motivation to challenge patriarchy and the norms it imposes on society.

While working in Afghanistan,[35] I met many women who discussed their experience with domestic abuse at the hands of their husbands as well as their in-laws. They suggested that this form of abuse had come to be viewed as an acceptable practice while the stigma attached to it prevented victims from talking about it or seeking assistance. We talked about how they thought domestic abuse could be combated, and they came up with many ideas including public education campaigns and stronger anti-violence laws and enforcement of those laws. But they felt that the most important initiative would involve changing family dynamics and the attitude that society and men have about women. They said it was time to train a new generation of young men. This was very interesting and exciting to hear. But when the question was raised, "well who raises these boys?" and "how do you treat your daughters-in-law?" there was silence followed by a discussion about the role of women as the primary educators of the next generation and how this power and opportunity could be harnessed for social change and development. Although this was an extremely empowering thought, patriarchy's strong hold in Afghanistan, and the many ways in which children learn about the roles, responsibilities and rights of men and women by observation, change will take time, and unfold when there is a clear commitment to foster change. This will be demonstrated in increased funding, social programs, education campaigns, laws and enforcement. But it will not happen when local and national governments are dominated by misogynistic warlords with a history of violence against women, who employ religion and culture to subjugate women and limit their rights and opportunities.

MILITARISM'S CONTRIBUTION

In the academic world, feminist writers have argued that gender inequality and the absence of women from public spheres of influence, promotes militarism and prevents sustainable peace. These authors, (Elshtain 1989, Enloe 1987, Peterson & Runyan 1999, Tickner 1992; Whitworth 2004) have sought to undermine prevalent myths, "including the assumption that the war front is separate from the home front or that women are always victims in times of conflict" (Afshar, 2004, 2). They argue that this simplistic approach to analysis fails to appreciate that

[c]onflicts can both empower and disempower women ... They may be both victims and agents of change – though they often have no effective choice in these matters. They may opt to be fighters and yet be attacked and raped; they may choose to provide back-up support and yet simultaneously find themselves and their homes in the firing line; they may be caught in transgressions – such as cross division marriages – that could have been bridges towards peace but may instead have become causes of hatred and war. Through the hardships they experience, many women do develop visions of peace that are rooted in their shared suffering, but that cannot translate into negotiations which are themselves anchored in hatreds and bounded by geographic, religious, and historical divisions that ignore the commonalities of experiences that women know so well (Afshar 2003, p. 2–3).

Presentations of war and violent conflict have tended to focus on the role of men as the active agents of violence, leaving women invisible and without agency. These representations ignore the fact that women are both victimized and galvanized in times of war. As Pankhurst argues, "Accounts of war, through news reporting, government propaganda, novels, cinema, etc., tended to cast men as the 'doers' and women as the passive, innocent victims ... stories of the courage and bravery of men as fighters has tended to eclipse the active roles which women have played" (Pankhurst, 2004, p. 13). Pankhurst further suggests: "As women's experiences have become more broadly known, it has become clear that there are many ways in which women live through and participate in war: as fighters, community leaders, social organizers, workers, farmers, traders, welfare workers, among other roles" (Pankhurst, 2004, 13). Conversely, until very recently, there has been very little discussion or acknowledgement that in times of war and other forms of violent conflict, it is quite common that the collapse of the country's infrastructure, such as health and education, as well as the deteriorating security situation, will adversely affect the women. Furthermore, once the conflict has formally ended and cease fires have been established, "it remains common for women's voices – either individual or organized – on all sides to be absent or marginal at the point when a settlement is reached" and beyond. (Pankurst, 2004, p. 17). As scholars and practitioners contribute to a more comprehensive understanding of the impact of armed conflict on women, and the many roles that women play in these conflicts, it becomes clear that women have a multiplicity of roles in situations of conflict. Yet, their activism and agency in times of war and conflict do not and should not mask the gendered forms of violence that contribute to women's suffering in situations of armed conflict.

In Afghanistan, women have been witnesses and actors at the forefront of the almost three decades of conflict. Their resistance and opposition to war and violence did not begin or end with the Taliban. They were vocal and active in both their support for and resistance against various regimes in the last 30 years. Evidence suggests that women were both the staunchest supporters as well as the greatest opponents of the Soviet occupation in Afghanistan. Supporters of the Communist government and their Soviet backers were largely Kabul-based educated and elite women who felt that the Communist government presented the greatest hope for gender equality in Afghanistan, and used the improving situation of women in Kabul to illustrate their point. One UN advisor stationed in the country during the Soviet occupation remarked:

During the occupation, women made enormous strides: illiteracy declined from 98% to 75%, and they were granted equal rights with men in civil law, and in the Constitution. This is not to say that there was complete gender equality. Unjust patriarchal relations still prevailed in the workplace and in the family with women occupying lower level sex type [sic] jobs. But the strides they took in education and employment were very impressive. I witnessed these gains first hand when the UNDP assigned me (1986–88) as senior advisor to the Afghan government for women's development ... In Kabul I saw great advances in women's education and employment. Women were in evidence in industry, factories, government offices, professions and the media. With large numbers of men killed or disabled, women shouldered the responsibility of both family and country.[36]

At the same time however, the Communist government and the Soviet occupation did not benefit all women. The regime is well known for its harsh crack down on political opponents, both men and women, and most families can say they've lost at least one loved one during this time. In addition to the deaths of thousands of women and children due to indiscriminate bombing campaigns by the Soviets "women along with men have been the victims of deliberate and arbitrary killings and 'disappearances'. In addition to this, women have been subjected to gender specific human rights abuses, such as rape and sexual assault, forced marriage and prostitution"

(Amnesty International, 1999, p. 1). Gendered forms of violence were not used only by the Soviet occupiers, but by government forces supporting the Soviets, and then later by Mujahedin forces, the Taliban, and most recently by Northern Alliances militias before and after the fall of the Taliban. As Amnesty suggests:

The violence directly against women during the Afghan conflict can be located on a continuum of human rights abuses that Afghan women have been, and continue to be, subjected to as a result of their status in society. Traditionally, the lives of Afghan women have been controlled by their male relatives. Notions of honour and shame underpinning cultural norms and practices emphasize female modesty and purity. During the last two decades, but particularly between 1992 and 1995, armed guards have used these norms as weapons of war, engaging in rape and sexual assault against women as an ultimate means of dishonouring entire communities and reducing people's capacity to resist military advances. (Amnesty International, 1999, p. 1)

The use of sexual violence in war is not new, nor limited to one region of the world. It is a universal strategy that has been recorded throughout the annals of history. As Liz Kelly (2000) suggests, "[s]exual violence as a deliberate strategy in war and political repression by the state is connected in a range of ways to sexual violence in all other contexts. Sexual violence is one of the most extreme and effective forms of patriarchal control, which simultaneously damages and constraints women's lives and prompts individual and collective resistance among women" (Kelly, 2000, p. 45). The insecurity that comes with militarism, and the use of rape and other forms of sexual violence against women sets the foundations for strengthening patriarchy, enforcing misogyny, and decreasing women's already limited access to public space.

Little wonder that many Afghan women were also at the forefront of opposition against the Communist regime and its Soviet supporters. In her book *Women of the Afghan War,* Deborah Ellis, who interviewed a large number of Afghan women for her research, shows that "much of the grass-roots opposition to the Soviet presence came from women. They were the first to organize huge demonstrations in the streets." Moreover, "[t]hey were the first to gather at the gates of Pul-e-Charki Prison in Kabul, demanding the release of political prisoners." (Ellis, 2000, p.7). And when they gathered in Shahrinau Park in Kabul in January 1983, many of the women who had lost male family members to the war began to protest and demand that the bodies of their loved ones be returned to the family and again reiterated their demand for the release of political prisoners. There is also evidence to suggest that women in the rural areas were actively engaged in supporting the Mujahedin in their war against Russian occupation. Women were sending husbands and sons to the battlefield, hiding fighters in their homes and providing food and supplies to the militias (Ellis 2000). Yet, women's support of the Mujahedin did not guarantee them security or improved rights and access during or after the Soviet occupation. Women were routinely targeted in kidnappings, forced marriages and rapes by opposing warlords' militia who used violence against women to terrorize and weaken their enemies. Amnesty International's 1995 annual report says:

Women and girls all over Afghanistan live in constant fear of being raped by armed guards. For years, armed guards have been allowed to torture them in this way without fear of reprimand from their leaders. In fact, rape is apparently condoned by most leaders as a means of terrorizing conquered populations and of rewarding soldiers ... Some women have attempted suicide to avoid being raped ... Fear of rape and other abuses has led many families to leave Kabul ... Torture of civilians in their homes has become endemic. Women and girls are treated as the spoils of war, being raped by armed guards or sold into prostitution. Unarmed civilians suspected of belonging to a rival ethnic group are routinely beaten and otherwise ill-treated. (Amnesty International, 1995, cited on RAWA website http://www.rawa.org/women9 .htm)

In fact, part of the initial popularity of the Taliban among some Afghan men related to the Taliban's harsh punitive laws which largely ended sexual violence by armed militia.[37] This came through very clearly in many of my conversations with Afghan men in 2003. Many of them explained that when villagers or townspeople would hear of an impending militia attack, many of the young women would commit suicide rather than wait to be kidnapped or raped by militia members. Unlike the men, women were not eager or relieved with the arrival of the Taliban. One of my friends who was a well-known human rights activist says that,

Afghan men, because they are very concerned about the honour of their
women, were feeling very insecure and concerned with the situation under
the Mujahedin. Even really intellectual and open minded men like my father
who were always supportive of their daughters' education and employment
wanted to try and protect their daughters and wives and were therefore initially happy when the Taliban initially came. But when they started to violate
women's rights, they changed their minds. Women on the other hand were
not happy with the Mujahedin nor with the Taliban. Women had lost their
hope and did not have emotional and psychological peace, and for us not
much changed between the Mujahedin times and the Taliban times, except
that under the Mujahedin we could work with some conditions, and go
shopping, but when the Taliban came, we could not work or go outside of
the house at all. So for us women we had this incremental change; between
transition between Soviet and the Mujahedin, and then the Mujahedin and
the Taliban.[38]

But as I've said before, violations of women's rights did not begin or
end with the Taliban. Even before the departure of the Soviets, there
was growing evidence of difficult days to come for Afghan women.
As Basu describes it:

As far back as 1988, I could see the early warning signs. Even before the Soviet troop withdrawal, 'shabnamas' or handbills warned of reprisals against
women who left their homes. Followers of Gulbuddin Hekmatyar started
throwing acid on women who dared to venture into the streets of Kabul in
trousers, or skirts, or short sleeved shirts. Ironically, the US favoured the
three fundamentalist resistance groups of 'freedom fighters' headed by Hekmatyar, Khalis and Rabbani over the more moderate Mujahedin groups."[39]

So, seven years before the arrival of the Taliban in Afghanistan, extremism was already becoming evident in Afghan politics, and
"[s]ince the Najibullah regime, which was still in power, was anxious
to accommodate the opposition under its National Reconciliation
Policy, women's rights were made the first offering" (Basu, 2001).
The results were immediately evident:

The backlash started in the Ministry of Islamic Affairs, which began dismissing women on the pretext of abolition of posts. A strict code of dress was
imposed, and lunch breaks which enabled women to meet, discuss problems,
and protest against unfair practices were stopped. So was co-education,
which still existed until sixth grade. With acute scarcity of resources it was

obvious that girls' schools would receive low priority and standards would drop ... (Basu, 2001)

And thus began the darkest period of Afghanistan's history in the past three decades. The fall of the Najibullah government in 1992 and the ensuing in-fighting between the Mujahedin brought the war to the neighbourhoods of Kabul, where over 50,000 civilians were killed in a three-year time period. Women's rights were violated with impunity, and in fact condoned by warlords who saw sexual violence as a means of intimidating opponents and rewarding supporters (Amnesty 1999, Basu 2001). Women from opposing ethnic communities were routinely abducted and detained, tortured, sexually abused and sold into prostitution. And while the world condemns the Taliban, there is very little discussion of the ways in which the Mujahedin undermined women's rights. "In addition to physical abuse, women were stripped of their fundamental rights to association, freedom of speech, employment and movement. The Supreme court of the Islamic State in 1994 issued an Ordinance on Women's Veil which decreed that women should wear a veil to cover the whole body, forbidding them to leave their homes." (Basu). And it is these very same actors who were hailed as the heroes of the war against the Taliban, invited to lead the discussions at Bonn, and today dominate the political scene in Afghanistan, with the backing of the United States and the international community.

The Mujahedin who were well known for their military prowess were surprisingly no match for the Taliban who very quickly gained control over 90% of the country by 1995. The Taliban brought their own brand of women's oppression in which women were virtually prisoners in their own homes, unable to appear in public without a male family member, forbidden from receiving an education or employment. Taliban edicts made women's lives increasingly unbearable and any infraction was met with strong and brutal punishment including lashings, cutting off of nail polished fingers and toes, stonings and shootings. The Taliban argued that their laws and edicts were an application of 'pure' sharia. Educated Afghans would disagree and support the view presented by Rashid (2000), Gagnon (2005) and others who argue that Taliban policies were rooted in extremely sexist, narrow, misogynistic interpretations of religious law mixed with an ultra-conservative application of pashtunwali, or the Pashtun code of conduct.

Despite international outcry, including UN resolutions against the

Taliban government,[40] there was no concerted effort to remove the regime until the tragedy of 9/11. In fact, the only notable effort to undermine the Taliban was a series of Security Council mandated sanctions which were shown to be unsuccessful and only deepened the suffering of the already miserable Afghan population.[41] The removal of the Taliban regime presented the first real opportunity for peace, security, and dignity for the Afghan people, and particular attention was paid to the women of Afghanistan who had suffered greatly during the conflict, and particularly under the Taliban. The international community not only used the plight of Afghan women to justify the so-called 'war on terror,' but they also made promises to Afghan women which are yet to be fulfilled.

THE BONN PROCESS AND ACCORDS

In the early days of post-Taliban Afghanistan, the removal of the Taliban – and the hope for the removal of the warlords - resulted in great hope and optimism about the new and active role that women would take in charting the course of their country's future. The first disappointment was almost immediate. The UN sponsored Bonn consultations on the future of Afghanistan was dominated by male delegates and the Northern Alliance forces who were complicit in the destruction of the country, and well-known for their fundamentalist and misogynistic attitudes and policies toward women. In fact, of the 60 delegates and advisors gathered at Bonn, only six were women, and of these only three were participating as full delegates while the other three were advisers to various delegations.[42] The three full delegates were Sima Wali and Rona Mansuri who attended as delegates of the Rome process, representing the former King Zahir Shah, and Ameena Afzali who was a delegate with the United Front delegation, also known as the Northern Alliance. Two other women attended Bonn as advisors to delegations, Seddiqa Balkhi as adviser to the Iranian backed Cyprus Group, and Fatana Gilani as adviser to the Pakistani-backed Peshawar Group representing the Pashtun leadership and refugee populations in Pakistan.[43]

The lack of participation by Afghan women in the Bonn Process was particularly disturbing and disconcerting given that these initial talks represented the forum for the forging of a new course in Afghanistan's history, and of particular significance for the women of Afghanistan who were marginalized from political decision making for over two decades. Their marginalization was also not surprising however, given that the Bonn Agreements were dominated by the Northern Alliance who have historically shown themselves to be fundamentalist and misogynistic in their approach to women's rights. International human rights organizations, Afghan advocacy groups, and citizens alike have attested to the brutality of these warlords against the Afghan population, and gendered acts of violence and human rights violations conducted by various militias and their warlord leaders against Afghan women. Despite this history of brutality, they were the main actors at Bonn consultations and ensured that the agreement acknowledged their 'heroism:'

The participants in the UN Talks on Afghanistan ... expressing their appreciation to the Afghan Mujahedin who, over the years, have defended the independence, territorial integrity and national unity of the country and have played a major role in the struggle against terrorism and oppression, and whose sacrifice has now made them both heroes of jihad and champions of peace, stability and reconstruction of their beloved homeland, Afghanistan.[44]

Clearly, the women had a difficult task ahead of them. Mansuri shared her feelings about her participation: "We're not starting at zero, but at a huge minus. I hope the fighters and Mujahedin leaders see that they've accomplished nothing by waging war and will listen to women's voices calling for peace and coexistence."[45] Her co-delegate Sima Wali was more assertive and argued:

We are not waiting any longer to be invited to sit at these tables where peace and the reconstruction of our economy is being discussed. We are the silent voices that need to be heard. I'm a constant presence to raise the issue of women. With the exception of the king, the previous leaders' records on human rights and gender issues are all cause for concern. With Rabbani talking about a willingness to defend the rights of women 'within the context of Islam' we are going to have to watch closely to make sure that all these statements about commitment to gender issues move beyond the rhetorical level. The most pressing problems of Afghan women are not the burqa, which Western women have tended to focus on, but extreme poverty and the number of widows who have no means to sustain themselves.[46]

Despite the lack of gender equality at Bonn, the Accords did produce several advances for the women of Afghanistan. The Accords "revived Afghanistan's 1964 constitution which secured equal rights before the law to all Afghan 'people' and gave Afghan women the right to vote in elections, serve in government, and be elected to parliament" (Sultan, 2005, p. 19), and two women were appointed to ministerial positions, Dr. Sima Samar as Minister of Women's Affairs and Suhaila Seddiqi as Minister of Health. These gains were hard won however, and, as my research indicates, mostly attributed to Sima Wali. For example, it was Ms. Wali who persuaded the King and former President Rabbani of the Northern Alliance to sign a statement supporting the right of women to fully participate in Afghanistan's political future. The establishment of the Women's Ministry has also been attributed to her tireless advocacy. It was also a difficult learning experience. For example, when Wali and the other women left the Bonn talks for a press conference, "the negotiated plan for a women's ministry was scrapped, forcing them to refight a battle they thought they'd already won" and making them realize that "being vocal was simply not enough. They had to be present and alert at every step of the negotiations to make sure their progress was not erased in their absence." (Sultan, 2005, p. 19)

To maintain the momentum on women's equality at Bonn, a three day meeting was organized in Brussels to coincide with the Bonn gathering. The meeting was arranged with the help of women's rights groups in Europe and the United States, and brought together forty prominent Afghan women – including the women delegates at Bonn. The women gathered at the Afghan Women's Summit for Democracy drafted and released a Call for Action Declaration which represented some of their hopes and demands for the new Afghanistan. The Declaration referred to as the *Brussels Proclamation* outlines recommendations in the areas of: education, media, and culture; health; human rights and the Constitution; and refugee and IDP women.[47] The delegation's specific demands included:

- The right for women to vote and to be entitled to equal pay and equal access to health care, education and employment
- An emergency plan for reopening schools by March 2002 for both girls and boys, a new curriculum, and training of teachers
- The inclusion of Afghan women lawyers in the development of a new constitution which would include the principles of non-discrimination
- The rebuilding of hospitals and provision of vital medicines, treatments and services, including psychological counselling and mother and child healthcare

- Central inclusion of women in the Loya Jirga
- The protection of women from forced underage marriages and sexual harassment.[48]

These demands highlighted ways in which gender specific programming and Afghan women's participation in post Taliban Afghanistan would contribute to improving the circumstances of Afghan women and ensuring their rightful place in the recovery of Afghanistan. The years following the fall of the Taliban were optimistic and positive ones for Afghan women activists. Following the preliminary successes – on paper – at Bonn, Afghan women's advocates were pleasantly surprised when the Interim President Hamid Karzai signed a document called the *Declaration of the Essential Rights of Afghan Women*. This document was actually drafted by Afghan women activists gathered in Tajikistan in June 2000, under the auspices of a Paris based NGO NEGAR-Support of Women of Afghanistan (Sultan, 2005, p. 19). The document which was drafted while the Taliban was still in power "calls for equality between men and women, equal protection under the law, institutional education in all disciplines, freedom of movement, freedom of speech and political participation, and the right to wear or not wear the burqa" (Sultan, 2005, 19).[49] Three years later in March 2003, the Interim government ratified the United Nations Convention on the Elimination of All Forms of Discrimination Against Women (CEDAW).

WHY ARE THESE REFORMS NOT IN PLACE?

Given all these promising efforts and indicators, how can we explain the continued resistance to and lack of progress towards gender equality in Afghanistan? Some of the answers are that constitutions, legal documents, declarations and promises, while important in promoting a culture of human rights and equality, do not address long-held attitudes, assumptions and prejudices which continue to determine the interpretation and application of laws. And moreover, in Afghanistan, gender dynamics are further complicated by the decades of war and violence, making the promotion of gender equality more difficult. Finally, a Mujahedin dominated political system is not conducive to promoting the advancement of women. In one of its reports, Amnesty writes that

Alongside the violence perpetuated against women by members of armed Mujahedin groups, all Afghan political groups have used the status of women as a political tool to claim legitimacy or popularity vis-à-vis other factions. The cultural constraints existing for women, which are bound up with interpretations of tradition and religion, have repeatedly been raised to the political level by Afghan armed groups. Invoking religion and Afghan culture, most armed groups have made pronouncements about appropriate behaviour for women, imposing restrictions on their freedom of movement and access to employment and education in areas they controlled. Women have been publicly harassed, intimidated and beaten for carrying out activities deemed by armed guards to be 'un-Islamic.' (Amnesty International, 1999, p.1).

Especially troubling is that a large portion of the women presently in parliament are also aligned with various Mujahedin factions and support the creation of an Islamic state where women's rights are defined and implemented according to very narrow and conservative interpretations of Islam. These women present the gender-friendly face of the new Afghanistan by filling in the required 25% quotas set by the Afghan Interim Government at Bonn, but the vast majority of them do not support a radical transformation of women's lives nor the change of the patriarchal structures that has impeded equality and justice for Afghan women. Political and family connections provide these women political strength and legitimacy, giving them little incentive to challenge the structures that also provide them with power and authority. These women stand in stark contrast to grassroots Afghan women activists inspired by radical feminist ideals, or Communist women who sought to advance women's equality by contesting patriarchy and promoting women's rights by challenging historical attitudes and behaviours toward women and seeking to drastically change these.[50]

   Militarism has intensified the politicization of gender equality, and has served to deepen patriarchy, misogyny and narrow and extremist interpretations of religious text while promoting the increased use of cultural practices such as under-age and forced marriages, bride price, exchange of daughters as a means of conflict resolution, and other traditional practices that violate women's rights.

BARRIERS TO GENDER EQUALITY AND PARTICIPATION
IN AFGHANISTAN

While religion and culture are often faulted for lack of progress on women's issues in Afghanistan, it is impossible and indeed inappropriate to attribute gender inequality in Afghanistan to a few simple matters. The roots of inequality relate to a plethora of complex factors, of which there are three main categories or clusters. The first is socio-cultural, referring to cultural and religious practices, beliefs, norms and customs that define, inform, determine and impact gender relations in Afghanistan. The second, socio-economic factors, relate to how poverty and illiteracy intersect with and shape socio-cultural factors. The third category are external factors such as militarism, armed conflict and the ways in which the presence and policies of foreign actors influence gender relations and impeded the advancement of women. These factors must be considered on their own and in relation to each other to develop an understanding of the complexities of attitudes and beliefs about women's rights and responsibilities. Understanding the root causes of gender inequality while appreciating the forces that exacerbate them are critical for contemporary peace-building and development efforts. Because Afghanistan is literally being rebuilt from the ground up, examining the factors that impede the advancement of gender equality in Afghanistan has important implications for long term transformation.

Discussing the root causes of gender inequality in Afghanistan is a difficult and intricate undertaking. They mix material conditions with social constructions, daily experience with historical memory and social, cultural, religious, economic, and historical realities as well as tribal, regional, and international politics that have dominated the Afghan landscape for centuries. More specifically, the promotion of gender equality has been impacted by the lack of access to universal education, political participation and economic independence, employment and poverty, long-term conflict, militarism and violence, and the impact of these on all the previous issues as well as on women's safety, security, freedom of movement and access to the public sphere.

Such inequalities have had severe effects on the health and welfare of Afghan women. Studies suggest that a vast majority of Afghan women, aside from having one of the world's highest maternal mortality rates and generally negative health indicators, also suffer from mental illness, including depression and anxiety, with a particularly high suicide rate. A recent study by Global Rights confirms that on average, 60% of Afghan women are victims of domestic abuse with variations across the country. Fawzia Raufi, an Afghan MP from Faryab province for example suggests that as many as 80% of the women in that province suffer from domestic violence, while rates in Kabul, Herat and Mazar-i-Sharif tend to be lower (Oates 2007).

At the most basic level, concepts such as 'gender' and 'equality' are contested in Afghanistan. First of all, there is no equivalent word for 'gender' in the Dari and Pashto languages. The descent of the international community into Kabul, and the focus on gender equality and women's advancement included an explosion of gender equality directed workshops that introduced the gender equality concept to the masses of women working for the advancement of women and into common discourse in Afghanistan. The vast majority of activists who have developed an understanding of the concept of gender as distinct from 'sex' and are exposed to alternative concepts of equality find them helpful tools for discussion and activism. There are others – both men and women – who strive to maintain the status quo. They completely reject these concepts as incompatible with Afghan culture and Muslim religious beliefs and practices, seeing them as largely Western in orientation, definition and application. The imposition of such Western values is seen as a new form of cultural imperialism. Resistance to these ideas has been manifested most vehemently in the rejection by Muslim and Arab states of international human rights norms and laws pertaining to the promotion and protection of women's rights and freedoms, such as the International Convention on the Elimination of All Forms of Discrimination Against Women, and other documents developed by the UN and the international NGO community. This opposition is seen by Muslim leaders as a necessary measure to protect Islam and Muslim populations from Western cultural and religious imperialism. There are also groups trying to mediate the competing commitments to advance gender equality and their devotion to Islam, and thereby to find ways to promote gender equality within the context of Afghan cultural and Islamic religious practice.

Gender is defined as "*socially constructed* roles, behaviors, activities, and attributes that a given society *considers appropriate* for men and women."[51] Each society has its own set of gender roles and responsibilities. These expectations are based on a number of factors including cultural, religious, social and economic realities among other things. One of the sources of tension and disagreement between Westerners and Muslims are their perspective on the role of religion in defining gender relationships. Ironically, both see religion as the source of the tension. Some non-Muslims and secular Muslims view Islam as patriarchal with laws that limit women's rights and freedoms. On the other hand, practicing Muslims see gender roles and responsibilities, as articulated and discussed in the Quran, are divinely ordained and incontrovertible.[52] Hence, by and large, 'gender' as a concept is misunderstood and contested by those who submit that notion of the roles, responsibilities, and social expectations of each sex are not simply social construction that have resulted within a vacuum. They see these as clearly defined elements revealed by God through Revelation in the Quran and Hadith. Hence in the Afghan context, it is the revealed word of God that is seen as defining each sex's roles, responsibilities and social expectations, and any deviation from this code is seen as contrary to Islam, disobedience against God, a sin, and a direct threat to social order and harmony.

The Western concept of 'equality' is also contested in Afghanistan, as it is in many Muslim, Asian and African countries. Muslim scholars argue that the Western notion of equality assumes, connotes and promotes sameness between men and women, and this is contrary to the parameters of Islamic law and practice. They argue that in Islam, men and women are indeed equal in the sight of God and have the same spiritual duties and responsibilities, but biological differences demand different roles and responsibilities that complement one another and allow for functioning families and societies. In Islam then, while men and women are believed to have spiritual equality (that is, they are equal in the sight of God and enjoy equal access to spiritual capacities) they are not seen as equal in the context of rights and responsibilities. According to the Quranic scholar Amin Ahsan Islahi, the Western notion of equality "champions a concept of equality which nurtures the idea that nature has bestowed women with the same kind of talents and energies with which it has blessed men; and whatever a man can do, a woman can inevitably do the same. Therefore, in the social set-up, the jurisdiction of a man and a woman should be the same, with an equality in their rights and responsibilities."[53] He argues that in contrast, Islam "propagates a concept of equality between man and woman which speaks of the fact that Allah has created both man and woman from the same matter ... and both have been created by Allah for their own specific purposes. Both have a right to be respected and honoured" but "in a society both man and woman should have responsibilities according to their talents and they should have all the rights according to their responsibilities."[54]

Hence, from a Muslim's perspective, gender roles, responsibilities and relations are clearly and irrefutably defined and described in religious texts and thereby non-negotiable over time and space.

Another criticism of the Western notion of equality is its emphasis on individualism and the West's preoccupation and commitment to individual rights which places the individual at the centre of the rights discourse. The Western notion of equality is based on the West's emphasis on the individual as the primary actor in society, with individual rights and freedoms being a natural extension. In this paradigm – theoretically, if not practically – all members of a society are seen as equal in rights and opportunities and enjoy equal freedoms regardless of race, sex, nationality, and without distinction. This 'individualistic' approach to understanding rights and freedoms attracts strong criticism from 'collectivist' societies where responsibility, obligation and duty predominate relational discourse. In collectivist societies, such as in parts of the Muslim world, individual rights are defined in terms of responsibilities, obligations and duties in the context of relationships with others in the family, tribe/clan, community and society. Responsibilities precede rights and any deviation against the status quo is perceived as undermining the health and well-being of family, community and by extension, society as a whole. This paradigm forms the basis of the 'cultural relativist' arguments posed by non-Western states who contend that the human rights discourse in principle is a Western concept because of its emphasis on 'rights' rather than 'responsibilities.' So the promotion of equality based on individual rights is perceived, or presented, as yet another Western imperialist threat to non-Western cultures and ways of life.

My interviews with women in Afghanistan in 2003 revealed that the vast majority of them do not oppose concepts of gender and equality. Like most Afghans, Afghan women are also devout, pious and view Islam as the centre of their lives, but many of them feel that culture and religion are used by fundamentalist forces in Afghanistan to maintain their supremacy over women. As one woman said to me in one of our training sessions, while Afghan women appreciate respect for the culture and religion of Afghanistan, they do not want Western feminists to be so careful and respectful of these so as to allow them to continue being used to perpetuate patriarchy. She saw political correctness on the part of Western feminists as tantamount to condoning the attitudes and structures that continue to keep women from achieving their rightful rights and freedoms within Islam and by international standards of human rights. This conversation was enlightening. There is a lesson here to be learned by women's rights activists about walking the fine line between promoting gender equality in a culturally sensitive manner while not upholding patriarchal structures or impeding the hard work of grass roots activists.

In this article, I have tried to show that gender equality efforts have been impeded by long term conflict and insecurity, which has plagued Afghanistan in the last thirty years. These efforts will continue to be impeded until Afghanistan is able to address internal challenges that fuel inequality and rising anti-Western attitudes, which are also contributing to heightened resistance to women's equality among policy makers and power holders. And in the final analysis, the advancement of women rights, and the promotion of gender equality will require the support and involvement of Afghan men who will serve a critical role in transforming existing gender relationships and power structures.

BIBLIOGRAPHY

Afshar, H. (2003). "Introduction War and Peace: What do Women Contribute?" in Afshar, H. & Eade, D. (eds.) *Development, Women and War: Feminist Perspectives*. Oxford: Oxfam.

Ahmed-Ghosh, Huma. (2003). "A History of Women in Afghanistan: Lessons Learnt for the Future Or Yesterdays and Tomorrow: Women in Afghanistan" In *Journal of International Women's Studies* Vol 4 #3 May.

Amnesty International, (1999). *Women in Afghanistan: Pawns in Men's Struggle for Power*. http://www.amnesty.org/en/report/info/ASA11/011/1999.

Bahgam, S. & Mukhatari, W. (2004). *Study on Child Marriage in Afghanistan*. Medica Mondiale.

Dupree, N. (1998). "Afghan Women Under the Taliban" in Maley, W. (ed.). *Fundamentalism Reborn? Afghanistan and the Taliban*. Pakistan: Vanguard Books.

Ellis, D. (2000). *Women of the Afghan War*. Connecticut: Praeger Publisher.

Elshtain, J.B. (ed.) (1990). *Women, Militarism, and War: Essays in History, Politics and Social Theory*. Maryland Rowman & Littlefield Publishers, Inc.

Emadi, Hafizullah, (2002), *Repression, Resistance and Women in Afghanistan*. Conneticut: Greenwood Press.

Emadi, Hafizullah, (2005), *Culture and Customs of Afghanistan*. Connecticut: Greenwood Press.

Enloe, C. (1987). "Feminist Thinking about War, Militarism, and Peace" in Hess, B. & Ferree, M. *Analyzing Gender: A Handbook of Social Science Research*. Newbury Park: Sage Publications.

Farhoumand-Sims, C. (2007). "Unfulfilled Promises: Women and Peace in Post Taliban Afghanistan" in *International Journal*, Vol LXII, no. 3, summer.

Gagnon, K. (2005). *I Is for Infidel: From Holy War to Holy Terror: 18 Years Inside Afghanistan*. New York: Public Affairs.

International Crisis Group (2003). *Afghanistan: Women and Reconstruction*.

Oates, L. & Nijhowne, D. (2008). *Living with Violence: A National Report on Domestic Abuse in Afghanistan*. Global Rights. (executive summary available on line at http://section15.ca/features/news/2008/07/04/afghan_women/)

Kelly, L. (2000). 'Wars Against Women: Sexual Violence, Sexual Politics and the Militarised State," in Susie Jacobs, Ruth Jacobson and Jennifer Marchbank (eds.) *States of Conflict: Gender, Violence and Resistance*. London: Zed Books.

Moghadam, V. (1994). "Reform, Revolution, and Reaction: The Trajectory of the Women's Question in Afghanistan" in Moghadam, V. (ed) *Gender and National Identity: Women and Politics in Muslim Societies*. London: Zed Books.

Moghadam, V. (1997). "Nationalist Agendas and Women's Rights: Conflicts in Afghanistan in the Twentieth Century." In West, L. (ed.) *Feminist Nationalism*. New York: Routledge.

Pankhurst, D. (ed.), (2008). *Gendered Peace: Women's Struggles for Post War Justice and Reconciliation*. New York: Routledge.

Peterson, V. S. & Runyan, A. S. (eds.) (1999). *Global Gender Issues*. Boulder: Westview Press.

Physicians for Human Rights (2001). *Women's Health and Human Rights in Afghanistan: A Population Based Assessment*.

Rashid, A. (2000). *Taliban*. New Haven: Yale University Press.

Rubin, B. (2002). *The Fragmentation of Afghanistan*. New York: Yale University Press.

Saikal, A. & Maley, W. (ed.) (1989). *The Soviet Withdrawal from Afghanistan*. Cambridge: Cambridge University Press

Schinasi, M. (1979). *Afghanistan at the Beginning of the Twentieth Century: Nationalism and Journalism in Afghanistan. A Study of Seraj-ul-Akhbar (1911–1918)*. Naples: Insituto Universitario Orientale.

Sultan, M. (2005). *From Rhetoric to Reality: Afghan Women on the Agenda for Peace*. Published by the Women Waging Peace Policy Commission, Hunt Alternatives. Report found at http://www.huntalternatives.org/download/18_from_rhetoric_to_reality_afghan_women_on_the_agenda_for_peace.pdf

Tickner, A. (1992). "Toward a Nongendered Perspective on Global Security" in Tickner, A., *Achieving Global Security*. New York: Columbia University Press.

Whitworth, S. (2004). *Men, Militarism and UN Peacekeeping: A Gendered Analysis*. Boulder: Lynne Rienner Publishers.

WEBSITES

Basu, R. "The Rape of Afghanistan." Published in *Z Magazine* and accessed at http://www.nowar-paix.ca/nowar/forum/209

Please see "Afghanistan's Bonn Agreement One Year Later: A Catalogue of Missed Opportunities.
http://www.cmi.no/pdf/?file=/afghanistan/doc/bonn1yr-bck.pdf

http://www.un.org/womenwatch/ianwge/taskforces/communique03.htm

NOTES

1 The author's observation is that while these generalizations hold among most Afghan communities and families, but it is not a universal reality. Many Afghan families support their daughters in their education and employment endeavours. However, cultural and community pressures demand that social mores – for example pertaining to marriage – be generally but not universally applied even among the most educated segments of society.

2 Please see Farhoumand-Sims, C. (2007)

3 International NGOs such as Amnesty International (2003, 2005), Human Rights Watch (2005), CMI (2005)

4 The last official census in Afghanistan was done in 1979, so these latest figures are largely based on estimations and not on formal census. This figure is found on CIA website, https://www.cia.gov/library/publications/the-world-factbook/print/af.html

5 World Fact

6 The land ruled by the ancient kings of the Persian empire fought against Arab-Muslim conquest for nearly a century before finally converting to Islam (Ghasemi, 1998, 447). This was followed by destructive invasions by Genghis Khan, the Moguls, and Alexander the Great. In more recent history, Afghans have been engaged in wars with the British (1842, 1878, 1919), the Soviets as Mujahedin fighters (1979–1988), among Mujahedin forces in a civil war (1992–1995) and between Mujahedin forces and the Taliban (1995–2001), before the Taliban's ongoing engagement with US and NATO forces (2001–present day) is the most recent of this scene of protracted conflict and violence. It was under British rule that the controversial Durand Line was drawn dividing Pashtun populations between Pakistan and Afghanistan which to this day is contributing to a porous border and escalation of conflict.

7 The PDPA split into two factions: Parcham (Flag) and Khalq (People)

8 Afghans often refer to the Mujahedin as jihadis

9 Although there are a large number of individuals whom Afghans refer to as warlords (jangsalar), the most powerful and famous include Gulbuddin Hekmatyar, Ustad Abdul Rasul Sayyaf, Rashid Dostum, Ismail Khan, Mohammad Fahim, Yunus Qanooni, and Yunis Khalis.

10 The vast majority of the Afghans I have spoken to will say that although living under the Taliban had its challenges, after the many years of fighting, bombing and human suffering, the 'security' they imposed through disarmament of militia and punitive measures against criminals allowed some 'peace.' One person I spoke to said it was a welcome change to be able to go to bed at night not worrying about militia breaking into one's home, raping women, stealing goods, and kidnapping and killing the men and boys. (Interview with male Kabul resident, June 2003).

11 Examples included the banning of music, kite flying and books other than the Quran, forbidding entertainment of any form (television, radio, movies) and regulation of personal issues such as men having to grow beards and spending a significant amount of their time at the local mosque.

12 These personal views are based on conversations with Afghans while working there in the summer of 2003, but confirmed also by Ahmad Rashid who shares the same perspective in his book *The Taliban* (2000, p. 32)

13 The four factions were the Rome Group delegation representing the King Zahir Shah; a delegation representing the United Front (Northern

Alliance), the Pakistani based Peshawar group and the Cyprus group
which was reported to be supported by Iran.

14 It is well documented that all parties to a conflict must participate in negotiations in order to increase the effectiveness of the peace agreement.
In Afghanistan, the challenge was that the US and its Northern Alliance
allies would not agree to include the Taliban, and in turn the Taliban
did not want to participate anyway because they saw the process as a
Western puppet process aimed at increasing US presence in the region.

15 Please see "Afghanistan's Bonn Agreement One Year Later: A Catalogue of Missed Opportunities.
http://www.cmi.no/pdf/?file=/afghanistan/doc/bonn1yr-bck.pdf

16 http://www.un.org/womenwatch/ianwge/taskforces/communique
03.htm

17 The Ministry of Women's Affairs has been under-resourced, marginalized and perceived among many Afghan women activists as a disappointment and largely unable to fulfill its mandate due to lack of
human and financial resources, capacity, and support.

18 Please see *Poppy Crackdown Gives Rise to Opium Brides*, on the
Afghanistan Conflict Monitor
http://www.afghanconflictmonitor.org/children/index.html and "More
Afghan Families Using Girls to Pay Debt" at http://www.newser.com/
story/22953/more-afghan-families-using-girls-to-pay-debt.html

19 This is a subject that could benefit immensely from more research.

20 Please see following reports for insight into the reality of Afghan
women's lives: Amnesty International Reports: *Afghanistan: Women
still under attack – a systematic failure to protect* (May 2005);
*Afghanistan: Noone listens to us and noone treats us as human beings.
Justice denied to women* (October 2003); Human Rights Watch reports: *Lessons in Terror: Attacks on Education in Afghanistan* (July
2006); *Campaigning Against Fear: Women's Participation in
Afghanistan's 2005 Elections* (August 2005), *The Forgotten War:
Human Rights Abuses and Violations of the Law s of War Since the
Soviet Withdrawal* (Feb 1991); *Campaigning Against Fear: Women's
Participation in Afghanistan's 2005 Elections* (August 2005); for a
complete list of remaining reports, please see http://www.hrw.org/cam-
paigns/afghanistan/1989-2001.htm, Oates 2006, *Taking Stock: Afghan
Women and Girls Five Years On* (2006) found at
www.womankind.org.uk/takingstockdownloads.html, and Oates
and Nijihowne, (2008), *Living with Violence: A National Report on
Domestic Abuse in Afghanistan.*

21 Mahrams are usually male members of the family related by direct blood or marriage such as father, brother, husband, son.

22 This report is available at http://www.crisisgroup.org/library/ documents/report_archive/A400919_14032003.pdf

23 In her book *Women of the Afghan War,* Deborah Ellis speaks of a woman in Ghazni who killed ten Russian soldiers before she herself was captured and killed. (2000, p. 8).

24 I recognize that there is a wide range of interpretations and applications of the Quran and what Islam does and does not permit. In this case I'm referring to clearly stated rights in the Quran such as the right to refuse a marriage, the right to inheritance, and the right to education and employment which are all clearly laid out in the Quran as explicit rights of women.

25 This is true of Amanullah's efforts in the early 1900's, Daoud's efforts in the 1960's, and the PDPA efforts during the Soviet occupation. In some cases, unnecessary reforms (ie. Amanullah's policy requiring everyone in Kabul to wear Western clothes) and implementation through force contributed to distress and fueled opposition in both the early part of the century as well as under Daoud and later the Communists. (Emadi, 2002, p. 64, 71).

26 http://topics.developmentgateway.org/afghanistan/ http://www.kabulguide.net/kbl-scenearticles.htm

27 http://www.dukenews.duke.edu/911site/dupree.html

28 Given Afghanistan's cultural norms, I imagine these efforts would have been highly contentious and contested, but I have not been able to find any written evidence to outline the outcome, consequence or reaction to these changes.

29 According to Ahmed-Ghosh, Tarzi was educated in Syria and Turkey and thereby greatly influenced by modern interpretations of Islamic jurisprudence, including the liberties accorded to women.

30 Ibid., pg. 11.

31 Human Rights Watch Report http://hrw.org/reports/2001/afghan3/ afgwrd1001-01.htm

32 Ibid.

33 Although this is generally true, the author and others have observed that there are variations in the degree of restrictions and inequality imposed on women among various communities. For example, the Pashtun are generally more conservative, while the Hazara tend to be more egalitarian in their beliefs and practices and significantly less conservative. (Per-

sonal observation, discussions on the subject with various friends in Afghanistan and Afghan Canadian friends, and also discussed Emadi 2002, and 2005, and Rory Stewart's talk at IDRC which can be found on line at http://www.idrc.ca/en/ev-110894-201-1-DO_TOPIC.html.

34 There are four schools of Islamic jurisprudence that have developed over the years. They are Hanafi, Maliki, Shafii, and Hanbali. Each school of thought is named after the Muslim scholar/thinker who developed this approach or interpretation of Islamic law.

35 In the Spring of 2003, I worked on two projects in Afghanistan. The first was with the Afghan Women's Organization where I provided women's human rights and peacebuilding advocacy training to Afghan women working in NGOs, within government Ministries, and with UNIFEM. My training included discussions of CEDAW and Security Council Resolution 1325 on Women, Peace and Security and their possible applicability and relevance within Afghanistan. The second project was with Rights and Democracy where I provided the same training for women jurists, judges and lawyers who were involved in the Constitutional reforms and consultations. In February 2008, I returned to Afghanistan to do some preliminary research on women's access to justice for a project I'm working on with The North South Institute which is looking at the relationship between gender inequality and state fragility in three 'fragile' contexts: Afghanistan, Occupied Palestinian Territories and Haiti.

37 Basu, Rasel (2001). *The Rape of Afghanistan.* http://www.zmag.org /basurape.htm

38 Please note that before long the Taliban was also using rape as a tactic of war against communities and groups who opposed them.

39 Female Afghan activist personal interview, July 15, 2008

40 Rasil Basu, "The Rape of Afghanistan." Published in Z *Magazine* and accessed at http://www.nowar-paix.ca/nowar/forum/209

41 UN Resolutions against the Taliban government of Afghanistan include Resolution 1189 of 13 August, 1998, Resolution 1193 of 28 August, 1998, Resolution 1214 of 8 December, 1998, and Resolution 1267 of 15 October, 1999, as well as resolutions by the Commission on the Status of Women

42 Secretary General's Report on Sanctions in Afghanistan.

43 Please note no women were invited to participate in the Peace and Unity conference held in Peshawar in November 2001, and a women's freedom march organized by women's activist Soraya Parkila to coin-

cide with the Bonn Agreements was banned by the Northern Alliance's
Interior Minister Younis Qanooni. http://findarticles.com/p/articles/
mi_qa3693/is_200112/ai_n9011748/pg_1

44 Please note that not all women are created equal. Sima Wali was the
most prominent woman delegate and much of the achievements on
behalf of women at Bonn have been attributed to her.

45 Please see full text of the Bonn Agreement at
http://www.un.org/News/dh/latest/afghan/afghan-agree.htm

46 *The Latest on Afghan Women: Off Our Backs,* http://findarticles.com/
p/articles/mi_qa3693/is_200112/ai_n9011748/pg_1

47 *The Latest on Afghan Women: Off Our Backs,*
http://findarticles.com/p/articles/mi_qa3693/is_200112/ai_n9011748

48 Afghan Women's Summit for Democracy, Brussels Proclamation:
http://www.un.org/womenwatch/afghanistan/documents/Brussels_
Proclamation.pdf

49 http://www.equalitynow.org/english/pressroom/press_releases/
summit_20011220_en.html

50 Please see http://users.erols.com/kabultec/declarat.html for full text of
the Declaration.

51 Based on interviews with Afghan women's rights activist September 25,
2008.

52 World Health Organization Website
http://www.who.int/gender/whatisgender/en/index.html

53 Please note there is wide variation of interpretations of the Quran with
Muslim men and women holding a wide range of views about the range
of rights given to women in the Quran.

54 Islahi is a prolific Islamic scholar who is well known and respected for
his contributions to Quranic studies. He was born in India, or present
day Pakistan, where he died in 1997. http://amin-ahsan-
islahi.com/?=58

55 Ibid

An Interview with Afghan MP Malalai Joya: Karzai Government Treats Women as Brutally as Did the Taliban

ASAD ISMI

Malalai Joya, 29, is the youngest female member of Afghanistan's parliament and has been elected twice from the western province of Farah. She is a popular women's rights activist and an outspoken critic of the government of Hamid Karzai and the Northern Alliance, which is now being defended by US, Canadian and other Western troops occupying Afghanistan. As a newly elected MP, Joya became famous in 2003 when, in her first speech to Afghanistan's Loya Jirga (Constituent Assembly), she denounced the presence of warlords and drug lords in that body. She also runs Hamoon Clinic in Farah province – the only health care centre in the area that offers free services, including medication, to its patients who are mainly women and children. Invited by BC Labour Against the War, Joya toured Canada in November 2007 to bring attention to the dire condition of women in her country, as well as to protest her expulsion from Afghanistan's parliament in May (her term runs until 2009). I spoke to her in Toronto.

One of the reasons the Canadian government uses to justify its invasion of and occupation of Afghanistan is that its troops are fighting the fundamentalist Taliban partly to protect women's rights. As Joya informs us, however, the Karzai government is as fundamentalist as the Taliban and treats women just as brutally. She denounces the Karzai government and parliament as a corrupt regime of warlords and drug lords who are guilty of many war crimes.

Q: Why were you expelled from the Afghan parliament?

JOYA: Because of comments I made during a television interview. I criticized the parliament for failing to accomplish enough for the Afghan people, saying, "A stable or a zoo is better [than this legislature]. At least there you have a donkey that carries a load and a cow that provides milk. This parliament is worse than a stable or a zoo." My specific crime was "insulting the institution of parliament." My expulsion is illegal, a restriction of free speech, and clearly shows that this is an undemocratic parliament. Today in Afghanistan, we have jungle law because of these Northern Alliance fundamentalists. Human Rights Watch has called for my immediate reinstatement and pointed out that members of the country's parliament have regularly criticized each other, but no one else has been suspended.

Q: How else have you been attacked?

JOYA: Since my election in 2003, I've been targeted by the criminals and drug smugglers in parliament because of my efforts to fight for women's rights. There have been four assassination attempts on my life, my house has been blown up, and I have to travel with bodyguards. In the parliament, I have been assaulted and my life has been threatened, with one of the members even saying, "We have to kill her by any means, even a suicide attack." I've also been threatened with rape and called a prostitute. The microphone has been turned off during my speeches.

Q: Who are the drug lords in the government among the important ministers?

JOYA: According to the media, at least three of them – Karim Khalili, Arif Noorzai, and Ismail Khan – are well-known drug lords. Most of the people who control the Northern Alliance, which runs the government, are drug lords. Also, according to Human Rights Watch, 80% of the members of the Afghan parliament are warlords, drug lords, and criminals. The drug lords are ministers, governors, com-

manders, MPs, and ambassadors; Karzai continues to put these criminals in high official posts and the Afghan people are hostages in their
hands. To give you one example: Izatullah Wasifi is an Afghan drug
lord who was jailed in the US for selling heroin in Las Vegas. After his
release, he returned to Afghanistan where Karzai made him governor
of Farah province. In this post, Wasifi engaged in drug trafficking and
corruption, and for this Karzai made him head of the government's
anti-corruption body in 34 provinces of Afghanistan – quite a promotion. This is why Afghanistan is the biggest producer of opium in
the world today, supplying 93% of the world supply. While the drug
dealers running the country enrich themselves, only a mere 2% of the
Afghan people have access to electricity, and 60% of them live below
the poverty line. [It is worth noting here that Karzai's own brother,
Ahmed Wali, is widely perceived to be involved in drug trafficking –
A.I.]

Q: Do Afghans support the Karzai government?

JOYA: Most Afghans do not support this warlord-drug lord government. In the parliamentary elections, most people did not vote because they wanted to show their anger at the results of the earlier
presidential election. A March 2007 survey conducted by Integrity
Watch Afghanistan revealed that 60% of Afghans think that the current administration is more corrupt than any other in the past two
decades. The people know that, as long as the Northern Alliance is in
power, there is no hope for positive social change. The main backers
of Karzai and the Northern Alliance are, of course, the US, Canada,
and other Western countries who are supporting a government of
drug dealers and criminals. Canada is following US policy which
makes a mockery out of democracy.

Q: Do you think the position of women in Afghan society is much
worse under Karzai than before?

JOYA: Yes, their position is catastrophic. The Northern Alliance
government is made up of fundamentalists, just as the Taliban were,
and they oppress women in horrendous ways. Women still cannot
get educated today, their movements continue to be restricted, and
they have very few employment opportunities. As a result, suicides
by women in Afghanistan are more numerous today than ever be-

fore. According to official figures, 250 female suicides were reported in just the first six months of 2007. Sumaya, an eighteen-year-old, hanged herself because she was to be sold to a sixty-year-old man. In Herat province, 104 women burned themselves in the Central Hospital.

According to an official survey, 80% of marriages in Afghanistan are forced, and 95% of women in the country suffer from depression. Every 28 minutes, a woman dies during childbirth. Life expectancy for Afghan women is only 45 years. According to OXFAM, a mere .05% of girls are enrolled in secondary education, and just 20% are in primary schools.

The Northern Alliance warlords, who today control much of Afghanistan, kidnap girls and women and rape them regularly. The shocking news of eleven-year-old Sorava, in Kunduz province, is enough to tell you about what is really happening to women in Afghanistan. She was the only daughter of an unfortunate widow; the local Northern Alliance warlords kidnapped her, raped her, and then exchanged her for a dog. There are many examples like this.

Q: Should Canada withdraw its military forces from Afghanistan?

JOYA: Foreign invasion is not a solution for the disastrous situation of Afghanistan. As our history demonstrates, we don't want occupation. Six years of Western military occupation clearly show that these armies have not come to provide us with security. The US and its allies, including Canada, are supporting the sworn enemies of our people. If they continue this wrong policy, one day they will be faced with the massive resistance of our people, as our history shows.

The Afghan people today are sandwiched between the Northern Alliance government, which is made up of pro- US terrorists and the Taliban, who are anti- US terrorists; Afghans want to be ruled by neither. My main message to the Canadian people is to please support the democratic-minded people of Afghanistan and pressure your government to end its support for the fundamentalist Karzai regime, which is a photocopy of the Taliban. Most of the money from the international community is going into the pockets of this corrupt government. We need the material support of Canadians for health and education in Afghanistan, not for the warlords, drug lords, and criminals. This is especially important for improving the position of women and children in my country, who are the main victims of the war. Canada needs to act independently and not blindly follow US policy.

We don't just want the withdrawal of Canadian and other foreign troops from our country. We also want the fundamentalists of both the Northern Alliance and the Taliban to be deprived of their power and resources. The possibility of a civil war happening once foreign troops leave Afghanistan can be minimized by the international community pressuring Pakistan, Iran, Uzbekistan, and others who support either the Taliban or the Northern Alliance, not to do so.

Q: Are there progressive forces in Afghanistan that could take over if the Taliban and the Northern Alliance were not there?

JOYA: Yes. We don't have only fundamentalists in Afghanistan; we also have a lot of democratic-minded people and parties. If I'm still alive today, it's because many, many people supported me and voted for me twice, in 2003 and 2005. Today, through OPAWC (Organization of Promoting Afghan Women's Capabilities), the non-governmental organization of which I am Director, we are promoting the social advancement of women. We've had health and education initiatives since the Taliban period in 1998 and we are still working inside Afghanistan. HAWCA [Humanitarian Assistance for the Women and Children of Afghanistan] is another democratic NGO which is very big. RAWA [Revolutionary Association of the Women of Afghanistan] is another women's political organization that's been fighting against fundamentalists in Afghanistan for more than 30 years. Their leader has been killed and the lives of their members are regularly threatened. We have democratic parties, as well, but they are very weak. They can't publish their magazines due to lack of money. I believe that, with the right kind of international solidarity, the Afghan people can defeat the warlords and drug lords ruining their country. As Bertold Brecht said, "Those who struggle may fail, but those who do not struggle have already failed."

A Visit to a Pashtun Village

ROSEMARIE WHALLEY

In April and May of 2005, I spent five weeks in a village in southern Afghanistan. I went to stay with a Pashtun family whose 2 adult children live here in Montreal. I paid my own expenses and represented no group or organization. The Pashtun tribe make up about 40% of Afghanistan's population.

The village, in a valley in Wardak province, was about an hour and a half south-west of Kabul, along the American-built Kabul-Herat highway and three to four hours from Kandahar. The household was of average size, about 15–18 people ranging from an old great aunt to a baby. It included the two family members from Montreal who speak English and translated.

The people in the village were extremely hospitable; I was invited for meals and tea to all the homes. Families came over the mountains to share the joy of the host family at having a guest. I was taken to a couple of villages to see relatives as well as to Kabul a few times. I kept up the schedule of a pop star. They were very conservative, practicing their culture of Pashtunwali- an ancient code of honour. One of the ideas of Pashtunwali is the importance of hospitality and sanctuary and I benefited from this.

I was very impressed by the way the people lived .In a climate like ours, but without any amenities, the people clung to their land, their lifestyle, their humanity. There was no running water; in fact, water was in short supply and most homes did not have a well. They lived without electricity, although a small generator had arrived in the village a few weeks before I did and was turned on for 2.5 hours in the evenings. Using the simplest equipment, shovels, a wheel barrow, a treadle sewing machine, or just their hands, they made everything: their carpets to sit on and sleep on, cushions, their blankets, clothes, they grew all their own food and prepared it, they baked fresh bread everyday. They built their own homes using the earth as building material and simple shovels and trowels. The women embroider clothes and household linen and they prepare wool which they weave and knit. Their houses, their compounds are well designed and comfortable.

The people were in an extremely distressed state because they lived in a state of terror, caught between two groups of religious fundamentalists: the Mujahedin, now called the Northern Alliance and sporting suits, led by Hamid Karzai, and the Taliban. They described themselves as hostages. The men, as well as the women cried as they recounted the 30 years of war, ... how their houses had been bombed, their land ruined by mines, how the Mujahedin, financed by the Americans had totally destroyed Kabul in 1992, they had dynamited each building. How the poverty and the loss had taken a toll on their lives ... how, young men are beginning to die of cancer – perhaps as a result of exposure to depleted uranium. Then came the euphoric few weeks when the American planes first flew overhead and they thought the Americans had come to liberate them because they cared about Afghans. The villagers thought the Americans would give them jobs and help alleviate their poverty, that with their advanced technology, the Americans would help clean up the war-ravaged countryside – get rid of the weapons left by the Russians and still used to settle grievances ... give the international aid that had been promised. They were sure that, in no time, clinics, schools, and roads would spring up and people would have a bit of material security, that they would enter a post conflict situation.

Instead, an ominous new problem, a catastrophe confronts the people of southern Afghanistan. The Americans (read Canadians, Dutch, British) have come as occupiers, not as liberators and the

Pashtuns will not be occupied. Stories begin to circulate ... of civilian casualties and humiliations – apparently, in some village, the Americans forcing village elders to undress ... the following day, they committed suicide. Dignity is everything. It's definitely not life at any cost.

In some areas, including the village in Wardak, the situation is worse than before. The boys' school has been damaged and the small informal primary school that the little girls attended has been closed, the UN textbooks destroyed. In the village of Oozra, where one of the married sisters lives, the girls' school closed after two bodies were found at the entrance.

The society is totally hierarchical and everyone has a clearly defined role to play. Yes, the women work really hard, but life is not easy for the men either. The young men have to bring home the food. Now, there are no jobs. The only work available for those guarding the homes and villages is fighting. The young boys, beloved sons, are forced to fight to feed their families. Both the Taliban and the Central government pay salaries, so, if you can, you fight for both sides and get double the money. Neither side is strong enough to topple the other and a protracted civil war, financed they believe by Washington will keep the country weak. Meanwhile, in Canada we hear gleeful reports of murdered Taliban; instead we should stop to reflect on who they are and think of the families mad with grief. We know how sad we are when our soldiers die. It's the same for these families, except that there's no government recognition of their grief. When they lose a breadwinner, there's no government compensation.

Even the locals are not sure who constitutes the Taliban. Some of them are local – indigenous Afghans who refuse the authority of the Western backed, highly corrupt government of Hamid Karzai. Others are fighting to protect their village, or as part of the honour system, still others are bandits, criminals, or victims of an insult or wrong of some kind who are seeking redress. Then there are those from the outside, from Pakistan (the villagers described them as intruders), and there are others from more organized fighting groups such as al Qaeda. There seem to be militia groups that fight each other.

Let's look at the 'good' guys ... the very corrupt government of Hamid Kazai supported by the NATO-led ISAF forces, the Americans and Canadians, all the contractors, the NGOs. So why is Canada there? How can our soldiers, young people from a materialistic culture, terrified of death, trained in traditional warfare, and into hockey and Tim Horton's ignorant about mountains and the Pashtunwali code even begin to understand the ancient culture of the Pashtuns and other ethnic groups in Afghanistan? We have no respect for the people, for their culture, their art, their lives. Given our Canadian culture of lots of geography and hardly any history, how can we relate to people who have lived in their area for 5,000 years. Imagine, if they came and bombed our homes, smashed our Mona Lisa's, killed our families and said that they were here to liberate us ? What are Canadian troops fighting and dying for in Afghanistan? Perhaps to help the Americans secure a route for their pipeline.

Like all the armed groups in Afghanistan, Canadians are contributing to a systematic campaign of terror perpetuated against unarmed people who are in no way a threat to Canada. Canadians are patronizing towards the dirty, illiterate and utterly poor citizens of southern Afghanistan. They don't see them as equals. The Western obsession with the veiled female figure only adds to feelings of Western superiority. Clearly, Canadians can feel superior, as they ride around in their armoured cars and tanks, really thinking that they are 'bringing democracy' to Afghanistan. But are they? Are these people really primitive and brutal and does the West really have the answer ?

During my conversations, it came up that we have homeless people in Montreal. My Afghan friends were appalled. Where were their families? Why didn't the homeless people knock on the doors of those with homes? Well, we don't open our doors to strangers. They were horrified. A penniless person could show up at your door and you would leave him standing on the step? We talked about the low status of elders in Canada ... how a lot of them live alone and/or in modest circumstances, how they are not respected. In the Pashtun village, old people are the most highly regarded members of the community: the men are community leaders and the women decide in the domestic sphere. They are treated with great tenderness and reverence.

The fighting is causing greater hardship than ever. More people are hungry, inflation is sky-rocketing and food prices have doubled in the last two years. Thousands and thousands of vulnerable people are living in bombed out buildings in Kabul in the terrible cold.

The poverty and human suffering is truly overwhelming and, in my opinion, whilst I recognize the work of certain NGO projects, the situation in southern and eastern Afghanistan is not improving. Enough Canadians have died to say nothing of the Afghans. The Canadian Armed forces should leave Afghanistan and Canadians should get beyond the brainwashing of the commercial media and learn all they can about the Pashtun culture which, for all its flaws, has much to teach us.

Afghanistan and Canada
Geo-politics and Energy

What Our Leaders Won't Tell Us: Afghanistan Vital to US as a Natural Gas Pipeline Route

JOHN FOSTER

As Canadians discuss a future role in Afghanistan, one fact is notably missing. In its regional setting, Afghanistan is an energy bridge. Its geography offers a link between the natural gas resources of Turkmenistan (immediately to the north) and the energy-starved economies of Pakistan and India.

Neighbouring countries and donors recognize this link. They plan the TAPI pipeline, named after the initials of the four countries involved: Turkmenistan, Afghanistan, Pakistan and India. The Asian Development Bank (cousin of the World Bank) is sponsoring the project. Canada is an active member of this bank.

Geopolitically, the route through Afghanistan is important in the rivalry for the energy resources of Central Asia. Turkmenistan has the world's second or third largest reserves of gas (an upgrade from fourth place after a 2008 audit of gas fields in the southeast). This gas flows out north through Russia; a pipeline is planned east to China; and a route is sought under the Caspian Sea west to Europe. Afghanistan offers a route to the south, a route the United States has long promoted.

At a donor meeting in New Delhi in November 2006, countries promised to accelerate planning of the pipeline and help Afghanistan become an "energy bridge." Canada had a high-level delegation at the meeting. Yet a report on Afghanistan issued shortly after the meeting by the Canadian Senate Committee on National Security and Defence failed to mention energy at all; and neither did the government-appointed panel on Afghanistan headed by John Manley.

The proposed pipeline could become Afghanistan's largest development project. It would pass through Helmand and Kandahar – provinces where security is a problem and where British and Canadian forces are supporting Americans under the NATO umbrella. Leaders in Pakistan and India speak publicly about their concerns for pipeline security. Hedging their bets, they are also promoting a pipeline to import gas from Iran, despite US opposition to that option.

In Canada, Afghanistan's potential as an energy bridge is omitted or belittled. We're told there's no pipeline. That's literally true. But the planning to *create* a pipeline corridor continues. We're told the NATO mission is not like Iraq; "It's not about oil." That's also literally true. In Afghanistan, the plan involves natural gas. Realistic or not, construction is planned to start in 2010. Afghanistan says the route will be cleared of landmines and Taliban by then. Canadian Forces, of course, are committed until 2011.

The United States has been supporting pipeline planning for more than a decade. When the Taliban ran Afghanistan, two consortia vied for the right to take on the project, one led by Unocal (an American firm) and the other by Bridas (an Argentinean firm). The US government supported Unocal. It was negotiating with the Taliban regime from 1997 to 2001.

US negotiations with the Taliban broke down in August 2001. Two months later, the US invaded Afghanistan and ousted the Taliban. Now the invasion has evolved into a NATO mission and an ongoing occupation, with Canada participating.

In their recent book *The Unexpected War*, Janice Stein and Eugene Lang say Canada put troops into Afghanistan to placate Washington. But what is the US motivation, seven years *after* 9/11?

Afghanistan is clearly a key part of US geopolitical strategies in Asia. In an interview with CBC Radio's *As It Happens* in January 2008, US Ambassador Thomas Pickering, co-chair of the blue-ribbon Afghanistan Study Group in Washington DC, said that "Afghanistan is of strategic importance ... it borders on producers of critical energy."

Central Asian reserves of both gas and oil are enormous. Pipelines are the only way to get them to market. Asian newspapers openly discuss the rivalry for control of these resources – the New Great Game among countries that want oil and gas to flow in directions under their control.

Energy Security was also prominent at the 2006 NATO summit in Riga. One US proposal at that meeting called for NATO to be involved in guarding pipelines and sea-lanes. Would that apply to the planned Afghan pipeline? If so, NATO troops could be in Afghanistan a very long time.

The Manley Panel noted that Canadian governments have failed "to communicate ... the reasons for Canadian involvement" in Afghanistan. Recent debates have focussed on how many troops and how long they should stay there. Completely ignored are key regional geopolitics and energy issues.

Since Afghanistan is widely perceived to be an energy bridge, why don't our leaders say so? Our troops, our citizens and our democracy deserve an explanation.

A detailed version (giving sources) is available at:
http://www.policyalternatives.ca/documents/National_Office_Pubs/2008/
A_Pipeline_Through_a_Troubled_Land.pdf

A Pipeline through a Troubled Land: Afghanistan, Canada, and the New Great Energy Game

JOHN FOSTER

Afghanistan's role as an energy bridge – a geographic link between Central and South Asia – has long been recognized, but rarely talked about in Canada. Speeches by the top ministers of the Canadian government omit Afghanistan's strategic importance in the geopolitical rivalry for control of the energy resources of Central Asia. At stake are pipeline routes to get energy resources to market, and power and wealth in the region.

In *Rising Powers Shrinking Planet: the New Geopolitics of Energy*, author Michael Klare writes that global competition over energy will be "a pivotal, if not central, feature of world affairs for the remainder of the century."[1] The US has its own geopolitical strategies in Asia, and Afghanistan is a key part of those strategies. US motivations in the region are complex, but the issue of establishing Afghanistan as an energy bridge underlies its ambitions.

Richard Boucher, US Assistant Secretary of State for South and Central Asian Affairs, said in September 2007: "One of our goals is to stabilize Afghanistan, so it can become a conduit and a hub between South and Central Asia so that energy can flow to the south ...

and so that the countries of Central Asia are no longer bottled up between two enormous powers of China and Russia, but rather they
have outlets to the south as well as to the north and the east and the
west."[2]

Light was also shed by US Ambassador Thomas Pickering, co-
chair of the blue-ribbon Afghanistan Study Group in Washington,
DC.[3] Interviewed on CBC's *As It Happens* (January 30, 2008), he
said: "Afghanistan is of strategic importance, a failed state in the
middle of a delicate and sensitive region that borders on a number of
producers of critical energy."

As part of both the NATO-led International Security Assistance
Forces (ISAF), and the US-led Operation Enduring Freedom, Canada
has been supporting US interests in Afghanistan.

In *The Unexpected War: Canada in Kandahar*, authors Janice
Gross Stein and Eugene Lang write that Canadian choices were repeatedly shaped by anticipated US reaction. When Canada joined
the US-led invasion of Afghanistan in 2001, Canadian leaders knew
little of Afghan tribal divisions or history of expelling foreign armies.
According to Stein and Lang, Canada went to Afghanistan to placate
the Americans.[4]

Deepak Obhrai, Parliamentary Secretary to the Minister of Foreign Affairs, affirmed in 2007: "Our relationship with the USA is central to our foreign policy ... The United States is our strongest and
most important ally, for domestic as well as international issues. It is
imperative that Canada support an engagement with the US on multiple fronts."[5]

Energy issues have not been part of official Canadian statements
on Afghanistan. Yet, in its regional setting, Afghanistan has a key
role in the quest for access to the immense energy resources of Central Asia.[6]

AFGHANISTAN AS AN ENERGY BRIDGE

Afghanistan's position between Central Asia and South Asia (Pakistan and India) enables it to serve as a link between the two. To the
north, Afghanistan borders three of the five countries that became in
dependent when the Soviet Union broke up. Turkmenistan, its immediate neighbour to the northwest, has immense reserves of natural
gas. Turkmenistan's petroleum minister told a meeting of pipeline

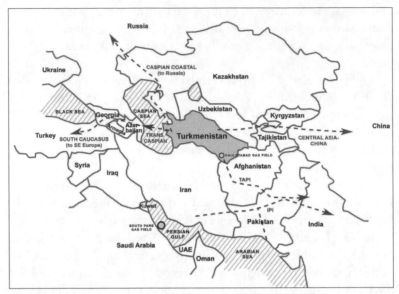

Proposed Central Asian Gas Pipelines

partners that "Turkmenistan has gas reserves of 8 trillion cubic metres."[7] Until recently, this gas flowed out only northward through Russia. But Turkmenistan wants to send its gas south to supply the growing markets in Pakistan and India.

In its regional setting, Afghanistan is an energy bridge, linking the gas resources of Turkmenistan and the energy starved economies of Pakistan and India. For more than a decade, the United States has been working towards a pipeline to move natural gas from Turkmenistan through Afghanistan to Pakistan and India.

When the Taliban was governing Afghanistan, two consortia vied for the right to take on the project, one led by Unocal (an American firm) and the other by Bridas (an Argentinean firm). The US government supported the Unocal consortium; it was negotiating with the Taliban regime from 1997 to August 2001, during both the Bill Clinton and George W. Bush administrations. The Bush administration saw the Taliban regime as a source of stability for the proposed pipeline, but demanded that the Taliban form a government of national unity that would include the northern tribes. Bridas took a different approach – they were negotiating separately with different tribes.[8]

US negotiations with the Taliban broke down in August 2001, just before the terrorist attacks of September 11, 2001. Shortly after, the US ousted the Taliban, with the assistance of the northern tribes. In December 2001, Hamid Karzai was appointed interim president of the Afghan Transitional Administration. Also that month, Zalmay Khalilzad was appointed US Special Presidential Envoy for Afghanistan. There are reports that Karzai had earlier consulted for Unocal.[9] Karzai and Unocal have denied such a relationship.

Khalilzad, while at the RAND Corporation in the 1990s, reportedly acted as liaison between Unocal and the Taliban regime. He has held key positions in the Bush Administration, most recently serving as US Ambassador to Afghanistan (2003–05), Iraq (2005–07) and the United Nations (2007–present).

Karzai was elected President in 2004, but Afghanistan continued to lack a government of national unity. The Pashtun – roughly 40 per cent of the population – are woefully under-represented in the Karzai government, which is viewed by many Afghans as corrupt and ineffective.[10] The insurgency, rooted in the Pashtun south with bases of support in neighbouring Pakistan, continues to thwart efforts by the Karzai government to extend its legitimacy across the entire country.

Throughout the period after Karzai assumed office, pipeline planning continued. In February 2002, Interim President Karzai and President Musharraf of Pakistan announced their agreement to "cooperate in all spheres of activity," including the proposed pipeline. In May 2002, Karzai signed a memorandum of understanding with the Presidents of Pakistan and Turkmenistan on the pipeline project.[11]

TURKMENISTAN-AFGHANISTAN-PAKISTAN-INDIA PIPELINE

The original plan for the gas pipeline linking Turkmenistan with southern neighbours extended only to Pakistan, through Afghanistan. But in April 2008, India officially joined and it became commonly known as the TAPI pipeline, TAPI being the initials of the four participating countries – Turkmenistan, Afghanistan, Pakistan and India. The United States strongly supports the project.

The Asian Development Bank (ADB) is coordinating the project. The ADB is a multilateral development bank headquartered in the Philippines, and is owned by 67 members, 48 from the region and 19 from other parts of the world. Canada is an active member of this re-

gional development bank. The four participating countries have regular steering meetings with the ADB as facilitator.[12]

In 2003 the ADB financed a technical feasibility study of the
pipeline.[13] The study envisioned the construction of a natural gas
transmission pipeline of about 1,700 kilometres to transport about
33 billion cubic metres (BCM) of gas annually through a 56-inch surface and underground pipeline. Reflecting each country's need for
imported gas, Afghanistan's share from the pipeline is estimated at
less than 5 BCM annually, compared with 14 BCM each for Pakistan
and India. Once the co-operating countries and other partners agree
on the project design, operating parameters and contractual agreements, the pipeline could take up to five years to construct.

The proposed TAPI pipeline follows an ancient trading route
from Central to South Asia. It will run from the Dauletabad gas field
in Turkmenistan along the main highway through Herat, Helmand
and Kandahar in Afghanistan; through Quetta and Multan in Pakistan; to Fazilka in India, near the border between Pakistan and
India. Helmand and Kandahar are the provinces where safety and security are problems and where British and Canadian forces, under
the NATO umbrella, are involved in combat alongside US forces.

Proposed Turkmenistan-Afghanistan-Pakistan-India (TAPI) Gas Pipeline

TAPI PIPELINE AND 2006 DONOR MEETING

The TAPI pipeline was high on the agenda of a major donor meeting held November 18–19, 2006, in New Delhi – the Second Regional Economic Cooperation Conference on Afghanistan. Representatives from 21 countries attended, including the United States; Russia; major NATO countries such as Canada, France, Germany, United Kingdom and Italy; and regional powers such as India, Pakistan and Iran, as well as Afghanistan. International institutions participating included the ADB, the International Monetary Fund, the United Nations, the European Commission and the World Bank.

Canada's delegation was led by the Parliamentary Secretary to the Minister of Foreign Affairs Deepak Obhrai, Conservative Member of Parliament for Calgary East. In a statement announcing Canada's participation, then foreign affairs minister Peter MacKay remarked: "Enhanced regional economic cooperation is important not only to Afghanistan's progress toward becoming a self-sustaining, prosperous state, but also in promoting regional stability."[14]

According to the official list of delegates, Parliamentary Secretary Obhrai was joined by David Malone, High Commissioner of Canada to India; Douglas Scott Proudfoot, Director of the Afghanistan Task Force in Foreign Affairs; and Linda Libront, First Secretary for Aid and Development.[15] The conference's final statement pledged: "Countries and organizations will assist Afghanistan to become an energy bridge in the region and to develop regional trade through supporting initiatives in bilateral/multilateral cross-border energy projects ... Work will be accelerated on [the] Turkmenistan-Afghanistan-Pakistan-India gas pipeline to develop a technically and commercially viable project."[16]

The conference statement exhorted: "Countries will encourage and facilitate transportation of energy resources within the region." It observed: "The proposed Turkmenistan-Afghanistan-Pakistan-India gas pipeline has the potential for new opportunities for regional energy cooperation, resulting in enhanced development, improvement in physical security and overall economic benefits."

The conference statement referred to the rising tide of violence in the region, noting: "Peace and economic stability in the region are dependent in large measure on the progress in stabilizing the security situation in southern and eastern Afghanistan." However, "cur-

rent conditions, despite the above mentioned security and other constraints, still represent a good opportunity to improve the welfare of
the peoples through ... joint promotion of infrastructure activities,
especially in all forms of transport and energy development."

RECENT DEVELOPMENTS ON THE TAPI PROJECT

In Canada hardly anyone talks about the pipeline, despite the fact
that it would run through the heart of the insurgency where Canadian troops are deployed. With notable exceptions, politicians and
press have remained silent.[17]

Even a major report on Afghanistan, presented in February 2007
by the Standing Senate Committee on National Security and Defence, failed to mention the pipeline, energy, oil or gas.[18] The silence
may reflect lack of knowledge on this issue. The Canadian government and media have focused mostly on short-term military operations and development.

Yet, if the pipeline goes ahead successfully, it could be Afghanistan's largest development project. According to the Ambassador
of Afghanistan to Canada, transit revenue could amount to US$300
million per year.[19] That's about one-third of the Afghan government's domestic revenue. This revenue is important to sustain
development efforts. Transit fees could help pay for teachers and
infrastructure. Afghanistan's domestic revenue, of course, is currently dwarfed by the aid from foreign donors (US$6.5 billion in
2008/09).[20]

There are regional benefits too. While helping to meet the energy
needs of Pakistan and India, and possibly other countries, the
pipeline would link Afghanistan with Pakistan and India in a way
that requires co-operation. So it's potentially good for peace. As the
Turkmen President said recently: "The pipeline between Turkmenistan, Afghanistan, Pakistan and India will be a weighty contribution
to the positive cooperation on this continent."[21]

Leaders in Pakistan and India speak publicly about their concerns
regarding pipeline safety and security. The former prime minister of
Pakistan admitted in February 2007 that the Afghan pipeline "would
have to pass through strifetorn Kandahar."[22] According to the Pakistani press (June 7, 2008), Afghanistan has informed stakeholders

that all landmines will be cleared from the pipeline route within two years, and the route will be freed from Taliban influence.[23]

Despite security concerns, the four participating countries signed formal agreements at a TAPI steering committee meeting on April 24, 2008, in Islamabad, Pakistan. The meeting, facilitated by the ADB, was attended by energy ministers from the four countries: Khawaja Asif (Pakistan), Baymurad Hojamuhamedov (Turkmenistan), M. Ibrahim Adel (Afghanistan) and Murli Deora (India). With India's signature on the Gas Pipeline Framework Agreement, the project officially became a four-nation initiative.[24]

At that meeting, the ADB presented an update of the feasibility study done three years ago. It noted that the estimated capital cost has doubled to $7.6 billion (2008 prices) but expressed willingness to submit the project to its Board for financing.[25] The cost increase was attributed to "(i) sharp increase in the price of steel; (ii) increase in construction cost, and (iii) increase in the cost of compressor stations." Turkmenistan promised independent certification of the gas available for the pipeline.[26]

According to reports, the Petroleum Minister of Afghanistan, Muhammad Abrahim, informed the meeting that more than 1,000 industrial units were planned near the pipeline route in Afghanistan and would need gas for their operation. He said 300 industrial units near the pipeline route had already been established, and the project's early implementation was essential to meet their requirements.[27]

Plans call for the line to be built and operated by a consortium of national oil companies from the four participating countries. A special-purpose financial vehicle is to be floated, and it is likely that international companies will join in laying and operating the pipeline.[28] Pakistan's new prime minister described the pipeline as a vital project for the development and progress of the region.[29]

A technical meeting of TAPI participants and ADB was held on May 30, 2008, in Ashgabat, Turkmenistan, to follow up on gas pricing and other issues.[30] It coincided with a three-day visit there by Richard Boucher, US Assistant Secretary of State. He called on the Turkmen President for talks on a wide range of issues, including energy co-operation.[31] He urged diversification of gas export routes from Turkmenistan.[32]

TAPI AND AFGHANISTAN'S NATIONAL DEVELOPMENT
STRATEGY

Afghanistan's new National Development Strategy (2009–2013) – presented at a donors' conference on June 12, 2008, in Paris – refers briefly to ongoing planning for the TAPI gas pipeline and to Afghanistan's central role as a land bridge connecting land-locked, energy-rich Central Asia to energy-deficient South Asia.[33]

• "Afghanistan is also participating in ongoing planning for a Turkmenistan-Afghanistan-Pakistan-India (TAPI) natural gas pipeline. A number of regional energy trade and import arrangements have commenced and will contribute to long-term energy security." (p. 81)
• "Enhanced regional cooperation provides Afghanistan an opportunity to connect land locked energy rich Central Asia with warm water ports and energy deficient South Asia. As a result of this expanded trade Afghanistan would be able to meet part of its energy demand. As a transit country, Afghanistan will realize increased revenue and enhanced economic activity, enabling it to better meet its main development challenges." (p. 143)

Interestingly, its table of Policy Actions and Activities (Appendix I) omits TAPI by name. It does mention the "promotion of regional cooperation to facilitate various projects under the energy sector," for which the expected outcome is "an enabling environment for private sector investment in energy sector." It goes on to specify various actions and activities that would facilitate the *utilization* of natural gas; viz., preparation of gas law and manual, establishment of new organizational structure for gas and oil management, design of gas pipeline grid to provinces, establishment of natural gas pricing regime. And finally, it includes planning for exploration activities, and for mapping and survey of minerals, oil and gas.

Meanwhile, Iran has separately offered an alternative to the route through Afghanistan – a pipeline to supply Iranian gas to Pakistan and India.

THE RIVAL PIPELINE: IRAN-PAKISTAN-INDIA PIPELINE

Iran is negotiating with Pakistan and India for a pipeline (called IPI after the names of the three countries) to supply Iranian gas along a relatively secure route. With an estimated capital cost of $7.5 billion, IPI is similar in cost to the TAPI project, and is seen as a potential rival to TAPI. The IPI pipeline would move Iranian natural gas to neighbouring Pakistan and on to India. The route would avoid strife-torn Afghanistan altogether.

The IPI pipeline would be 2,670 kilometres long, with about 1,115 kilometres in Iran, 705 kilometres in Pakistan, and 850 kilometres in India, and would take four years to build. It would be constructed by the three nations separately, rather than by a single, co-operative venture along the lines that the TAPI partners propose.[34] The purpose of this separate approach is reportedly to avoid raising the United States' ire and potential sanctions for co-operating with Iran.[35]

Russia's Gazprom has expressed willingness to help build the IPI line.[36] Pakistan is considering inviting bids by oil and gas companies to build the section in its territory, and BP has publicly expressed interest.[37]

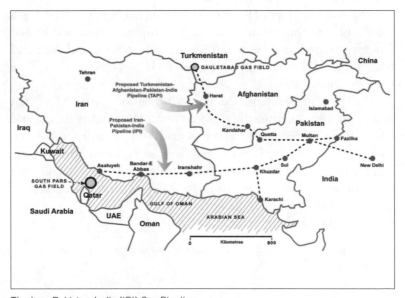

The Iran-Pakistan-India (IPI) Gas Pipeline

In 2007, a senior State Department official, Steven Mann, stated that the United States is unequivocally against the deal. "The US government supports multiple pipelines from the Caspian region but remains absolutely opposed to pipelines involving Iran." Washington fears the IPI pipeline deal would be a blow to its efforts to isolate Iran. The Bush administration has been trying to pressure both Pakistan and India to back off from the pipeline.[38]

This has resulted in the TAPI pipeline being viewed as a US-backed initiative to aid in its isolation of Iran. Local leaders are sensitive to this accusation, given widespread popular aversion to the Bush administration. In response to a reporter's question this April, Pakistan's petroleum minister categorically denied that talks on TAPI were held in Islamabad under US pressure to block the Iran-Pakistan-India deal.[39]

Until recently, India's participation in IPI was uncertain. In a significant breakthrough, oil ministers of India and Pakistan met on April 25, 2008, in Islamabad (just after the TAPI meeting) to resolve a pricing squabble and clear the way for signing agreements.[40] The President of Iran visited Islamabad and New Delhi the following week for talks on the pipeline. This breakthrough happened despite strong US pressure on India and Pakistan to abandon the project and go for the line through Afghanistan.[41]

Assistant Secretary of State Richard Boucher admits the US has a "fundamental strategic interest" in Afghanistan "as a conduit and hub for energy, ideas, people, trade, goods from Central Asia and other places down to the Arabian Sea." He predicts the US will be there for a long time.[42]

The US strategic interest extends to its relationship with Pakistan and India. Both countries are regional powers, wooed by Russia and China. India has become a major power in Asia (not just South Asia). As Evan Feigenbaum, Deputy Assistant Secretary of State, points out, the US looks at "the role of India, China and Japan ... and their relations with each other in this larger Asian space."[43] Geopolitically, the ties Pakistan and India have with other countries – and their pipeline links – are important to the US.

THE CANADIAN CONNECTION IN TURKMENISTAN
AND THE REGION

Canada's energy sector is active in the region. In 2005, there were 35 Canadian energy companies in Kazakhstan and 4 in Turkmenistan.[44]

On February 12, 2008, former prime minister Jean Chrétien travelled to Turkmenistan to meet with President Berdimuhamedov, along with executives of Buried Hill Energy, an Omani-Canadian company with offices in Calgary. According to the Turkmen state news service, Mr. Chrétien said "the international community showed intense interest in Turkmenistan and its leader, whose policy of the progressive reforms had won the country the recognition and high prestige worldwide."[45]

At that meeting, Roger Haines, Chairman and Chief Executive Officer of Buried Hill Energy, gave an update on his company's activities in Turkmenistan, including seismic work in the offshore Serdar gas field. Buried Hill Energy signed a production-sharing agreement with Turkmenistan in late 2007 to explore and develop this field in the Turkmen sector of the Caspian Sea.[46]

Thermo Design, a Canadian engineering and manufacturing company, also has contracts in Turkmenistan. It built and maintains an LPG (liquefied petroleum gas) recovery plant for the state firm Turkmengas in eastern Turkmenistan.[47] Canadian firms could be awarded construction contracts if the TAPI pipeline moves forward. Afghanistan is already Canada's largest recipient of foreign aid and Canadian troops have taken a disproportionately high level of casualties, so Canadian firms would be well positioned politically to win contracts from the Afghan government.

But the deteriorating security situation makes it unlikely that any Canadian firm would want to have employees working in the region. Unless the risk of attacks is greatly diminished and the security position improves enough to allow construction and operation to proceed, it's unlikely that Canadian firms will benefit from the TAPI pipeline.

NATO PROPOSALS

Energy has become an issue of strategic discussions at NATO, and the issue was reviewed at the 2008 NATO Summit in Bucharest. The Summit Declaration affirmed that NATO will support the protection of critical energy infrastructure, and stipulated that a progress report on energy security be prepared for the 2009 Summit.[48]

Two years earlier, the 2006 Summit Declaration avowed support for a coordinated effort to promote energy infrastructure security.[49] At that Summit, held in Riga, Latvia, the US made several proposals to commit NATO to energy security activities,[50] but the Summit reached no decision. The Europeans were wary of tasks they might come to regret. However, these proposals could come up again, and they merit close scrutiny.

One proposal at the 2006 Summit called for NATO to guard pipelines and sea lanes. Would that apply to the Afghan pipeline? If so, NATO troops could be in Afghanistan for a very long time. Pipelines last until they're decommissioned – that may be 50 years or more. Would guarding sea lanes apply to the Persian Gulf? Would the Canadian Navy be part of a sea lane protection service?

A second US proposal called for energy security to be a NATO Article V commitment (an attack on one is an attack on all). That would make threats to energy security tantamount to an attack on a member country, and that, in turn, would require a response from all members.[51] Does Canada wish to have this responsibility outside the North Atlantic area?

At the 2007 EU-Canada Summit, Prime Minister Harper referred to energy security as requiring "unprecedented international cooperation ... protecting and maintaining the world's energy supply system."[52] Foreign Affairs and International Trade Canada (DFAIT) recognizes "the re-emergence of energy as a major foreign policy consideration," and has resurrected its Energy Secretariat "to analyse key energy security and related issues."[53] That's despite severe budget cuts and twenty or so years with no energy secretariat. NATO proposals could have enormous consequences for Canada, especially if NATO's role is extended to include energy security worldwide.

RIVALRY IN CENTRAL ASIA: THE NEW GREAT GAME

"Energy Security" is the current buzzword in Western capitals. No country talks about playing the New Great Game – what leaders talk about is achieving energy security. These two words have crept into the mission statements of governments and international agencies, including Canada, the United States and NATO.

The New Great Game in Central Asia is a geopolitical game among the world's Great Powers for control of energy resources. The geopolitical game is openly analyzed in US think tanks, such as Brookings Institution,[54] Johns Hopkins University's School of Advanced International Studies,[55] and Heritage Foundation.[56] It is well reported in the Asian press. It is hardly visible in Canada.

The term Great Game dates back to the 19th century, when it was popularized by Rudyard Kipling in his novels of British India.[57] At that time, the rivalry was between the British and Russian empires. The epicentre of conflict was Afghanistan, where the British fought and lost three wars. Throughout history, tribal loyalty in Afghanistan has remained paramount, making life difficult for invaders.

North of Afghanistan are the five countries of Central Asia: Kazakhstan, Kyrgyzstan, Tajikistan, Turkmenistan and Uzbekistan. Until 1991, they were part of the Soviet Union. They became independent when the Soviet Union broke up. These five "Stans" of Central Asia are sandwiched between the Caspian Sea to the west, Russia to the north, China to the east, and Iran and Afghanistan to the south.

When the countries of Central Asia were within the Soviet Union, their oil and gas flowed only to the north through Soviet-controlled pipelines. After 1991, competing world powers began to explore ways to tap these enormous reserves and move them in other directions.

Kazakhstan is by far the largest Central Asian country – about the same size as western Canada. It has the largest oil reserves in Central Asia. They are said to be three times those of the North Sea. One discovery alone – Kashagan in the Caspian Sea – may be the world's most important oil find in 40 years, since Alaska. According to the International Energy Agency, Turkmenistan has the world's fourth largest reserves of natural gas. A recent audit of fields in the southeast suggests Turkmenistan's gas reserves may advance to third or even second place in the world.[58]

Turkmenistan and Kazakhstan border the Caspian Sea, as do three other countries – Iran, Azerbaijan and Russia. The Caspian Sea is the world's largest inland body of water; it is about 20 times the size of Lake Ontario. All littoral countries are looking for their share of the oil and gas riches under the Caspian Sea. That makes it a prime target for rivalry among competing world powers.

Countries playing the New Great Game want energy to flow in directions under their control: north to Russia, west to Europe (bypassing Russia), east to China, south through Afghanistan. The players are USA, China and Russia; regional powers such as Pakistan, India, Turkey and Iran; and NATO countries, and by extension Canada through its NATO membership.

The Central Asian countries are far from the world's oceans and tankers, so they must rely on pipelines to get their oil and gas to market. Pipelines are fixed and inflexible. Without a pipeline, the oil and gas remain locked in the ground. The pipeline route is critical; the oil or gas can only go where the pipeline goes.

Pipeline routes are important in the same way that railway lines were important in the 19th century. They connect trading partners and influence the regional balance of power. When a pipeline crosses more than one country, each country becomes a stakeholder. The countries are bonded physically, economically and diplomatically.

Russia is expanding its imports of Turkmenistan's gas treasure. Turkmenistan currently exports virtually all its gas via Kazakhstan to Russia. However, the pipeline infrastructure is aging, and the route was originally designed to supply other Soviet republics rather than European countries. In December 2007, ministers from the three countries signed an agreement to construct a new gas pipeline that will parallel the older one and augment the export system's capacity. President Putin of Russia and President Nazarbayev of Kazakhstan oversaw the signing and conferred by phone with President Berdimuhamedov of Turkmenistan.

The pipeline is expected to come on line in 2010 and have an initial capacity of 20 BCM annually. The gas is destined for countries of the European Union.[59] When this project was first announced in May 2007, during a visit by President Putin to Turkmenistan, US Energy Secretary Samuel Bodman voiced concern about European dependence on Russian energy. He said the proposed pipeline was "not good for Europe."[60]

On May 27, 2008, President Berdimuhamedov visited the Dauletabad gas field to inaugurate a new gas compressor station that will increase the capacity of the pipeline connecting Turkmenistan with Kazakhstan and Russia.[61] The ceremony took place one day before Richard Boucher's visit to Ashgabat mentioned above.

China is tapping into Turkmenistan's gas treasure too. It has started building a 2,000-kilometre gas pipeline from Turkmenistan east through Kazakhstan to China's western province Xinjiang. There it will join a proposed west-east pipeline, stretching to Shanghai in the east and Guangzhou in the south. The total length of both lines will exceed 7,000 kilometres.[62]

Pipeline	Route (Source & recipient)	Length, Volume	Cost US$ bn	Comp-letion Date	Partners	Financing	Support	Oppose	Certainty of Supply
TAPI	Turkmenistan, Afghanistan, Pakistan, India	33 BCM 1,700 km	$7.6	2015	Special venture company held by national companies. May bring in private partners	ADB	USA	Russia	Security problems
IPI	Iran, Pakistan, India	33 BCM 2,670 km	$7.5	2015	Iran, Pakistan, India (may subcontract in private companies)	Partners separately	Russia	USA	Political problems - US opposition
Caspian Coastal	Turkmenistan & Kazakhstan to Russia	20 BCM initially		2010	Turkmenistan Kazakhstan Russia	Partners separately	Russia	USA	Good
Central Asia-China	Turkmenistan & Kazakhstan to China	30 BCM 2,000 km	$7.3	2011	Turkmenistan Kazakhstan China	Partners Separately	China, Russia		Good
South Caucasus	Azerbaijan-Georgia - Turkey	8.8 BCM expandable to 20 BCM 692 km	$1.2	2006	Consortium of companies led by BP & Statoil	EBRD	USA	Russia	Phase 1: OK Phase 2: gas additional to Azerbaijan (Iran, Turkmenistan)
Trans-Caspian	Turkmenistan-Azerbaijan	30 BCM	$5.0	n.a.	n.a.	n.a.	USA	Russia, Iran	Hurdle: Russian opposition
South Stream	Russia to Italy & Austria via Black Sea	31 BCM 900 km		2013	Led by Gazprom and ENI		Russia	USA	Good
Nabucco	Turkey-Austria	3,300 km Rising to 31 BCM	$12.0	2013	Project company owned equally by companies of Austria, Hungary, Romania, Bulgaria, Turkey, Germany		EU, USA		Hurdle: gas additional to (Iran, Turkmenistan)

Pipeline projects for natural gas from central Asia

The Great Power rivalry continues with plans for new gas lines to Central Europe. The Russians plan to bring gas under the Black Sea to Bulgaria, thence forking to Italy and Austria, in what is called the South Stream project. It would bypass Turkey and Ukraine.

The EU is backing a rival plan, called the Nabucco project, to bring gas from Turkey to Central Europe. It would connect to the line from Azerbaijan, but Azerbaijan can't supply enough gas. So Turkey wants to get additional gas from Iran and Turkmenistan.

For its part, Washington wants pipelines built under the Caspian Sea to bring Central Asian oil and gas to Azerbaijan. They would link with the recently built pipelines to Turkey. The Russians oppose that, but the Americans are persistent. In the first nine months of 2007, the US government sent fifteen delegations to Turkmenistan.[63]

In January 2008, over a three-week period, three high-level US officials called on the Turkmen President to discuss economic and energy sector co-operation. In turn, they were Senator Richard Lugar, senior Republican on the Senate Foreign Relations Committee; Admiral William J. Fallon, at that time in charge of US Central Command; and Ambassador Steven Mann, Coordinator for Eurasian Energy Diplomacy.

Ambassador Mann returned in late February and early June for further discussions on energy issues and bilateral relations.[64] President Berdimuhamedov of Turkmenistan has reiterated his commitment to multiple routes for export of gas: to China, to Russia, to Pakistan and India via Afghanistan, as well as a possible route to Europe via the Caspian Sea.[65]

Significantly, in April 2008 during the NATO Summit in Bucharest, Romania, he met with President Bush to discuss gas export policy,[66] and with President Karzai to review the TAPI project.[67] Mr. Bush wrote to President Berdimuhamedov: "I enjoyed seeing you in Romania during NATO Summit. I enjoyed our discussions, and I look forward to continuing to work with you on important issues facing the United States and Turkmenistan."[68]

ENERGY SECURITY – CANADA AND RUSSIA

In the context of Turkmenistan, Assistant Secretary of State Richard Boucher defines energy security as not being dependent "on any one route, on any one customer, or on any one investor." He maintains that European energy security is important to the United States as well as to Europeans and that it "is based on having multiple sources."[69]

Author Michael Klare asserts the rivalry in Central Asia is "part of a global struggle over energy."[70] Canada's role in this struggle is unclear.

At the 2006 G-8 Summit, Prime Minister Harper and President Putin issued a joint statement welcoming "cooperation between Canadian and Russian energy industry players." They agreed to promote international trade between Canada and Russia, "particularly in the area of liquefied natural gas (LNG)." They affirmed such development "will play an important role in enhancing global energy security."[71] Announcements in May 2008 indicate planning is underway to deliver Russian gas to eastern Canada. A Canadian consortium, Rabaska (Gaz Metro, Enbridge, Gaz de France), plans to import natural gas from Russia into Quebec, thence to eastern Ontario. The gas would come from Gazprom's giant Shtokman field offshore the Russian Arctic in the Barents Sea. It would be liquefied in the Russian Arctic, shipped to Quebec, and re-gasified at Lévis east of Quebec City.[72]

Currently, Quebec and Ontario receive natural gas from Alberta down the Trans-Canada pipeline. But the gas market continues to grow; and the flow of a pipeline can be reversed. How the plan to deliver Russian gas to Eastern Canada relates to Canada's energy security has not been elaborated. It would, of course, free up Alberta gas for the US market.

CONSOLIDATING CONTROL IN THE MIDDLE EAST

The Middle East is a sensitive region – strategically, economically, politically, culturally and religiously – not least because of its oil and gas. The United States has acknowledged its vital interest in Middle East oil since the 1940s.

The British have done so since before the First World War. But the Bush administration put a new twist on the Great Game.[73] It pushed for global domination through overwhelming unilateral power and sought to reshape the Middle East by force. There may be more than one motive for the US invasion of Iraq and for its bellicosity towards Iran. But one major reason is energy.

The Middle East accounts for 60% of the world's proven oil reserves and 40% of its gas. It is of vital importance. Saudi Arabia

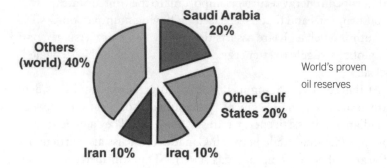

alone accounts for 20% of the world's oil reserves, and the Gulf States (Bahrain, Kuwait, Oman, Qatar, United Arab Emirates) another 20%. Iraq accounts for an additional 10%. (Oil and gas data in this article are drawn from the BP *Statistical Review*.[74])

The US military umbrella dominates these countries, ensuring a measure of control over more than 50% of the world's oil reserves. And Iran has a further 10% of the world's oil reserves.

A brief look at Iran reveals ongoing strategies. Iran is a regional player in the New Great Game – a place of enormous strategic importance. Its proven reserves of oil are the world's third largest in size, and those of natural gas rank second.

Where are Iran's oil and gas reserves? Some are in the Persian Gulf – heavily patrolled by the US navy. But 90 per cent lie in Khuzestan province, just across the Shatt al-Arab River from Iraq. Saddam Hussein crossed the Shatt al-Arab River in the Eight-Year War and tried to seize Iran's oil. He destroyed the Abadan refinery, once the largest in the world.

Iran is surrounded by US bases. It's another flashpoint among the Great Powers – a whole story in itself. The United States claims that Iran has plans to develop nuclear weapons. Thus far, ongoing inspections by the UN International Atomic Energy Agency support Iran's claim that it is developing only nuclear power for electricity, but investigations into specific allegations continue.[75] As a signatory of the Nuclear Non-Proliferation Treaty, Iran is allowed to develop civilian nuclear power.

The Iranians remember that the US has interfered for regime change before. Iran had a democracy in 1951; that government nationalized the Iranian assets of the Anglo-Iranian Oil Company, a UK company that later became British Petroleum. Foreign companies blackballed Iran, and no oil flowed for 18 months. Then, in 1953, the CIA engineered a coup.[76] Democracy ended, and the Shah was reinstalled. A foreign oil consortium came in, and oil flowed again.

In 1979, the foreign oil companies were thrown out. Since then, US oil firms have remained out of Iran – for about thirty years. Iran reopened the door to investment after its crippling war with Iraq. European and Asian companies signed huge contracts, but the White House blocked American companies from Iran.[77] Now the US and others have imposed new sanctions against Iran. There is much more to the tussle than the question of nuclear energy.

What's been going on in the Middle East involves increasing control over energy resources. This provides insight into what's going on in Central Asian countries as well. They are at the northern end of the so-called Oil Corridor, which runs from the Gulf states through Iraq and Iran to the Caspian Sea. The New Great Game is a serious competition for energy resources. It's a big game, and a ruthless one.

CONCLUSION: CANADA AND AFGHANISTAN POLICY

Canada's stated objective is to help Afghanistan become a stable, democratic and self-sustaining state.[78] Over the years, the public has been presented with numerous other reasons for Canada's presence in the country, such as helping to provide for Afghanistan's development needs, liberating women, educating girls, seeking retribution for the attacks of September 11, 2001, and even keeping NATO from failing.[79]

Government efforts to convince Canadians to stay in Afghanistan have been enormous. But the impact of a proposed multi-billion dollar pipeline in areas of Afghanistan under Canadian purview has never been seriously debated.

Even so, the Canadian government participates in donor meetings where Afghanistan is discussed as an energy bridge – a pipeline corridor.

The TAPI pipeline proposal could have positive or negative impacts on Canada's role in the country. Yet, during parliamentary deliberations over whether to extend the Canadian mission in Kandahar to 2011, the debate focused on how many troops to send and how long they should stay there – details rather than the big picture. It ignored regional geopolitics and energy issues.

The decision to extend the mission was reached hot on the heels of the report of the Independent Panel on Canada's Future Role in Afghanistan (the Manley Panel). The report said that Canadian governments have failed "to communicate ... the reasons for Canadian involvement."[80] It focused on four military options for Canada's role in Afghanistan but gave little attention to a political settlement, which is how most conflicts end. It ignored Central Asia, regional geopolitics and energy issues, although at least one submission (made by this author) brought these matters to the panel's attention.[81]

Canadian policy makers and the public cannot ignore the fact that the US clearly asserts the geopolitical importance of the region. Assistant Secretary of State Richard Boucher, in recent testimony to the US House Committee on Foreign Affairs, stressed the importance of Central Asian states to the "long-term stability of Afghanistan."[82] He noted the US has "ambitious policy objectives in the region." These ambitions clearly involve energy. He said the US is "working to facilitate multiple oil and gas export routes" and "has been active in promoting private energy sector investment in the Region." How much these objectives are shared by Canada, and how US ambitions will affect Canada, remain to be clarified.

The importance of oil and gas in the region was stressed at a Council of Foreign Relations panel discussion in 2007 in New York.[83] Steve LeVine, journalist and author, noted: "US policy is pipeline-driven within a strategy ... to make this area a pro-western swath of territory between Russia and Iran, driven by the establishment of an independent economic channel. Everything else is really – I hate to call it window-dressing – but it's secondary to that." Carter W. Page, CEO for Energy and Power, Merrill Lynch, observed: "From an economic perspective, oil and gas are far and away the largest place for both investment and trade ... Energy and power are really the main game."

Informed decisions on Canada's future role in Afghanistan and NATO require attention to energy issues and to our allies' designs on the resources and routes in the region. Afghanistan must be seen in its geopolitical setting and in terms of the rivalry for the energy of Central Asia. Since Afghanistan is perceived to be an energy bridge, why don't our leaders say so? Our troops, our citizens and our democracy deserve an explanation.

NOTES

1 Michael T. Klare, professor of peace and world security studies at Hampshire College, MA, "Rising Powers Shrinking Planet – the New Geopolitics of Energy," Metropolitan Books, Henry Holt & Co, New York NY, 2008.

2 Richard Boucher, Assistant Secretary of State for South and Central Asian Affairs, Speech at the Paul H. Nitze School for Advanced International Studies, 20 September 2007. http://www.state.gov/p/sca/rls/rm/2007/94238.htm

3 Ambassador Thomas Pickering and General James A. Jones, *Afghanistan Study Group Report*, Center for the Study of the Presidency, Washington, DC, January 2008. http://www.thepresidency.org/pubs/Afghan_Study_Group_final.pdf

4 Janice Stein and Eugene Lang, *The Unexpected War: Canada in Kandahar* (Toronto: Viking Canada, 2007), pp 260-265.

5 Deepak Obhrai, Parliamentary Secretary to Minister of Foreign Affairs, speaking notes, Canadian Institute of International Affairs Parliamentary Forum, 14 May 2007. http://www.deepakobhrai.com/media/speeches/2007/14May2007_Speech.pdf

6 Lutz Kleveman, *The New Great Game: Blood and Oil in Central Asia* (New York: Grove Press, 2004). http://www.amazon.ca/s?ie'UTF8&search-type'ss&index'books-ca&field-author'Lutz%20Kleveman&page'1

7 "Delay in TAPI project doubled its cost: ADB," *Daily Times*, Lahore, Pakistan, 24 April 2008. http://www.dailytimes.com.pk/default.asp?page'2008%5C04%5C24%5Cstory_24-4-2008_pg5_2

8 Ahmed Rashid, *Taliban: Militant Islam, Oil and Fundamentalism in Central Asia* (New Haven: Yale University Press, 2001).

9 Françoise Chipaux, Le Monde, "Hamid Karzaï, une large connaissance du monde occidental," Paris, France, 6 December 2001. http://www.thedossier.ukonline.co.uk/Web%20Pages/LE%20MONDE_Hamid%20Karzai,%20un%20Pachtoune%20nomme%20president.html

10 "Afghanistan is moving backward," *Asia Times Online*, Hong Kong, 3 July 2007. http://www.atimes.com/atimes/South_Asia/IG03Df01.html Eric Margolis, "Bogus Elections in Kabul," 13 December 2004. http://www.ericmargolis.com/archives/2004/12/bogus_elections.php

11 Alexander's Gas and Oil Connections, "Turkmen-Afghan-Pakistani gas pipeline accord published," 27 June 2002. Http://

www.gasandoil.com/goc/news/nts22622.htm

12 "Asian Development Bank and Turkmenistan," 2007 Fact Sheet on
    Turkmenistan, p. 2. http://www.adb.org/Documents/Fact_
    Sheets/TKM.pdf

13 Regional Technical Assistance: 37018-01, RETA-6153 REG: Turk-
    menistan-Afghanistan Pakistan Natural Gas Pipeline (Phase II),
    December 2003. http://www.adb.org/projects/project. asp?id'37018

14 Peter Mackay, "Parliamentary Secretary Obhrai to Represent Govern-
    ment at Second Regional Economic Cooperation Conference on
    Afghanistan," 17 November 2006. http://w01.
    international.gc.ca/MinPub/Publication.aspx?isRedirect=True&
    publication_id=384585&Language=E&docnumber=136

15 List of Delegates, Second Regional Economic Cooperation Conference
    on Afghanistan, New Delhi, India, 18-19 November 2006.
    http://meaindia.nic.in/srec/frame.php?s'internalpages/ dlist.pdf

16 New Delhi Declaration, Second Regional Economic Cooperation
    Conference on Afghanistan, New Delhi, India, 19 November 2006.
    http://www.mfa.gov.af/Documents/ImportantDoc/ newdelhi_declar
    ation.pdf

17 "Parliament is ignoring 'New Great Energy Game' in Afghanistan,
    says MP," *Hill Times*, Ottawa, 14 April 2008. http://www. thehilltimes.
    ca/html/index.php?display'story&full_path'2008/
    april/14/energy_bridge/&c'2

18 Standing Senate Committee on National Security and Defence, *Canadi-
    an Troops in Afghanistan – Taking a Hard Look at a Hard Mission*,
    Ottawa, February 2007. http://www.parl.gc.ca/39/1/ parlbus/com
    mbus/senate/com-e/defe-e/rep-e/repFeb07-e.pdf

19 Omar Samad, Ambassador of Afghanistan to Canada, Letter to *Globe
    and Mail*, 'Just another war for oil?," Ottawa ON, 20 July 2008.
    http://www.afghanemb-
    canada.net/en/news_bulletin/2008/june/19/index.php

20 Government of Afghanistan, *National Development Strategy*, Kabul,
    2008, page 50. http://www.ands.gov.af/ands/final_ands/src/final/
    Afghanistan%20National%20Development%20Strategy_eng.pdf

21 Kazinform, "India to produce gas in Turkmenistan," Kazakh News
    Agency, 7 April 2008. http://www.inform.kz/showarticle.
    php?lang'eng&id'162723

22 "Agreement on Iran gas pipeline close, Pakistan says," Reuters, Lon-
    don, UK, 19 February 2007.

23 "Kabul to clear mines on TAPI gasline route in 2 yrs," Daily Times,

Pakistan, 7 June 2008. http://www.dailytimes.com. pk/default.asp?page=2008\06\07\story_7-6-2008_pg7_30

24 "Pakistan, Afghanistan, India agree on gas supply from Turkmenistan," *Pakistan Times*, Pakistan, 24 April 2008. http:// www.pak-times.com/2008/04/24/afghanistan-pakistan-indiaagree-on-gas-supply/

25 "Delay in TAPI project doubled its cost: ADB," *Daily Times*, Lahore, Pakistan, 24 April 2008. http://www.dailytimes.com. pk/default.asp?page'2008%5C04%5C24%5Cstory_24-4-2008_pg5_2

26 "India facilitated to join TAPI: GSFA signed," *Business Recorder*, Islamabad, Pakistan, 25 April 2008. http://www.brecorder. com/index.php?id'727446&currPageNo'1&query'&search'&te rm'&supDate'

27 "Delay in TAPI project doubled its cost: ADB." http://www. daily-times.com.pk/default.asp?page=2008%5C04%5C24%5Cst ory_24-4-2008_pg5_2

28 Financial Express, *GAIL to lay TAPI pipeline*, India, 28 April 2008. http://www.financialexpress.com/news/GAIL-to-lay-TAPIpipeline/302677/

29 "TAPI gas pipeline pact signed," *Daily Times*, Lahore, Pakistan, 25 April 2008. http://www.dailytimes.com.pk/default.asp?page '2008%5C04%5C25%5Cstory_25-4-2008_pg1_4

30 State News Agency of Turkmenistan, "Trans-Afghanistan Pipeline to take shape," Ashgabat, 30 May 2008. http:// www.turkmenistan.gov.tm/_en/?idr=5&id=080530a

31 Embassy News, "Assistant Secretary of State Richard A. Boucher reviews growing bilateral relationship during visit to Turkmenistan, " US Embassy, Ashgabat, 28 May 2008. http://turkmenistan. usembassy.gov/pr20080528.html

32 "U.S. urges Turkmenistan to diversify gas exports," Reuters India, Ashgabat, 29 May 2008. http://in.reuters.com/articlePrint ?articleId=INL2982498920080529

33 Government of Afghanistan, *National Development Strategy*, Kabul, 2008, pages 81 and 143. http://www.ands.gov.af/ands/ final_ands/src/final/Afghanistan%20National%20Development %20Strategy_eng.pdf

34 "IPI Gas pipeline to be built in parts," *Pak Tribune*, Pakistan, 7 March 2007. http://www.paktribune.com/news/index. shtml?171124

35 "IPI Gas pipeline to be built in parts." http://www.paktribune.

com/news/index.shtml?171124

36 "Gazprom confirms interest in Iran-India gas pipeline," Reuters, London, UK, 5 May 2007. http://uk.reuters.com/articlePrint?ar ticle Id'UKDAH53558120070505

37 "BP keen to lay IPI pipeline in Pakistani territory," *Daily Times*, Lahore, Pakistan, 20 January 2008. http://www.dailytimes.com. pk/default.asp?page'2008%5C01%5C20%5Cstory_ 20-1-2008_pg5_2

38 "Iran-Pakistan-India Pipeline: Is it a Peace Pipeline?," MIT Center for International Studies, September 2007. http://web.mit. edu/CIS/pdf/Audit_09_07_Maleki.pdf

39 "India facilitated to join TAPI: GSFA signed," *Business Recorder*, Islamabad, Pakistan, 25 April 2008. http://brecorder.com/index. php?id=727446&currPageNo=1&query=&search=&term= & supDate=

40 "Energy crisis forces India to join Iran gas pipeline project," *Dawn*, Pakistan, 26 April 2008. http://www.dawn. com/2008/04/26/top1.htm

41 "Iran-Pakistan-India Pipeline: Is it a Peace Pipeline?" http://web. mit.edu/CIS/pdf/Audit_09_07_Maleki.pdf

42 Richard Boucher, Assistant Secretary of State for South and Central Asian Affairs, Briefing on the International Conference in Support of Afghanistan, Washington DC, 10 June 2008. http:// www.state.gov/p/sca/rls/2008/105793.htm

43 Evan Feigenbaum, Deputy Assistant Secretary of State for South and Central Asian Affairs, "Strategic Context of U.S.-India Relations," Briefing to Harvard University Weatherhead Fellows, Washington DC, 7 April 2008. http://www.state.gov/p/sca/ rls/2008/103809.htm

44 "Where in the World are Canadian Energy Companies?" Embassy Report, Ottawa, 2 November 2005. http://www. embassymag.ca/reports/2005/110205_em.pdf

45 "President of Turkmenistan receives Buried Hill Energy top managers," Turkmenistan – the Golden Age, 13 February 2008. http://www.turk-menistan.gov.tm/_en/?idr'1&id'080213c

46 "Buried Hill Delegation Meets President of Turkmenistan," *Buried Hill News*, 14 February 2008. http://buriedhill.com/ news/index.php?m=02&y=08&entry=entry080215-141113

47 Thermo Design, "Bagadja Gas Sweetening & Turbo Expander LPG Recovery Plant," Edmonton Alberta. http://www. thermodesign.com/turnkey_plants.html?Plant=Bagadja

48 NATO, Summit Declaration, Bucharest, Romania, 3 April 2008. http://www.summitbucharest.ro/en/doc_201.html

49 NATO, Summit Declaration, Riga, Latvia, 29 November 2006.

http://www.nato.int/docu/pr/2006/po6-150e.htm

50 U.S. Senator Lugar, Opening Speech, NATO Summit Conference, Riga, Latvia, 27 November 2006. http://www. rigasummit.lv/en/id/newsin/nid/239/

51 NATO, *The North Atlantic Treaty*, Washington, DC, 4 April 1949. http://www.nato.int/docu/basictxt/treaty.htm

52 "2007 EU-Canada Summit Statement," Berlin Germany, 4 June 2007, Office of the Prime Minister website. http://pm.gc.ca/eng/media. asp?id'1683

53 Foreign Affairs and International Trade Canada (DFAIT), "Energy Security," Ottawa, 1 October 2007. http://geo.international. gc.ca/ cip-pic/library/energy_security-en.aspx.

54 Johannes F. Linn, "Central Asia: A New Hub of Global Integration," Wolfensohn Center for Development, Brookings Institution, Washington, DC, 29 November 2007. http://www. brookings.edu/articles/2007/1129_central_asia_linn.aspx

55 School of Advanced International Studies, Johns Hopkins University, "The Politics of Pipelines: Bringing Caspian Energy to Markets," Silk Roads Study Program, Washington DC, 2005. http://www.silkroad-studies.org/new/inside/staff_publications/ articles.htm

56 Ariel Cohen et al., "The Proposed Iran-Pakistan-India Gas Pipeline: An Unacceptable Risk to Regional Security," Heritage Foundation, Washington, DC, 30 May 2008. http://www. heritage.org/Research/Asi-aandthePacific/bg2139es.cfm

57 Peter Hopkirk, *The Great Game: The Struggle for Empire in Central Asia* (New York: Kodansha Globe, reprint edition, April 1994). http://www.amazon.ca/Great-Game-Struggle-Empire-Central/ dp/1568360223

58 *All Business Magazine*, "Turkmenistan's Gas Reserves May Exceed 38 TCM," 20 Oct 2008. http://www.allbusiness.com/mining-extraction/ oil-gas-exploration-extraction-oil/11666006-1.html News Central Asia, "Massive Gas Reserves: Dangers Ahead for Turkmenistan," 20 Oct 2008. http://www.newscentralasia.net/Articles-and-Reports/379.html

59 AFP, "Russia, Kazakhstan, Turkmenistan sign Caspian pipeline accord," Moscow, 20 December 2007. http://afp.google.com/ article/ALeqM5hZznE4ux89gRJzlgVm5CSruCQ5bg

60 "Eurasia: Europe Urged To Diversify Oil, Gas Supplies Away From Russia," Radio Free Europe website, Prague, 15 May 2007. http://www.rferl.org/featuresarticle/2007/05/ac33fof2-f167- 4d27-9d42-do46ce5e73a3.html

61 State News Agency of Turkmenistan, "President Gurbanguly
   Berdimuhamedov visits the Dovletabad gas field," Ashgabat, May 27,
   2008. http://www.turkmenistan.gov.tm/_en/ ?idr=4&id=080527a

62 "China's Pipeline Diplomacy," *Asia Sentinel*, Hong Kong, 7 September
   2007. http://www.asiasentinel.com/index.
   php?option'com_content&task'view&id'686&Itemid'32 UPI, "Analysis: China and Turkmen energy," 4 January 2008.
   http://www.upi.com/Energy_Resources/2008/01/04/Analysis_
   China_and_Turkmen_energy/UPI-43231199460342/

63 Evan A. Feigenbaum, Deputy Assistant Secretary of State South and
   Central Asian Affairs, "'Turning the Page' in US-Turkmenistan Relations," Carnegie Endowment for International Peace, Washington,
   D.C., 17 September 2007, U.S. Department of State website.
   http://www.state.gov/p/sca/rls/rm/2007/92861.htm

64 U.S. Embassy News, "U.S. Senator Richard Lugar Visits Turkmenistan," Ashgabat, Turkmenistan, 12 January 2008. http:// turk-
   menistan.usembassy.gov/pr20080112.html
      U.S. Embassy News, "Commander of U.S. Central Command returns
   to Turkmenistan," Ashgabat, Turkmenistan, 28 January 2008.
   http://turkmenistan.usembassy.gov/pr20080125.html U.S. Embassy
   News, "U.S. Coordinator for Eurasian Energy Diplomacy Visits Turkmenistan," Ashgabat, Turkmenistan, 29 January 2008. http://
   turkmenistan.usembassy.gov/pr20080129.html
      U.S. Embassy News, "Return Visits of U.S. Officials Advance Cooper-
   ation in the Energy Sector," Ashgabat, Turkmenistan, 28 February
   2008. http://turkmenistan.usembassy.gov/ pr20080228.html
      U.S. Embassy News , "US Energy Envoys Examine Energy Coopera-
   tion in Turkmenistan," Ashgabat, Turkmenistan, 4 June 2008.
   http://turkmenistan.usembassy.gov/pr20080604.html

65 "Hydrocarbon Development Policy of Turkmenistan," News Central
   Asia, 15 March 2008. http://www.newscentralasia. net/print/263.html

66 "NATO: Uzbek, Turkmen Presidents Offer Cooperation," Radio Free
   Europe website, 4 April 2008. http://www.rferl.org/ featuresarti-
   cle/2008/04/c2cc94b7-3c23-4d4c-bff8- 186da4b14106.html

67 "President of Turkmenistan has meeting with President of the Islamic
   Republic of Afghanistan," Turkmenistan – the Golden Age, 4 April
   2008. http://www.turkmenistan.gov.tm/_en/ ?idr'1&id'080404b

68 U.S. Embassy News, "A Note from President Bush to President
   Berdimuhamedov," Ashgabat, Turkmenistan, 2008. http:// turk-
   menistan.usembassy.gov/note20080523.html

69 Richard Boucher, U.S. Assistant Secretary for South and Central Asian Affairs, "Turkmenistan: Change and the Future," Ashgabat, Turkmenistan, May 29, 2008. http://www.state.gov/p/sca/rls/2008/105714.htm

70 Michael T. Klare, *The Nation*, "The New Geopolitics of Energy," New York NY, 1 May 2008. http://www.thenation.com/doc/20080519/klare

71 Joint Statement by Prime Minister of Canada Stephen Harper and President of the Russian Federation Vladimir Putin on Canada-Russia energy cooperation, St Petersburg, Russia, 15 July 2006. http://pm.gc.ca/eng/media.asp?id=1248

72 Gazprom and Rabaska, "Gazprom US Based Subsidiary And Rabaska Reach Agreement," press release, May 2008. http://www.enbridge.com/investor/pdf/2008-05-15-Gazprom- Rabaska-nr.pdf
   Globe and Mail, Rhéal Séguin and Shawn McCarthy, "Gazprom picks Quebec plant for LNG foray," Quebec and Ottawa, 16 May 2008.

73 Michael T. Klare, *Blood and Oil* (New York: Henry Holt & Company, 2004).

74 British Petroleum, BP Statistical Review of World Energy 2007, London, England, 2007. http://www.bp.com/productlanding.do?categoryId'6848&contentId'7033471

75 UN IAEA, Reports by the Director General, "Implementation of the NPT Safeguards Agreement," Vienna, Austria, 22 February and 26 May 2008. http://www.iaea.org/Publications/Documents/Board/2008/gov2008-4.pdf http://www.iaea.org/Publications/ Documents/Board/2008/gov2008-15.pdf

76 Stephen Kinzer, *All The Shah's Men: An American Coup and the Roots of Middle East Terror* (Hoboken, New Jersey: John Wiley & Sons, 2007). http://www.chapters.indigo.ca/books/All-Shahs-Men-American-Coup-Stephen-Kinzer/9780470185490-item. html?pticket'uetzgbf5qflzaq55mbviqlmoXmmuBMjHVYdVKDD%2fGJZD7bIoMlo%3d

77 Herman Franssen and Elaine Morton, "A Review of US Unilateral Sanctions Against Iran," *Middle East Economic Survey*, Nicosia, Cyprus, 26 August 2002. http://www.mafhoum.com/press3/108E16.htm

78 Government of Canada, "Canada's Approach in Afghanistan," 7 May 2008. http://www.canada-afghanistan.gc.ca/cip-pic/ afghanistan/library/mission-en.asp

79 Haroon Siddiqui, "Come clean on why we are in Afghanistan," *Toronto Star*, 20 January 2008. http://www.thestar.com/ printArticle/295478

80 Independent Panel on Canada's Future Role in Afghanistan, *Final Report*, Ottawa, January 2008, p. 24. http://www.independent-panel-independant.ca/pdf/Afghan_Report_web_e.pdf

81 John Foster, "Submission to the Independent Panel on Canada's Future Role in Afghanistan," Kingston, Ontario, 30 November 2007. http://www.independent-panel-independant.ca/pdf/ Submission-161.pdf

82 U.S. Embassy News: Testimony by Assistant Secretary Richard Boucher http://turkmenistan.usembassy.gov/testimony20080408. html

83 Steve LeVine, journalist and author, and Carter W. Page, CEO for Energy and Power, Merrill Lynch, *The Pursuit of Black Gold: Pipeline Politics on the Caspian Sea*, panel discussion, Council of Foreign Relations, New York, 13 November 2007. Steve LeVine covered Central Asia for *New York Times* and *Wall Street Journal*, and is author of *The Oil and the Glory: The Pursuit of Empire and Fortune on the Caspian Sea*. http://www.state.gov/p/sca/rls/ rm/2007/97957.htm

Afghanistan and Canada
What Can Be Done?

Canada's Honourable Role
as a Peacekeeping Nation

A. WALTER DORN

Note: the views represented herein do not necessarily represent the views of the Government of Canada or the Department of National Defence. Dr. Dorn used his contractually-guaranteed freedom of expression as an academic in matters pertaining to his area of expertise, to voice his own opinions before the House of Commons Standing Committee on Foreign Affairs and International Development in 2007. This is an updated transcript of what he said.

Thank you for the honour of appearing before this Committee. I will offer a constructively critical and comparative perspective of Canada's current engagements in Kandahar, Kabul and various UN missions around the world. When I teach officers at the Canadian Forces College, I use this approach, believing that our soldiers should view their work from differing and critical perspectives weighing the pros and cons of different strategies. During training, soldiers usually learn how to think the same. During education, they should learn how to think differently. "Diversity in Unity" or "Unity in Diversity" is a key principle of our participatory democracy, indeed of our Parliament, as parliamentarians well know.

My research and experience has focused on UN peacekeeping and peace operations, so I am positioned to compare our actions in Kandahar and Kabul to many peacekeeping missions, some of which I experienced first-hand. Canada has a long, strong and proud tradition of peacekeeping; we have a tradition of war-fighting as well, in the "right wars" until now, in my opinion.

The first consequence of our current deployment in Afghanistan is that Canada is currently at a historic low in its UN peacekeeping contribution. Ironically, this comes at a time when UN peacekeeping is at an historic high. We currently deploy merely 55 soldiers under the UN blue flag at a time when the UN has over 70,000 soldiers in the field. The police forces of Canada contribute 50% more than the Canadian Forces. Our military makes up less than 0.1% of UN forces, a hundred times less than the 10% average for Canada during much of the history of UN peacekeeping.

Canada has often ranked as the number one peacekeeping nation since Pearson proposed the first peacekeeping force 60 years ago, a concept which has thrived and evolved internationally as he hoped it would. As you will see from Graph 1, Canada ranked in the top ten until 1996. Then we began the great slide. One of the largest drops (to one quarter strength) occurred two months after the Conservative government of Stephen Harper took office in February 2006, when we closed out our mission in the Golan Heights. 190 logistics specialists left the UN mission, largely because of the pressures of Kandahar, and we have provided the UN with nothing remotely comparable since.

It is clear that one of the casualties of our large Afghanistan deployment is our contribution to UN peacekeeping. This is not only in the field, but also at UN headquarters, which has to guide over 100,000 military and civilian personnel in the field. There is not a single Canadian officer serving in the UN's Department of Peacekeeping Operations (DPKO) in New York, which has some 70 officers in its military division. The UN has, since 2000, experienced a surge in demand for its peacekeeping services (see Graph 2), with important missions in 18 war-torn areas, including Haiti, the Congo, Liberia, and Lebanon. But the UN has stopped coming to Canada for contributions, knowing that the answer will be a polite "no" with a finger pointing to Afghanistan.

This is doubly tragic because robust peacekeeping, which the UN has evolved over many decades, points the way, in my opinion, to a long-term solution in Afghanistan. The time honoured and tested principles of peacekeeping have led to the resolution of many seemingly intractable conflicts, including intrastate conflicts in Cambodia, Mozambique, Liberia, Sierra Leone, the former Yugoslavia, and East Timor. Former combatants finally relinquished the simplistic labels of "enemies" and "terrorists" to adopt a peace agreement, the only thing that a lasting peace could be based upon. When peacekeeping has deviated from its principles, as it did in Somalia in 1993, it has resulted in disaster.

The three central principles of peacekeeping are impartiality, consent, and minimum use of force. Let us see how these principles apply to Kandahar today.

1. IMPARTIALITY

Impartiality does not exist in Kandahar. We have a declared enemy, given to us by President Bush when he said in September 2001 that the US would make "no distinction between the terrorists who committed these acts and those who harbour them." At the time many of us recognised this as a recipe for an expanding and endless war. Instead of isolating al Qaeda, the Bush administration widened the war to the country's regime, giving us the first regime change in the Global War on Terror. The US has not sought and did not receive UN authorization for its war on terror nor the operation designed to carry out this war, "Operation Enduring Freedom" (OEF). Unlike ISAF, OEF has no UN-sanction. Yet Canada entered Kandahar under the banner of OEF and from that moment on, we could not be labelled as impartial or objective or as having the population's interest foremost in mind. Around the world, we are increasingly identified with the US effort to find and defeat enemies in American national interest. We became one of the conflicting parties and we remain so to this today, even though we are currently serving under NATO.

2. CONSENT

There is no peace agreement. We do not have the consent of the main parties to the conflict for our deployments in Kandahar. Even the consent of the local population is in doubt in many areas. We do have the consent of the Government of Afghanistan, though many inhabitants see President Karzai as a leader hand-picked by the US and legitimized by an election in which they did not vote.

Without winning the hearts and minds of the locals we can never win either the war or the peace, nor obtain their consent to our presence. Canada has for decades urged parties in vicious conflicts around the world to come to the peace table. But we seemingly cannot practice this advice ourselves.

3. MINIMUM AND DEFENSIVE USE OF FORCE, AS A LAST RESORT

Finally, we are clearly on the offensive in Kandahar. The posture is not one of self-defence or protection of civilians but is rather characterized by "search and destroy" missions and large scale offensives, in which civilians are all too often unfortunate casualties. We seem to be producing as many enemies as we are killing, as angry brothers, sons, clan members, and other displaced people fill the ranks of the fallen.

We are losing our young and courageous too: namely the 111 soldiers and one diplomat dead on the fields of Afghanistan (as of March 2009) (The diplomat – whose job, incidentally, I was offered and declined, coincidentally, the day before he died in an "Iraq"-style suicide attack on his convoy. I chose, instead, to serve UN peacekeeping.)

We have lost as many soldiers in Afghanistan than in all UN peacekeeping operations in over 60 years. This was not because Canada did not take risks in peacekeeping operations. As you can see from Table 1, Canada has the second highest level of fatalities in the history of peacekeeping. But the stance the Canadian Forces chose in Kandahar under Operation Enduring Freedom and then NATO, has meant that to many we appear as aggressors not defenders.

We deviate from the three principles of peacekeeping – impartiality, consent, and minimum use of force – at our peril.

So what is the alternative? There is no use criticising unless a better way is possible.

Robust peacekeeping of the type the UN has practiced so successfully in recent years is the better way. In the Eastern Congo, Sierra Leone and Liberia, this approach has given us lessons:

(1) Serve the local population first and foremost, not only to "win hearts and minds" to our cause but to make sure that their interests become our common cause.
(2) Narrow the list of spoilers, rather than broadening it.
(3) Negotiate for peace and always give a way out to those committing vio-

lence, except for the most egregious crimes which should be referred to the International Criminal Court or to a special tribunal.

(4) Do not lump together all who oppose the international presence. In Afghanistan, this means recognition that not all who oppose the Canadian presence are "Taliban terrorists." There are many former Mujahedin from various clans that the West once supported during the war against the Soviet invaders, who are motivated by defence of their country, not love of the Taliban. They long to live and die like the heroes of their folklore, whether it be heroes from the time of British colonizers or Soviet invaders, and they are willing to sacrifice themselves for their tribe or country.

In contrast to prudent peacekeeping policies, the recent model of the Canadian Forces, originating from US Marine Corps commandant Charles Krulak, is the "ThreeBlock War" concept, in which the first block states: "Canada will engage in a high intensity fight against the armies of failing states," to use the words of a recent Army poster. The Three-Block War model is unworkable and fatally flawed because we cannot simultaneously fight offensive high-intensity combat and carry out effective humanitarian and reconstruction tasks. (See the article by Stephen Cornish in this book.) This is the case in Kandahar, though in Kabul we had a working peacekeeping-type model.

The UN uses force as a last resort ("combat if necessary, but not necessarily combat" to use a quintessentially Canadian phrase), when all negotiations and warnings have failed. I saw this in the Eastern Congo in November 2006 when the renegade 81 and 83rd Congolese brigades tried to capture the city of Goma. The UN gave a firm order to these forces to halt in Sake and when this warning was not heeded the UN and government forces stopped the advance, using advanced helicopter gunships flown by India. Canada, the US and NATO have not even started talking or negotiating with their opponents in Kandahar or other conflict-ridden parts of Afghanistan.

The UN tries to create a working model for a broad-based central government of national unity ... From this "city on a hill" model, it is much easier to win hearts and minds. People will strive to become part of a working society. And to a great extend NATO succeeded with its Peace Support Operations in Kabul and some of the provinces. But this progress is being jeopardized by the US' and NATO's provocative measures in other provinces.

This alternative model, sometimes known as the "ink blots" model, suggests that you spread out only when you can succeed. As hearts and minds are won, people will flock to the safety and security of protected areas, to places where their voices are heard, their rights respected (especially their right to peace) and their votes permitted. We have to build capacity not dependency, unity not animosity, in Afghanistan. This is what is working in the Democratic Republic of the Congo and this seems to me to be the only model that can work in the long-term in Afghanistan.

CONCLUSION

Some may dismiss the UN's sixty years of peacekeeping as outdated and out-moded, but today's UN operations are, in fact, the result of steady evolution, learning from past lessons on the under-use and overuse of force. A balance has finally been achieved in many UN operations. But in the mountains of Afghanistan, we seem to be re-learning these lessons the hard way.

There are three possible approaches: the hawk, dove and owl approaches. The hawk is, in my mind, too aggressive to establish a long-term stability and peace. The dove is too weak to deal with the messy problems in harsh war zones. The owl has the wisdom to know when and where to engage. We should move to an owl approach, knowing when to expand our operations in the "ink blot" model, the ink will spread when the time is ripe.

If we want to restore Canadian leadership in the world, a goal that Foreign Minister Peter Mackay enunciated to this Committee, then we should start where we are able and universally recognized to have provided solid leadership in the past: peacekeeping missions. Of course, we should still make substantial contributions to NATO and NORAD but if there is an activity where we stand out in the eyes of the world, it is peacekeeping. We need not compete with South Asian nations for "boots on the ground," but we should be innovative, using our specialized expertise and equipment to make UN peacekeeping more effective and the world safer. We have the technology and skilled personnel that are so needed in UN peacekeeping today. With UN peacekeeping booming, it is the place to be. It is the model to use.

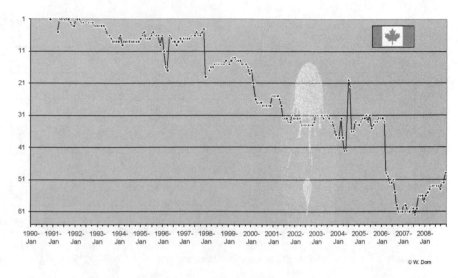

Graph 1: Canada's rank among nations by contribution of uniformed personnel to UN peacekeeping, 1991 to 2008

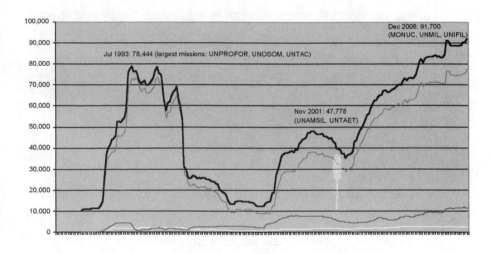

Graph 2: UN uniformed peacekeepers (military and police), number deployed 1991–2008

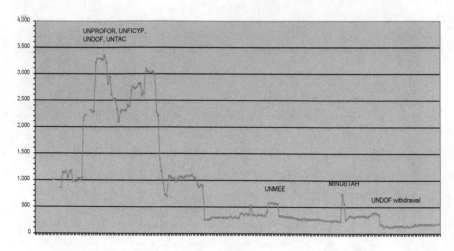

Graph 3: Canadian uniformed personnel (military and police) in UN PKO, 1991–2008

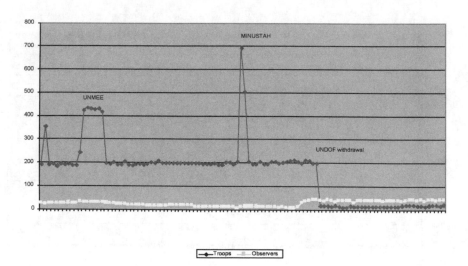

Graph 4: Canadian uniformed personnel (troops, observers, police), 2000–2008

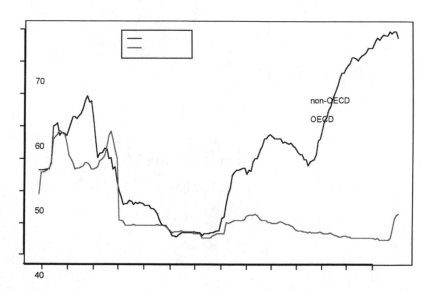

Graph 5: Develped (OECD) and developing (Non-OECD) country contributions to PKOs

COUNTRIES WITH THE MOST FACILITIES IN UN PEACEKEEPING, 31 DECEMBER 2006 (first 30)

Nationality	Fatalities
India	120
Canada	114
Ghana	109
France	95
United Kingdom	95
Pakistan	94
Ireland	89
Bangladesh	80
Nigeria	80
Zamabia	68
Sweden	65
United States of America	62
Nepal	57
Ethiopia	52
Denmark	48
Poland	47
Fiji	45
Finland	45
Italy	45
Austria	42
Kenya	41
Norway	41
Russian Federation	38
Indonesia	29
Jordan	28
Senegal	24
Belgium	23
Malaysia	23
Morocco	23
Netherlands	23

Data Sources:

Fatalities: Casualties Database, Situation Centre, Department of Peacekeeping Operations (emails in November 2006 and January 2007). Some of these data are available online at www.un.org/Depts/dpko/fatalities

Personnel contribution numbers: Peace and Security Unit, Department of Public Information. Some of these data are available online: Military and police – national contributions: www.un.org/Depts/dpko/contributors Civilian personnel statistics: www.un.org/Depts/dpko/dpko/archive.htm

Canada and the Crisis in Afghanistan

PIERRE BEAUDET

As we know, the Canadian involvement in Afghanistan, in its military as well as humanitarian aspects, began in 2001, right after the events of September 11. Canadian involvement began under the Liberal government of Jean Chrétien, continued under his successor, Paul Martin, and was reconfirmed by Stephen Harper and his minority Conservative government, which was elected in January 2006. The involvement was further legitimized in early 2008 by the so-called "independent" Report of John Manley (former Liberal Minister of Foreign Affairs), which went out of its way to call itself "non-partisan."[1]

More recently, Stephen Harper, reelected in October 2008, has vowed to commit 2,545 Canadian soldiers in Kandahar province in the combat zone until 2011. (According to Steven Staples' article, the current number is approximately 2,300.) At the same time, Canadian aid to Afghanistan (largely through CIDA) has increased considerably, by $100 million a year for five years, and in principle and fact has become one of Canada's major international engagements. The purpose of the following article is to explain how and why this astonishing evolution came about.

BACKGROUND

After 9/11, the United States declared "a war without end on terrorism." President George W. Bush declared "the right" of the United States to intervene unilaterally and "preventively" against any country or para-national force. The attack and invasion of Afghanistan was planned quickly, and carried out in late 2001, resulting in the fall of the Taliban regime. Invoking the UN charter, the United States got the support of member-countries who, together, put in place a military force in order to consolidate the occupation. This action, in fact, was "discussed" by the UN, but was not endorsed. At the same time the United States and its allies pushed through an international process to establish a temporary Afghan government to organize elections (which led to Hamed Karzai as president), and to begin a reconstruction program in the country. The first contingents of the Canadian military arrived in 2001 under the sponsorship of NATO allowing the US military forces to pursue the war in contested zones in the south and east. From 2006, however, faced with the lack of military success by the occupation forces, the decision was taken to extend the radius of NATO's action.

"War without end" and "Redefine"

The principle motive of the Chrétien government in becoming involved in this war was to support the United States, to act as an important economic and political partner, as a member of NATO, and to behave like a victim of aggression. This position has remained at the centre of Canada's involvement. The United States is our principle ally, so their war is our war. As Stephen Harper has repeated many times, our involvement in the war in Afghanistan is to "defend the interests of Canada." Much later, as the "War without end" expanded, mainly in Iraq, Washington's discourse evolved. The goal of the military intervention had now become, according to George W. Bush, one of "regime change," interfering in the internal functioning of countries throughout Central Asia and the Middle East. This "regime change" was defined as putting into place "democratic" governments based on certain American values, principally in the economic realm, such as free trade, privatization and openness to foreign ownership.

The Support of the Allies

The arguments supporting "regime change" were more or less endorsed by the member countries of NATO even though there were from the beginning concerns from Europe as well as Canada as to whether this was the best way to proceed. As we know, the United States pushed very hard, at the special session of the UN Security Council in February 2003, to convince its allies and the majority of the member nations of the UN as to the necessity of invading Iraq. However, the concerns of these countries were focused more on the "how" rather than the"why" of such an invasion. Paris, Berlin and the other major world capitals believed that the way the invasion was planned would lead to major chaos. This concern was also held by a large part of the American elite class, including well-known General Colin Powell, Secretary of State of the US government at the time. All of those concerned, US as well as European, were convinced that the Bush-Rumsfeld-Cheney trio was about to commit a grave error.

The Geopolitical and Geo-economic Issues

To understand this process we have to refer back to the US policy of "regime change," which coalesced in the Middle East and in Central Asia with new energy in 2001, and has recreated the serious problems we see today. For a long time, the United States has pushed to maintain its position of power in this area of the world, which contains the world's major energy resources situated in the geographic crossroads between Europe and Asia.

After the demise of the Soviet Union, Washington saw the opportunity to strengthen its control in the Middle East, and at the same time make inroads into Central Asia, previously the purview of Russia. This drive for control used opportunities as they arose, and grew substantially with the first invasion into Iraq when one of the US allies, Saddam Hussein, made the mistake of invading Kuwait. We know the rest. Saddam was deposed; hundreds of thousands of American troops were sent to the region. This strategy, which was quite rational from the point of view of American interests, consolidated Washington's interests to the detriment of European concerns. While other "emerging" powers (notably Russia and China) were in no position to challenge American military, political and economic strength, the leadership in Washington consolidated its hegemony in a vast arc across Asia, an area Western countries have called, ever since being so named by the British Empire, the Middle East.

The arrival of the Neo-Cons

In a sense, the coming to power of the neo-conservatives in 2000 in the form of a Republican administration represented both a continuity and a rupture with the strategy we have just described. George W. Bush wanted to consolidate the American Empire in the region and prevent Russia (and eventually China) from threatening the interests of the United States and the Western world. He saw himself as continuing the policies of the preceding administrations, including those of Bill Clinton. However, Bush and his ideological neo-cons of the Project for a New American Century did not want to stop there. Their objective, which was more or less explicit, was to unilaterally place the American military in such a way as to be ready for any new and serious conflict. At the same time the Bush administration massively increased its spending on military hardware which sent a message to the rest of the world that it was reversing the modest decline (largely during the 1970s) in military spending in order to make it clear that no other power (read Russia or China) could successfully compete with the United States.

Washington-Ottawa Convergence

Under the Liberal government of Jean Chrétien, and then Paul Martin, Canada fell in line behind these new priorities. Certainly, as we have just pointed out, there were tensions, notably over the timing and planning of the Iraq invasion. But basically, the priority of the Canadian government was to "consolidate relations" with the United States which was stated explicitly in a revised foreign affairs document adopted by the Martin government in 2005, several months before the election of the Conservative minority government of Stephen Harper. The result of this was to move Canada toward a re-oriented policy toward Afghanistan, to support in a non-military way the intervention in Iraq, and to reinvest in military spending. All of this was certainly accelerated starting in 2006. Stephen Harper, who had supported the 2003 invasion of Iraq, saw himself as the "best friend" of George W Bush. The re-stationing of the Canadian military into conflict zones, along with the considerable increase in spending on military hardware, was a clear sign of this new strategy.

THE CHAOS IN AFGHANISTAN

Today, eight years later, where are we? Afghanistan, like several other countries in the region, is in a much worse situation than it was eight years ago.

The Return of the Taliban

According to recent studies, the Taliban insurrection has both expanded and decentralized, and has developed the techniques needed to fight a modern guerrilla war in the mountains. Military leaders on NATO's side have often said that this war is not "winnable" using military tactics. However, the current success of the Taliban cannot be explained only by military or tactical efforts. Rather, an important portion of the population recognizes its legitimacy by default. We have to remember that when the Taliban first took power in 1995, they brought relative peace to a country ravaged by a brutal civil war that had created several factions, some of which are now established in the present Afghan government.

A Delinquent Government

Meanwhile, it is not a secret that a substantial number of the members of the current Afghan government, chosen and supported by the Bush administration, are a big part of the problem. So, not only is the Afghan government weak and discredited due to its close relationship with Washington, but it cannot even exercise real authority because the "warlords" who were the principal allies of the United States in the war against the Taliban, continue to function as "a state within a state," and do this even though their chiefs are formally members of the central government. In its 2006 Annual Report the NGO Human Rights Watch estimates that more than half of the new Parliament deputies are closely aligned to groups with ties to the warlords.[2] Not only do they exercise total control on the central government, but they are also responsible for the corruption, murders and systematic violations of the legal systems, and they function with impunity. Their predatory behaviour is tolerated by the NATO occupation because they continue to be the bulwark against the Taliban. Faced with this distressing situation, the political improvements put in place since 2001 – the election of the government with its new constitution recognizing human rights and equality for women before the law – have lost their power. Faced with this situation, many Afghans find themselves caught between two evils. They don't believe in the government and are not willing to fight to defend it. At the same time they fear the return of the Taliban. Meanwhile, the social and economic situation continues to deteriorate.

The Questionable Value of International Aid

According to the human development index of the United Nations Development Program, Afghanistan is classed 169th of 174 countries in the world. 60% of its population lives on less than a dollar a day. Meanwhile, the international community is involved in a huge reconstruction project of more than $10 billion under the aegis of the World Bank and several UN organizations.[3] The current aid program is divided among security, governance, law and human rights, as well as economic and social development, all of which are used to build the basic infrastructure, the social and education services, and the economy (largely toward the private sector). All of this is conceptualized and coordinated from the outside with little involvement from Afghans.[4] The aid is also divided among several programs, defined in such a way as to respond to the needs of the donor countries, oriented far too much toward the cities (when the majority of the population is rural), and more often co-opted by the people with privileged relations with the various aid agencies, foreign armed forces and the Afghan government itself.

Humanitarian Militarization

On the other hand, reconstruction aid is often re-channeled by short term military demands. Thus in combat zones, the aid is co-opted by the NATO military according to the model developed by the Pentagon's "Provincial Reconstruction Teams" (PRT), a model used by the army to supposedly "win the hearts and minds" of the population by being involved in the distribution of humanitarian aid and the construction of infrastructure. According to most experts, this co-optation of aid has negative political consequences since it ends up being used by the local military forces. (For a thorough discussion of this essay, see article by Stephen Cornish)

Meanwhile in the rural areas, agriculture, the traditional economic support of the majority of the population, is floundering and disorganized, opening agriculture to the drug traffickers who easily recruit the peasants to grow poppies for opium (showing a 49% growth since 2005).

Canadian Contribution

Canada's contribution to this reconstruction is significant. At more than $100 million a year, it is Canada's largest aid program, on par with the aid programs of other countries, including the United States. A substantial part of it goes through the World Bank. According to independent analysts a large part of the budgets of these programs returns to the donor countries in the form of contracts given to consultants or to foreign companies. The Canadian military also receives a certain amount of this Canadian aid budget thanks to its involvement in its PRT in the province of Kandahar. Such projects are chosen based on their use to the military, for example, in order to consolidate the Canadian presence in a certain region. Even though such projects can serve to build schools or dig wells, they don't really have the long-term effect of allowing the Afghan population to run their own affairs.[5]

There are certain CIDA projects that are well-managed and respect official principles, but on the whole the picture is discouraging.

The Afghan Crisis and Its Regional Implications

It is clear to anyone who can read a map that the conflict in Afghanistan is taking place in a very complex region. Pakistan, whose northern provinces are immediately adjacent to Afghanistan and are home to the same ethnic population (the Pashtuns), is in the epicentre of the crisis. Thanks to the Afghan crisis (if we can use that phrase), Pakistan has been substantially militarized in the last two decades. The Pakistani armed forces have become a state within a state, hot and cold in its management of the Afghan conflict, one time on the side of the government, another time on the side of the Taliban. Amongst the Pakistani population, many political fractures are at play. A very large segment is extremely hostile to the American presence and intervention in Afghanistan, especially because, more and more, this tends to be directly in Pakistan itself. Many Pakistanis are also not comfortable with the jihadist movement in Afghanistan or in Pakistan and would rather take their country out of the crisis through democratization and peace. The continuing influence of Iran and the former Soviet republics north of Afghanistan doesn't help. And finally the Afghan conflict is strongly felt throughout the entire region, firing up the "sacred cause" and legitimizing the vast anti-American jihadist movement.

Recently the United States has intensified its military operations into Pakistan where they claim to be finding the hidden bases of the Taliban. In reality this regional spread of the war makes it more difficult than ever to end George W. Bush's "war without end."

THE FUTURE: WHAT ARE THE POSSIBILITIES?

Let's remember the words of President Bush after the events of 9/11; he called them "an opportunity." We know that immediately after the events there was a heartfelt coming together of the populations of many countries in spite of the complexity of the situation, and both local and international opposition, to say nothing of the costs involved. However, today everywhere in the world as well as in Washington, this feeling of partnership is lost. This is the dilemma facing the new president Obama. We can understand why it is important to him to repair this damage by proceeding to make important changes in the current strategy.

A New Regime in Washington?

Now that the new president, Barak Obama, plans to launch a new era, the debate continues. Regarding Iraq one thing is clear: the original plan of the Bush administration to create a new Western-style neo-liberal society is a complete dead-end. It is probable that the United States under Obama will continue the military involvement, but on a reduced level, consolidate the permanent military bases scattered throughout the country, and then pull out, leaving a weak Iraq state torn by civil war. For the moment the neo-con dream of reorganizing the whole region, including Iran, under the American umbrella, has had to be put aside. Obama has no choice but to forge a more realistic approach.

The "Good War"

In Afghanistan, however, Obama has committed himself to continuing this so-called "good war," which concretely means an intensification of military operations and consolidation of the occupation, the details of which could evolve over time. In Iraq, the US and its local allies have succeeded, to a certain extent, in controlling the insurrection, transforming it, at least partially, from an anti-occupation war to a civil war, relieving the pressure on occupation forces. The US General who was in charge of that shift in Iraq is now in Afghanistan. Another of the reasons for this new direction in Afghanistan is the current world economic crisis.

In addition, in terms of world-wide opinion, Obama represents the current majority opinion in the United States, which believes that he must rebuild a multilateral consensus, starting with NATO allies. This reorientation also calls for more emphasis on "humanitarian development," an idea pushed by Canada and several European countries in the last several years. There is no question that the United States is still interested in maintaining its involvement in Afghanistan for all of the geopolitical and geo-economic reasons we have discussed above. Even with Obama's tactical military shifts, like the pull-out of Iraq, there would be a logic to continuing the "war on terror without end" in Afghanistan, Iraq, Palestine, eventually in Syria, and above all in Iran. The long-term goal is to prevent the stabilization of the region, which might give an advantage to certain European countries and the Chinese, who would have easier access to the region's energy resources.

Damage Control

There is, however, another way we can look at this impasse in Afghanistan. Obama and his allies could impose on Afghan society a kind of agreement, a cease-fire among the warring factions. As a beginning Washington could distance itself from all the individuals most heavily implicated in the corruption, principally President Karzai. Then they could begin indirect negotiations with the Taliban or some of the factions of the Taliban who could agree to abandon their ties with al Qaeda in exchange for immunity from persecution. It is not unreasonable to suppose that the majority of the Taliban leadership would be open to such an agreement, at least for the reason that their government would then be free of Western interference. However, Washington and some of its allies would never admit defeat and abandon the country to the Taliban.

But in the short-run, such a compromise would be an improvement, if for no other reason than that it would end the misery and destruction caused by the military conflict.[6]

And in the long-run the United States could still maintain its influence and preserve its local military capacities in such a way as to stay well-positioned in this part of the world, where the stakes are so high.

What Are the Options for a Canadian Policy?

We'll have to wait to know what effect the new Washington administration will have on Canada. The neo-conservative alliance between Bush and Harper will certainly be gone. A "new strategy" from Obama could still entail the continuation of a strong military presence in central Asia, which could work well for our second conservative minority government. Or it could mean that the mode of Canadian involvement would be called upon to change. Faced with mounting public pressure, and the growing accumulation of facts, Ottawa could cause a policy change, including a reduction of Canadian troops in the combat zones. Meanwhile the moral tone of the debate ("our troops are there to protect the Afghans") may continue, with Harper repeating his mantra that Afghanistan remains the "good" war, which we have to win.

Are There Any Alternatives?

Now that Canada, like its allies, is involved in Afghanistan and in adjacent regions, it will not be easy to make any substantial change. But nothing is impossible.

There will also be no lasting solution as long as the United States and its allies continue to pour oil on the fire. Their dream of recolonizing the region, one way or the other, has to be abandoned. This means an end to all the military involvements, such as the recent one with India and Pakistan (the United States just signed a new accord with India regarding the military use of nuclear energy.)

In the first place, the aspirations of the Afghan people for peace and democracy cannot be pushed aside. In addition, as we have seen throughout, this conflict is a regional conflict, and any solution will have to take into account the regional players. Together with certain European countries, Canada could create a strategy to reduce the violence and begin negotiations with all the actors involved: this means the Taliban, as well as Iran and Pakistan.

Demilitarization and De-nuclearization

At the same time, we have to work toward a reduction in the military capacities of the countries in the region (Israel, India and Pakistan already have nuclear weapons.) Finally we have to strengthen the role of the United Nations in the region, begin to withdraw NATO troops from Afghanistan, and bring in a peace-keeping force, "the blue berets."

None of this is magic; it cannot be carried out without a long-term perspective which involves, in a synchronized way, the establishment of peace, the creation of legitimate institutions, and social and economic reconstruction. Without a commitment to this difficult perspective, the war in Afghanistan will continue and will ruin not only the lives of the Afghan people, but the illusions of those who think that we can save the country by intensifying the war.

NOTES

1 In fact, during the last federal election in October, 2008, only the NDP clearly opposed the conclusions of this Report.

2 http://hrw.org/wr2k6

3 This figure may seem huge, but in fact it amounts to only $60 per Afghan citizen. It is much less than the amount sent to Bosnia ($760 per capita) or East Timor ($223 per capita)

4 According to Astri Suhrke (Reconstruction as Modernization: the post-conflict' project in Afghanistan Third World Quarterly, Vol. 28, No. 7, 2007), 75% of the aid budgets are directly administered by the agencies mandated by the donors and not by the Afghan government

5 See Omar Zakhilwal and Jane Murphy Thomas, "Afghanistan: the role of rural development in peace-building" in Stephan Baranyi, The Paradoxes of Peace Building Post 9/11, UBC Press and North/South Institute, 2008.

6 There are several international precedents for such negotiated ends to military conflicts based on a local and international consensus; think of Mozambique or Angola, or even South Africa.

Afghanistan:
A Disastrous Situation

CLAUDE CASTONGUAY

Throughout 2008 violence and a lack of security increased substantially in Afghanistan. With the death of some 290 soldiers and more than 4000 civilians, 2008 was a bloody year. Nothing indicates 2009 will take a turn for the better, on the contrary. The Canadian Minister of National Defence, Peter MacKay, confirmed recently that we can expect the insurgency to intensify and the Taliban to have clear advantage in their efforts to erode democratic functioning in their society.

Faced with this situation, the new US President, Barack Obama announced his intention to transfer another 30,000 soldiers, making Afghanisan the main front in the War on Terror. For the Americans, contrary to the situation for Canadians, the struggle is not to establish a democracy, but rather is a real fight against terrorism.

The involvement of Canada in Afghanistan dates back to 2002, and at the beginning was supposed to end in 2009. Following the Manley report last year, Stephen Harper gained an extension until 2011. Because of the weak Parliamentary opposition, there was no debate on this extremely important question. In prolonging the Canadian mission in Afghanistan, Prime Minister Harper was hoping to curry favour with President Bush, who had not been pleased with Canada's refusal to participate in his Iraqi mission.

In the next few weeks, we can expect intense US pressure to extend the schedule for Canadian withdrawal in 2011. However, in the current political context created by the fall 2008 election, the Prime Minister won't be able to commit Canada to the mission in Afghanistan without a serious debate in Parliament. Such difficult decisions will only be made by Parliament and by the government after this debate; thus we have to think carefully while there is still time.

Since 2002, over 100 Canadians have lost their lives and many hundreds have been wounded. Among those there are several hundred who will remain invalid for the rest of their lives. Let us also not forget the growing number who will live scarred by the nightmares of the horrors they have witnessed. All of us Canadians are paying a heavy price for our presence in Afghanistan. We must ask ourselves whether the results obtained and foreseeable are worth the price.

THE INCREASING VIOLENCE

Evidence shows the Taliban are winning territory throughout Afghanistan, despite enormous efforts deployed to contain them. Even Kabul is becoming less and less secure. The Taliban are showing that they are capable of moving freely nearly everywhere, right to the heart of the capital. On the ground the NATO military commanders foresee an increase in violence and weakening security well into 2009.

It is becoming more obvious that the Taliban enjoy support, even if it is only passive, from a large part of the Afghan population. How else would the Taliban be able to plant home-made bombs in populated areas, and then melt away, disappearing into the countryside? The tribes and their powerful leaders control the majority of the territory. And finally, the poppy cultivation and the trafficking of heroin continue to be the main economic activity. Even if we take into account progress in the areas of education and the human rights of women, the overall picture is a disaster.

This assessment should remind us once more that you cannot impose the development of a secular culture in a society by means of a foreign military. No society changes because of an outside pressure, and certainly not by force of arms. The British were powerful colonizers, but they failed dismally in Afghanistan in the 19th century. The Russians in the 1980s had to yield before the Taliban, who, let us not forget, were strengthened thanks to American aid. What makes us think we can now succeed where the others have failed?

I often think of a conversation I had in 2002 with a young Afghan recently arrived in Canada. He was categorical: the invasion of the United States and its allies was destined to fail. The very idea of believing that they could change the ancient culture of the Afghans and introduce democracy was a deception.

Granting that the situations are different in some respects, the Americans find themselves in the same situation as in Vietnam and in Iraq. In fact, sending American troops from Iraq to Afghanistan is simply a face-saving way of leaving Iraq. But Canada, fortunately, has nothing to do with this dreadful tragedy in Iraq.

NEGOTIATE WITH THE TALIBAN?

Put bluntly, Canada has no justification for extending its military presence in Afghanistan beyond 2011. This doesn't mean that Canada should abandon Afghanistan. Since the new year the idea of starting negotiations with the Taliban has come to the surface. We must follow that route.

Since the end of World War II, Canada has always opted for negotiation and the pursuit of peace; it should return to that role. For the new Liberal leader, Michael Ignatieff, this would be the occasion to show that he can lead his party in the long Canadian tradition of working for peace.

At the same time, Canada should lead the way in withdrawing its military while continuing its active participation in programs of reconstruction and development. This is the objective that Canada should be following in this country that has been devastated by decades of war.

And I say to the parents, spouses and friends of the soldiers who have been killed or wounded in Afghanistan, this approach would not mean that they have suffered in vain. On the contrary, they contributed substantially to the fact that the Taliban now feel obliged to negotiate, to compromise and accept reconstruction. For this country, that would be real progress.

This question contains an aspect which though indirect, cannot be ignored. The impending debate on Afghanistan has to be situated within the context of the world financial and economic crisis. The military withdrawal would have the effect of reducing the enormous costs of the Canadian mission (See article by Steven Staples in this book). At a time when the government is being required to incur heavy fiscal deficits, a reduction in military spending would greatly ease the problem.

An Alternative to the
Manley Report

RICHARD PRESTON

The Report of the Independent Panel chaired by John Manley is now, and will continue to be, a pivotal statement in governmental debate and decision-making. There is widespread unity in Canada, including the government, the military, the public, and now the Manley Panel, that the overall goal of our presence in Afghanistan is to bring peace and better living conditions to one of the poorest and most fragile nations in the world. As the Manley Report says,

The essential questions for Canada are: how do we move from a military role to a civilian one, and how do we oversee a shift in responsibility for Afghanistan's security from the international community to Afghans themselves?

The specific steps for these changes are also specified in the Manley Report: developing local and national government institutions that are respected and not corrupt; recruiting and training Afghan soldiers and police; reclaiming of agricultural lands from mines and opium poppy crops; and building roads, bridges, electrification. With the exception of recruiting and training soldiers and police, these are activities that the NATO military are not suited to perform.

Diplomacy and development requires other people with non-military abilities, yet the solutions proposed by the Manley Panel focus almost exclusively on the need for increased military resources. This focus on war rather than on peace-making and rebuilding is a concern for several reasons:

• First, the field of political influence that is operative in the Afghanistan War is broad. Canadians need to clearly understand the leading role of the US administration in their Afghan adventure. I refer to US initiatives that converted what was a policing task of containing and diminishing al Qaeda into a US-escalated War on Terror. Several commentators claim that Canadian troops are in Afghanistan because of a perceived need to make amends for refusing to go with the US into the Iraq War.
• Second, the level of Canadian, NATO and especially US moral responsibility for substantially increasing the level of violence in Afghanistan needs recognition. In escalating the extent and level of conflict, NATO has taken on the role of increasing the level of armament of the region, with the Taliban and others reciprocating with their own increased armaments, much of it coming through Iran. This echoes the US arming of the Mujahedin and Taliban to drive out the USSR, and more distantly echoes what happened when the French left Vietnam to the US. The escalation of the technical capacity for violence makes the possibility of reducing violence and negotiating an end to war much more difficult, and the result is a sharp rise in people wounded and killed. In Vietnam, the USSR armed the Viet Cong to counter the American forces, the level of destruction sharply increased, and the US lost the war. In the Soviet invasion of Afghanistan, US armament matched the Soviet armament, the USSR withdrew, and left a potential for destructive violence that we have been witnessing in the current war.

Most of the other NATO nations have been loath to commit battle troops, and this should tell us something about the nature of this adventure. The US administration's position is one of unilateralism and pre-emptive strike. This extraordinary self-image as the single global superpower is not shared by the other NATO member nations, who regard it as dangerous and unrealistic, especially in the light of the Soviet failure in Afghanistan and US failures in Vietnam and Korea.

It is now quite possible that NATO, and the UN, and the US will all be seen to have failed again, and to have left Afghanistan in civil war with the bloody local purging of those suspected of having supported the US.

The comparison with the Korean War, including Canada's level of participation is instructive. I was there, with the First Marine Division, for the winter of 1951–52. A half-century later, I still do not understand why I was there. Sure, South Korea is wealthy now. And North Korea is poor and nuclear now. The US did not win, and in the long (nuclear) run, may be seen to have lost in terms of global security. Will we wind up with two nations – a Northern Afghanistan that is developed, and a Southern Afghanistan that is militantly theocratic, with nuclear Pakistani neighbours?

A strength of the Manley Report is its recognition of leadership limitations both within Canada, and more broadly, within NATO. A striking phrase in the Report says that Canada is in Kandahar Province "for whatever reason." Mr. Manley told us, via the CBC, that the person(s) responsible for this sustained commitment is not known even to the Independent Panel. The military leadership may be making decisions and operating without sufficient political leadership – as argued in Janice Stein and Eugene Lang's recent book, *The Unexpected War*.

Afghanistan was the first real test of the 3D policy – Defence, Development and Diplomacy – and officials from all three departments do not think that Canada has done as well as it could. The 3D s are not working well together and some are not working well alone. In Ottawa, words like dysfunctional, debilitated, and broken are common descriptions of the institutions at the centre of Canadian foreign policy. These descriptions come not from hostile outsiders but from people who have spent years working within one of the three big departments – Defence, Foreign Affairs and CIDA – that are Canada's face to the world. The balance among those three departments has shifted markedly in the last three years. Defence has been reinvigorated under strategic and focused leadership, while the other two have largely lost their way.

We are encouraged by the recommendation that a high-profile UN special representative should be appointed to coordinate the NATO and other participants, since the poor coordination of Canadian policy is mirrored in the poor coordination of the Afghan government,

NATO participants, the International Security Assistance Force (ISAF) and Canada. It is the UN's responsibility to address the ownership of the Afghanistan project.

We note that the Report faults both the Martin and Harper governments for lacking honesty and full disclosure. It recommends that the PM take a personal leadership role and establish a special Cabinet Committee with a mandate for political oversight of the Afghanistan project. Currently, oversight of this and other projects is hindered by lack of coordination within and between Canadian governmental departments, especially Defence and Foreign Affairs.

DEPARTMENT FOR PEACE

The establishment of a Canadian Department for Peace would provide an inter-departmental coordination structure with focus on peace-building strategy and project funding. An attempt at a coordinating structure has begun with START – the Stabilization and Reconstruction Taskforce. Foreign Affairs chairs the group. START is an interdepartmental body that attempts to coordinate and implement activities of the 3D policy of the government.

However, START can only achieve part of the overriding task of peace-building. We propose that a full Cabinet-level Minister and Department of Peace, in place alongside Defence and Foreign Affairs, would be the best coordinating re-structuring plan to respond effectively to the diverse needs involved in reconstruction and helping establish a long-lasting peace in Afghanistan.

The Manley Report states, on several occasions, that there is currently no role for peacekeeping in Afghanistan because there is currently no peace to keep. This view is reactive rather than proactive and fails to recognize that peace is a process, not a stagnant state. This is precisely the time for active peace-making and peace diplomacy, leading to a large-scale peace-building effort.

In a recent Environics poll, 60 per cent of Canadian respondents said Canada is a country that exerts a positive force in the world. There is deep public support for a major, forward-looking peace initiative led by the establishment of a Canadian Department of Peace. Afghanistan is the current challenge, but certainly will not be the last. Canada needs to anticipate the larger challenge of reducing violence in the global world and at home.

The CDPI now enjoys the support of such prominent Canadians as Sen. Doug Roche, the Hon. Lloyd Axworthy, the federal NDP Caucus and the Green Party. Discussions have been held with many Liberal members, who have also shown a great deal of interest. Borys Wrzesnewskyj (Etobicoke Centre-Liberal) is reported in Hansard to have called for a Cabinet Minister of Peace, April 24, 2006.

The overall mandate of a Minister of Peace would be conflict resolution by peaceful means, consistent with the UN Declaration and Program of Action for the International Decade for a Culture of Peace and Non-violence for the Children of the World (2001–2010), of which Canada is a signatory. The proposed Department of Peace would have the overall responsibility for the coordination and timely implementation of peace-related policy and would be composed partly of existing offices that are now spread across several Federal departments, relocated to ensure coordination of their activities. The department would act as a sensor for the early warning of potential violent conflict, serve as an incubator of creative responses to violent conflict, and design effective long term peace-building projects responding to the root causes of violence.

Back to the "Peace" in Peacebuilding: An Old/New Role for Canada

PEGGY MASON

We need to step back from the debate over the use of force in Afghanistan. Drawing on the wealth of experience from the 63 UN-led peacekeeping operations and the handful of UN-authorized, but not UN-led, peacekeeping, peace support, and crisis stabilization operations since the end of the Cold War, we need to focus instead on what we have learned about how it *should* be done. How do we, the international community, help *resolve* the armed conflict and start to build a sustainable peace? So my starting point is a distillation of key lessons learned in relation to internal armed conflict, or at least, lessons identified, since "learning" implies that we will act on these experiential insights.

WHAT IS PEACEKEEPING

UN peacekeeping was never meant to supplant the peaceful resolution of disputes. It was never meant to replace the central tool of conflict resolution – the negotiated settlement. "Traditional" or "classical" peacekeeping, what Canadians claim was invented by Lester Pearson but which the Swedes credit to their countryman Dag

Hammerskjold when he was UN Secretary-General, was based on a negotiated ceasefire agreement and a separation of military forces (which the UN peacekeepers would monitor) to allow a window of opportunity for the negotiation of an overall comprehensive peace settlement. Cyprus is the quintessential example of this approach and is often cited as a *military* peacekeeping success (the opposing Greek and Turkish Cypriot military forces generally having been kept on their respective sides of the famous "green line" of separation for over 40 years) but a diplomatic peacemaking failure, there as yet having been no achievement of a comprehensive political settlement.

Post Cold War *comprehensive* peacekeeping broadened the scope of the heretofore largely military peace operation to encompass all those *civilian* actors and elements necessary to help the parties implement a comprehensive peace settlement.

So let's go back to the starting point – the negotiation of a comprehensive peace agreement that addresses all relevant issues underlying the conflict. Ideally the agreement will seek to lay the political/security and socio-economic foundations for a sustainable peace including the disarmament, demobilization and reintegration into civil society of former combatants, the strengthening of the rule of law (police, judges, courts, penal system); technical assistance for democratic development including notably the holding of free and fair elections within inclusive political structures; improving respect for human rights, reform of the military, rehabilitating economic infrastructure and ultimately when the situation is sufficiently stabilized, promoting sustainable development. A particularly important aspect of the negotiation process will be the identification of mechanisms and procedures, down to the grassroots level, to allow the post-conflict society to find the right balance between justice and reconciliation processes.

I have briefly outlined some of the fundamental elements that typically need to be addressed in a comprehensive peace agreement, each one of which contains many issues to be resolved (type of political structures, constitution, legal framework and so on.) External facilitation will generally be critical to help the parties negotiate this type of agreement, and here the UN has considerable expertise.

So the first lesson is the need for as comprehensive a peace agreement as possible, addressing all relevant issues and, in turn, the importance of *impartial* and *expert* third party facilitation to this end.

A comprehensive peace agreement presupposes not only that the

full range of issues will have been put on the table but that all necessary parties to the conflict will have been involved in the negotiation.
This will include all the various factions engaged in the conflict (government and rebels, all sides of the civil war). There may be some "ir-
reconcilables," but if there is to be any chance of achieving a comprehensive and sustainable agreement, they must be kept to a
minimum. The more factions left *outside* and not included in the negotiation, the less chance of the peace plan succeeding.

But it will not be enough for the peace talks to involve political
and military leaders. The negotiations must be informed by an inclusive consultative process down to the grassroots level if it is to replace
elitist, exclusionary forms of governance, with pluralistic, inclusive
political institutions and mechanisms. And what a powerful demonstration effect on war-weary publics when the peace process itself is
emblematic of the democratic goals being sought!

Once again, expert, impartial third party facilitation will be key
to creating the minimum conditions of trust in order to get all parties
to the table and underpin the formal negotiations with broader consultations.

But relevant parties that need to be part of the overall negotiating
framework go well beyond the *internal* factions in a civil war. Typically there will be a number of external parties actively aiding one
side or the other. They may have military forces within the country
(in the Democratic Republic of Congo at one point, armies from
eight different neighbours were directly engaged in the conflict in
support of one faction or another or in pursuit of natural resources).
At a minimum they must agree to withdraw their forces and to cease
other forms of assistance to one or the other internal parties to the
conflict. In all likelihood, there will be a host of related issues to resolve as well, from border and resource disputes to treatment of ethnic minorities with ties to the external actor, to issues of political influence and trade relations. In short, the external actors are involved
in the conflict for a variety of reasons relating to their own perceived
interests. and it is unlikely these intertwined issues can be resolved
without a negotiating framework expressly designed to do so.

If the peace agreement is to receive the blessing of the UN Security Council, then the veto-wielding "Permanent 5" (China, France,
Russia, UK and USA) must see it in their interest (or at least not
against their interest) to support the agreement. This in turn means
that, where one or more of the P5 have specific interests, they must be

satisfactorily addressed. It is precisely in those cases where individual members of the UNSC have their own vested interests and agendas that it will be critically important for the negotiation to be facilitated by an impartial, competent third party. At the same time, the more important the vested interest, the more difficult it will be for these powerful actors to step back and allow such disinterested mediation. There is much evidence that US control of the negotiating process that led to the Dayton Accords (in relation to the Former Republic of Yugoslavia) produced a highly problematic agreement that proved very difficult to implement. The Quartet mechanism in the Middle East peace process is allegedly a mechanism to bring into play both the UN Secretary-General and, to a somewhat lesser extent, the EU, as honest brokers, counter-balancing US and Russian special interests, but the evidence to date suggests that its main effect has been to dilute the voices of moderation and balance.

All of which is to say that one of the most vexing negotiation challenges is how to satisfactorily address concerns of powerful external actors without totally unbalancing the agreement so it then doesn't meet the needs of the main parties to the conflict.

Once achieved, the comprehensive peace agreement must be implemented and this is where the modern, multidisciplinary peace operation comes into play with a UN mission under the overall political and diplomatic direction of the SRSG, (Special Representative to the Secretary General) and typically comprised of military, police, judiciary, corrections and rule of law components, a humanitarian coordinator, human rights and development components, an electoral assistance unit, a civil affairs unit, child protection experts, and a gender advisor.

Note that the type and scope of third party implementation assistance must be negotiated as well, ideally as part of the overall peace negotiation. And it is here that we have perhaps one of the starkest examples of powerful third party interests impeding a robust implementation capacity. I refer of course to the example of Darfur and Chinese reluctance, because of its dependence on Sudanese oil, to bring the necessary pressure to bear on Khartoum to secure its agreement to a robust implementation force.

In addition to all of the elements *within* the UN peacekeeping operation, there will be a diverse array of more or less independent actors operating *outside* the mission and focused on humanitarian relief or on other aspects of the post-conflict peacebuilding process, broadly defined. They come from the family of UN funds, programmes and agencies (UNHCR, UNICEF, WFP, UNDP for example), from the international financial institutions, notably the Conflict Prevention and Reconstruction (CPR) Unit of the World Bank, from the donor community (CIDA, DFID, USAID) and from the international non-governmental community (CARE, World Vision, Oxfam, Médecins sans Frontières) and from the unique and independent International Committee of the Red Cross (ICRC). And all of these external actors will in turn be interacting with a multitude of local, national, governmental and non-state actors from the post-conflict country itself, from the neighbouring countries and sub-regional groupings, increasingly from regional entities (such as the African Union, NATO and the European Union), which may be mandated by the Security Council to assist in the peace implementation process.

Slowly and painfully, this extraordinarily diverse array of international 'intervenors' is coming to understand that, for such a complex effort at social engineering to have any chance of working, an agreed multilateral framework is necessary for the international community to work within, ideally reflecting a comprehensive approach, freely negotiated and agreed by the parties, and which addresses all aspects of the governance "failure" that led to the conflict in the first place.

Simply put, the mandate for the peacekeeping operation must be based on the comprehensive peace agreement.

The UN may or may not be the lead entity in the peace negotiation process, and UN-led "blue helmets' may or may not be the military force that is providing security assistance during the peace implementation phase. But only the UN Security Council can mandate a multidimensional peace operation under UN civilian leadership to oversee and facilitate implementation by the parties of the peace agreement. In other words, only the UN can mandate a comprehensive multilateral peace implementation *framework* legitimizing international action, and within which governments need to work to identify and agree on their areas of action and specific programmes and projects within those areas of action, including identifying how those projects and plans support the overall strategy. And equally important, only the UN can even notionally *lead* the *overall* peace implementation process, if only because no other single entity is acceptable to the international community.

THREE FUNDAMENTAL COMPONENTS

There are three fundamental components here – the consent of the parties, the comprehensive framework and the coherence of the international assistance effort.

And now we turn to Afghanistan and the indescribably sad, frustrating and inexcusable fact that *none* of these essential factors for success has been put in place.

There has been no peace negotiation whatsoever, let alone a comprehensive one. Key parties to the conflict, notably the southern Pashtuns, the largest single tribal group in Afghanistan were lumped in with the Taliban, who were in turn lumped in with al Qaeda and then left out of the agreement. The Bonn Agreement (Background to the Bonn Agreement can be found in articles by John Warnock, TariqAli, and Chesmak Farhoumand-Sims.) which created Afghanistan's elected bodies, was almost entirely developed by external parties and was never the subject of negotiation by Afghans. The framework developed at the London Conference at the end of January 2006 – the Afghanistan Compact – was developed by an even narrower group of foreigners – and then "presented" at the Conference. The lower house of the Afghan National Assembly, which has the power under the new Constitution to ratify treaties and international agreements, was given no role in developing or approving the Compact.

Afghanistan has long-standing conflicts with Pakistan over relations with India: the border, ethnic issues and transit trade. Iran is a vital economic partner for landlocked Afghanistan. The issue of Taliban insurgents receiving safe haven in the tribal areas of Pakistan is inextricably intertwined with core issues of governance in those areas. All of which is to say that these are fundamentally *political* issues that cannot be resolved by hectoring the President of Pakistan into sending yet more troops into Baluchistan or North Waziristan. Yet no serious attempt has been made to bring these parties to the negotiating table.

No provision was made in the Bonn Agreement for an overarching, coherent framework for peace implementation. With the United States in its heyday of unilateralism, the UN was initially confined to a narrow humanitarian coordination role, while key peacebuilding tasks were parceled out to a series of lead nations, utterly unequipped to handle them.[1]

Later, when the election planning ran into serious problems, the UN role was expanded to cover elections, but President Karzai consistently opposes any overarching UN role. The new Afghan government-led coordination mechanism (the Joint Coordination and Monitoring Board (JCMB)), established under the London Compact, is too unwieldy to be effective and, in any event, key activities take place completely outside its orbit, notably the Provincial Reconstruction Teams (Background to these PRTs can be found in the article by Stephen Cornish), each one unique to the international military force that created it.

Just as the international *political* leadership in Afghanistan is fragmented, so is the military effort. From the beginning there have been two distinct and fundamentally incompatible military efforts: the US-led Coalition, Operation Enduring Freedom (OEF); and the North Atlantic Treaty Organization (NATO)–led International Security Assistance Force (ISAF). The Coalition, whose primary mission is defined as counterterrorism and counterinsurgency, and which enjoys freedom of action under the United States' right of self defense, came to Afghanistan to assure first the security of Americans from al Qaeda and then of the Afghan government from the insurgency. ISAF's mission is to help the Afghan authorities provide security according to the Bonn Agreement, relevant UN Security Council resolutions, and a bilateral agreement with the Afghan government.

ISAF, as a UN-authorized but NATO-led post-conflict stabilization force, was meant to be a robust peace operation, loosely modeled on those deployed in the former Yugoslavia to help implement the Dayton Accords, and in Kosovo, while a comprehensive political settlement was to be worked out. But during the critical *immediate* post-conflict phase, when the Taliban government had been routed, ISAF was mandated to operate only in and around Kabul, giving the US-led OEF freedom of action in the rest of the country to track down al Qaeda and Taliban insurgents, operate on the basis of overwhelming force, make deals with local warlords when it was deemed expedient to do so. In the process, this put the security needs of ordinary Afghans constantly at risk.

And what in the end happened was the worst of all possible worlds – the expansion in late July 2006 of ISAF into the south (under relentless pressure of the US, who sought to free up American troops for Iraq) when the insurgency there had not been quelled but had steadily grown in strength, with the result that ISAF too was sucked into the counterinsurgency quagmire.

A word about the structure of Canadian Forces in the south is in order. The multinational brigade headed by General David Fraser and constantly referred to by then Defence Minister O'Conner and Prime Minister Harper as a "Canadian mission" authorized by the UN, was in fact a subordinate unit of Combined Joint Task Force 76 (CJTF 76) – commanded by Major-General Benjamin Freakley of the 10th Mountain Division of the US Army and was therefore neither Canadian nor operating under a UN mandate. Despite the fact that this information is clearly stated on the website of the Canadian Forces, the media – from Mike Blanchfield in the *Ottawa Citizen*, to Jeffrey Simpson in the *Globe and Mail*, to the editorial board of the *Toronto Star* – constantly and erroneously referred to Canada as leading NATO operations in the Kandahar region. When challenged directly on the fact that Canadian soldiers were not wearing the characteristic large green ISAF shoulder patch in English and Arabic when given proof positive that we were not then part of the NATO forces – they responded by going silent about this aspect of the mission, until ISAF forces finally did arrive in the south in mid-summer of 2006 and Canadian forces transitioned to NATO command.

If Canada were trying to pursue a course of action designed to obliterate the difference between the ISAF stabilization mandate and the OEF anti-terrorist effort, they could not have chosen a more effective means. As I wrote in an online article for the *Globe and Mail* in May 2006, whatever Canada's actual motivation, the course of action followed by Canadian Forces in Kandahar province has made it virtually impossible for the ordinary Afghan to distinguish between the war-fighters and the peacebuilding forces.

AIM OF A PEACE OPERATION

The aim of a peace operation – however robust – is not to go to war with the parties but to help them build the democratic institutions and processes that will enable them to manage societal conflicts in a non-violent way. A robust force can deter violations, effectively address them when they occur and thus build confidence in the peace process. But this presumes that all or most of the key players want peace more than war, such that individual spoilers can be effectively isolated and dealt with. Without a credible peace process, the international military force, as it seeks to take action to address violations, risks becoming just another party to the conflict.

On June 12, 2007 the ICRC (The International Committee of the Red Cross), which has had an uninterrupted presence in Afghanistan since 1987, gave a press briefing entitled *"Afghanistan: three decades of war and no end in sight."* Their statement emphasized that the conflict between Afghan and international forces on the one hand and armed opposition groups on the other had "significantly intensified," and had spread over the previous 12 months, no longer confined to the south, but spreading to parts of the east, west and north.

The September 21, 2007 Report of the UN Secretary General to the Security Council stated that 2007 was turning out to be the worst year in security terms for Afghanistan since 2001, with an average of 548 insurgent and terrorist-related incidences a month – a 20 per cent increase in violence since 2006.

The ICRC and UN reports, when released, were but the latest in a long, grim list dating back to at least late 2004, with each one documenting a *further* deterioration in the security situation in Afghanistan. (And there have been many more since, including one by the Atlantic Council, whose authors included former NATO Supreme Allied Commander General Jones.)

NATO military commanders themselves know that there is no military solution to Afghanistan's myriad problems. According to respected analyst, Paul Rogers of Bradford University, "there is a widespread and bleak consensus among NATO commanders: unless there is a significant change in policy, foreign forces will remain in the country for decades, tied down in bitter counter-guerrilla operations."

Fighting the Taliban, al Qaeda and other disaffected groups loosely aligned with them involves tactics, most notably heavy reliance on air power and aggressive search and destroy missions, that lead to at least as many civilian casualties by international and allied Afghan forces as by opposition groups, breed hatred against foreign forces and, in the south, build support for the insurgents. Equally problematic, the use by the military of humanitarian aid as a tool in their information campaign against the Taliban carries the grave risk of making humanitarian workers themselves a target, as well as the civilians they seek to assist. (See article by Stephen Cornish in this book.)

Fighting the Taliban *et al* also means that military forces cannot focus on helping build and support the institutions that the Afghan people desperately need for long term security, particularly a professional, accountable police service and national army, together with the disbandment of armed groups, the end to government corruption and to impunity for abuses.

The Canadian military and other NATO forces in the south are in an impossible situation. They cannot help build a secure environment without ending the war and they cannot end the war by military means.

HOW CAN THE WAR BE ENDED?

Without a decisive victory by one side or the other, history tells us that the only way to end such internal conflicts is through a negotiated settlement.[2]

The optimum time to negotiate with the Taliban was when they were defeated and routed by the US military action in late 2001, a strategy that would have had the added benefit of separating them from al Qaeda, rather than pushing them closer together.

Now they are infinitely stronger, whatever short term tactical gains – at such human cost – are made by ISAF and by the OEF on the battlefield.

President Karzai, an array of Afghan Parliamentarians and even former high profile members of the Taliban have realized there is no other way forward, but, incredibly, the Harper government first opposed and ridiculed negotiations and then as *ad hoc* efforts began to increase, became silent about them – surely the most powerful evidence ever that Canada had become part of the problem, not the solution.

But let me be clear: what is needed in Afghanistan is not another backroom deal forged by elites to save their political hides. Yet this is what will happen, indeed, what is already underway, if a new direction is not taken by the international community.

What is urgently needed is a UN-led broadly-based political dialogue in Afghanistan engaging all sectors of society and communities of interest. And Canada has a key role to play – one we have bought with the blood of young Canadians – in securing support within NATO for a comprehensive peace process to build the political consensus that is now absent.

Let us now turn to the Manley Panel Report[3] to see what contribution it has made, if any, to a fundamental rethinking of Canada's failing Afghanistan strategy.

What is new in the Manley Report is more honesty in the narra-
tive than we have seen from the Harper Government on how bad the
situation really is in Afghanistan, particularly in the south. On page
12 of the report there is a recognition that the security situation is
getting worse, not better. There is an admission on page 17 that the
current fighting is a continuation of the thirty-year civil war and a
grudging acknowledgement of the need for an "eventual political
reconciliation," and for Canada to support *ad hoc* efforts to this
end.4 On page 27, there is recognition of the key role of regional actors and of the many complexities of the situation:

Beyond its own borders, Afghanistan is surrounded by a violence-prone region. The mountainous western reaches of Pakistan, along the boundary
with Afghanistan, harbour Afghan insurgents who are reinforced by recruits
from countries around the Gulf and further abroad. Pakistan's own domestic political upheavals and recurring crises – and its concerns about India's
growing economic and political presence in Afghanistan – complicate the region's geopolitics. Iran, to Afghanistan's West, has been a source of arms
trafficking into Afghanistan. The actions of regional powers require focused
consideration as policy-making proceeds. Canada, in concert with key allies,
should adopt a coherent diplomatic strategy that addresses regional risks
and engages all the region's actors, in particular Pakistan, to establish a more
stable security environment.

And on page 33 there is a call for a "comprehensive political-military
strategy."
    So all of this seems promising.
    But what of the recommendations contained in the Manley Re-
port. Having concluded that more of the same will lead to failure in
Afghanistan, what do they urge Canada to do next?
    They call for more frankness from the Harper government about
the difficulties the mission is facing as well as for clear "benchmarks"
and "criteria" to evaluate progress. They also say NATO must provide 1,000 more soldiers and some medium-lift helicopters if Canada is to *extend* its current military role until the job is done.5 As for
their earlier call for a comprehensive strategy, apparently they didn't
actually mean a *new* strategy, just better coordination of the existing
one, with the head of the UN political mission in Afghanistan to be
given the lead role in such coordination. WFM (World Federalists
Movement – Canada) President Warren Allmand, while welcoming

the Panel's call for a high-level civilian representative of the UN to take the lead, went on to say that, "... [h]e or she should be tasked with more than ensuring civilian-military coherence. The UN is best suited to galvanize international support for a truly inclusive peace process."

Incredibly then, the only advice in the Manley Report on the central challenge of moving towards a sustainable political solution in Afghanistan is for Canada to pursue "ad hoc" efforts towards "eventual political reconciliation."

With respect to the need to address the complex regional dimensions of the conflict, the Panel recommends that Canada, in concert with key allies, should press for "(f)orceful representations with Afghanistan's neighbours, in particular with Pakistan, to reduce the risks posed to regional stability and security by recent developments in that country."

In other words, the incredibly complex nexus of regional issues bedeviling the Afghan conflict is to be addressed through increased diplomatic pressure on Pakistan to solve its security problems. Clearly, such empty exhortations must be replaced with international support for processes that address the deep democratic deficit that is at the root of Pakistan's insecurity; but the Manley Panel Report is silent on any meaningful diplomatic engagement with Afghanistan's neighbours.[6]

What about the strategic review of Afghanistan policy still ongoing in NATO at the time of the Manley Report's release, the results of which were to be announced at the Bucharest Summit in April 2008?

The Manley Report is silent on any inputs by Canada to this review other than to push for greater military-civilian coherence (an impossibility without a comprehensive strategy to align with), focusing instead on the idea that the Harper government should concentrate its efforts on getting NATO to agree to the additional soldiers and helicopters as a condition for Canada's continued participation in the south.

Rather than caving in to the Conservative government's motion to extend the Canadian combat mission, what Parliament *should* have done was to issue a strong call to the Harper government to actively and creatively engage in the NATO strategic review, using Canada's hard won influence and credibility to convince the Alliance's 26 member states (comprising many of the key donor countries and troop contributors in Afghanistan) of the need for a new, overarching political framework for international engagement in Afghanistan, under a UN leadership that is mandated to begin the urgent work of creating the conditions for a comprehensive peace process.[7]

UPDATE/ADDENDUM IN FEBRUARY 2009

After seven years in Afghanistan, the Western coalition does not have much to show in terms of progress. All available data indicate a general failure in security and state building: increased civilian and military casualties, expansion of the guerillas, unfavorable perceptions of foreign troops by the local population, absence of functioning national institutions, and growing destabilization of the Pakistani border, which threatens NATO's logistical roads, essential for resupplying NATO forces. Most of the two provinces south of Kabul are under the control of the Taliban.[8]

Against this backdrop of continuing failure and the sad milestone of over 100 Canadian soldiers having died in the Afghanistan conflict along with thousands of Afghan civilians, there is one small piece of good news. The new Obama administration has instituted a "root and branch" review of its Afghanistan policy with the stated intention of putting more emphasis on diplomacy and a regional strategy. At the same time, however, the US has announced its intention to deploy a further 17,000 American soldiers to southern Afghanistan. Secretary of Defense Robert Gates used the February meeting of NATO Defense Ministers in a largely futile attempt to persuade other NATO members to deploy greater numbers of combat troops. Some analysts like Paul Rogers believe that the US "surge" is less to seek outright military victory than to exert sufficient force to bring cooperative elements of a weakened Taliban into negotiations. Yet, the addition of more foreign troops may, in itself, provoke increased Afghan resistance as well as encouraging yet more foreign fighters from Iraq and elsewhere to join the fray.[9]

The new head of the UN mission in Afghanistan, Kai Eide of Norway, an extremely able and experienced diplomat with both UN peacekeeping and NATO postings under his belt, has pushed his coordination mandate to the limit, asserting that what is needed is a "political" surge. When asked in a press conference if that meant talking to the Taliban, he responded, "If you want an agreement that matters, then you have to talk to who matters." The beleagured President Zidari of Pakistan is doing just that, desperately trying to reach local agreements to stabilize the border areas at whatever cost to good governance and human rights. This demonstrates once again that the choice has always been between backroom deals and a comprehensive political solution.

President Obama has appointed Ambassador Richard Holbrooke as his special envoy for Afghanistan and Pakistan. Let us fervently hope that Holbrooke has at long last learned from his many, many past mistakes, not the least of which was his strong support for redirecting American military and intelligence assets away from the region in 2002-2003 in order to invade and occupy Iraq.[10]

Canada in the meantime is still holding to its latest deadline of February 2011 for the withdrawal of its combat forces, while pledging further increases in our development efforts. Without improvements in security, increased development will be impossible. Without a new political strategy, there will be no improvements in security. Michael Ignatieff, Leader of the Liberal Party of Canada, told reporters shortly before the American President's arrival in Ottawa on February 19th, that he believed Obama would listen to what Canada had to say about Afghanistan. After his short meeting with the President, he said that he had welcomed the American review of its Afghanistan strategy since it was clearly "adrift" and he had urged more attention to diplomatic efforts. If Mr. Ignatieff meant to imply by these comments that he supports greater efforts towards a political resolution of the long and bloody conflict in Afghanistan, then why did he not just say so?

Why is it so hard for Canadian leaders to forthrightly champion what used to be our bread and butter - creative, committed efforts to build a just and lasting peace through sustained, impartial, inspired diplomatic engagement?

CONCLUSIOINS

To be an effective peacemaker, Canada must situate its efforts at resolving conflict and helping build a sustainable peace within a whole-of-government peacebuilding policy that is itself embedded in a UN-led international strategic framework; this is where Canada should be focusing its efforts.

And this means, in turn, giving pride of place in our foreign policy – together with the eradication of poverty and the promotion of fair trade – to the peaceful resolution of disputes, to the prevention of conflict through "deep prevention" efforts focused on systemic change and the promotion of human security, and to a sustained commitment to post-conflict peacebuilding. Embedding Canadian peacebuilding activity in a UN-led international strategic framework also means a rededication by Canada to the principles of the UN Charter, to one set of rules for all, fairly applied to all, to the principle that the security of *each* state is *equally* important and can only be truly safeguarded and enhanced by means of the twin objectives of human and common security – and therefore to the paramount need for Canada to work tirelessly to support and strengthen UN institutions and capacities for peacebuilding.

NOTES

1 The UK took the lead on poppy eradication, Germany on police training, Italy on reform of the judiciary, Japan on the disarmament of ex-combatants and the US on the training of the new Afghan national army.

2 See the 2008 study by the Rand Corporation, *How Terror Groups End,* which analyzed 648 groups in existence during the period 1968 to 2006. They found that "… a transition to a political process is the most common way in which terrorist groups ended … and, conversely, that military force has rarely been the primary reason for the end of such groups."

3 "Independent Panel on Canada's Future Role in Afghanistan," January 2008.

4 Why "ad hoc" efforts instead of concerted, systematic, coordinated efforts?

5 Nothing demonstrates the fundamentally political character of this document more than the absurd recommendation that 1000 additional soldiers from other NATO countries should be a key determinant in whether Canada extends its combat mission beyond the February 2009 deadline. Did the Panel actually believe that this tiny number of additional forces would turn the tide and, if so, why wouldn't they urge Canada to come up with the additional soldiers so we could save the day for NATO and Afghanistan?

6 A call for such diplomatic engagement was included in a joint press release from a range of non-governmental organizations including Peacebuild, which Peggy Mason chairs, in response to the release of the Manley Report.

7 NATO, as a military alliance can only review its own strategy. The UN Security Council would have to mandate any new UN role.

8 "Focus and Exit: an Alternative Strategy for the Afghan War," Report of the Carneigie Endowment for International Peace, page 2 (January 2009).

9 The Carnegie report, *op cit*, makes this observation as does Paul Rogers in his always cogent analysis at < www.opendemocracy.net >.

10 For a sobering analysis of Richard Holbrooke's career, see "Holbrooke: Insensitive Choice for a Sensitive Region," FPIF Commentary, January 29, 2009 at http://www.fpif.org/fpiftxt/5826.

Author Biographies

TARIQ ALI is a British-Pakistan novelist, historian, filmmaker, and commentator. He is a member of the editorial committee of the New Left Review political journal. He regularly contributes to *The Guardian, Counterpunch*, and the *London Review of Books*. He is the author of several books, including *Pirates Of The Caribbean: Axis Of Hope, Bush in Babylon, Clash of Fundamentalisms: Crusades, Jihads and Modernity*, and the recently published *The Duel: Pakistan on the Flight Path of American Power*. His article first appeared in the *New Left Review*, March-April, 2008.

IRA BASEN is a Canadian radio producer and author. He joined CBC Radio in 1984 and was a senior producer at *Sunday Morning* and *Quirks and Quarks*. He has written for *Saturday Night, The Globe and Mail*, and *Walrus*. He taught at the University of Toronto, the University of Western Ontario, and Ryerson, and is a co-author of the Canadian edition of *The Book of Lists*.

PIERRE BEAUDET is an organizer, writer, teacher and a professor of sociology at the University of Ottawa. He has been active for 25 years in international development, as a manager of various programs in Africa, Asia and Latin America, and as consultant for

CIDA, the United Nations Development Programme (UNDP) and several Canadian and International NGOs. He was a founder and one-time director of the Montreal-based NGO Alternatives, which conducts work in Afghanistan.

CLAUDE CASTONGUAY is a Canadian politician and businessman. He taught at the University of Laval before being elected to the National Assembly of Quebec in 1970, where he served in the Robert Bourassa's cabinet. In the 1980s, he was president of the Laurentian Bank of Canada. He served as Chancellor of the University of Montreal from 1986 until 1990 and was appointed to the Senate as a member of the Progressive Conservative caucus in 1990 before resigning in 1992. He headed a task force on Quebec health care for the Liberal government in Quebec in 2007. His article first appeared in *Le Devoir*, 14 January 2009.

STEPHEN CORNISH is the Policy & Advocacy Advisor at CARE Canada, where his special responsibility is dealing with CARE's work in Afghanistan. After ten years in the field with Médecins sans Frontières, he worked as a program manager for the Canadian Red Cross. He has also worked with aid organizations in Chechnya, Sierra Leone, Sudan, Rwanda, Colombia and Haiti. His article is exerpted from a longer version which first appeared in the *Journal of Military and Strategic Studies*, Fall, 2007, Vol. 10, Issue 1.

D'ABORD SOLIDAIRES (SOLIDARITY FIRST) is a non-partisan citizen-based collective involved in political education, in particular that which strengthens democracy, whether representative, participative, or deliberative. Their article was submitted as a brief at the Public Hearings for the Withdrawal of Canadian Troops from Afghanistan, 9 February 2008, Montreal.

MURRAY DOBBIN has been a journalist, author, broadcaster, and media analyst for more than thirty years. His books include *Preston Manning and the Reform Party*, *The Politics of Kim Campbell*, *The Myth of the Good Corporate Citizen*, and *Paul Martin: CEO for Canada?* He is a research associate and board member of the Canadian Centre of Policy Alternatives and is a past executive board member of the Council of Canadians. His two articles first appeared in the *CCPA Bulletin*: November, 2006 and September 2008.

WALTER DORN is Associate Professor of Defense Studies at the Canadian Forces College and Royal Military College of Canada, and holds academic positions at Queen's University and the Pearson Peacekeeping Centre. He is a scientist by training, receiving a Ph.D. in Chemistry from the University of Toronto, and has assisted with the negotiation, ratification and implementation of the 1993 Chemical Weapons Convention (CWC). He has extensive experience in field missions, serving in UN missions in East Timor and Ethiopia, and has served as the UN Representative of Science for Peace, a Canadian NGO. His article was presented as testimony before the Standing Committee on Foreign Affairs and International Development, 22 March 2007, Ottawa.

ÉCHEC À LA GUERRE is a large Montreal-based anti-war coalition that was formed in 2002 to oppose the pending war on Iraq. Échec à la guerre (Stop the War!) is composed of peace and human right groups, student and labour unions, community organizations and many others. Their article in this anthology was originally published in French, December 10th, 2006, as a 50-page document.

CHESHMAK FARHOUMAND-SIMS is an Assistant Professor in the Conflict Studies Program at Saint Paul University in Ottawa. She has done research on conflict resolution, human rights and the UN, reconciliation processes in identity conflicts, the impact of armed conflict on women, and since 2002, women's human rights and peace-building efforts in Afghanistan, where she worked in 2003 and 2008. She is a research associate on a North South Institute project investigating women's access to justice in Afghanistan, Haiti, and the Occupied Palestinian Territories.

JOHN FOSTER is a retired petro-chemical engineer and energy economist with 40 years of international experience in energy and development. He has worked with British Petroleum and Petro-Canada, and the World Bank and Inter-American Development Bank. He currently lives in Kingston, Ontario and collaborates on research and editorial work with his wife, Millie Morton. His first article first appeared in the CCPA *Bulletin*, May 2008. The second article first appeared in Foreign Policy Series, Vol. 3, No. 1, 19 June 19 2008, published by the *Canadian Centre for Policy Alternatives*.

ASAD ISMI is the international affairs correspondent for the *Canadian Centre for Policy Alternatives Monitor*. He has written extensively on US policy towards Afghanistan and is the author of two books, many reports and articles, and four radio documentaries. His website is www.asadismi.ws. Malalai Joya's website is www.malalaijoya.com. His article first appeared in the CCPA *Bulletin*, December 2007–January 2008.

LIGUE DES DROITS ET LIBERTÉS is an independent, non-partisan, non-profit organization founded in 1963. Its objectives are to defend and promote the universal and indivisible rights entrenched in the International Bill of Human Rights. The Ligue des droits et libertes, a member of the International Federation for Human Rights (FIDH), is one of the oldest rights organizations in the Americas. Their article was submitted as a brief at the Public Hearings for the Withdrawal of Canadian Troops from Afghanistan, 9 February 2008, Montreal.

LUCIA KOWALUK graduated from McGill University's School of Social Work with an MSW. She immediately became involved in a wide range of community issues, including the peace movement of the 1960s. She helped organize the community base of the Milton-Park cooperative housing project, the largest of its kind in Canada as well as other non-profit housing projects including Benny Farm. She was an editor of the journal *Our Generation* from its inception. Awarded the Therese Daviau prize in 1994 by the City of Montreal, she continues to work from the local to the international. She is co-editor of this book.

PEGGY MASON is Chair of the Canadian Peacebuilding Coordinating Committee, a senior fellow at the Norman Patterson School of International Affairs, and a faculty member of the Pearson Peacekeeping Centre, where she has trained NATO officers. She served as Canada's Ambassador for Disarmament from 1989 through 1994 and served on the UN Secretary-General's Disarmament Advisory Board from 1993 to 1997. She has acted as an advisor to the Canadian Foreign Ministry on the control of small arms and light weapons. She is active with a number of NGOs, including as a Senior Advisor to the Ottawa-based Rideau Institute and a member of the Council of the World Federalist Movement-Canada. Her article was presented at a public lecture in Montreal, 8 March 2008.

DAVID MACDONALD is the president of Embryonic, an economic consulting firm for progressive organizations. Over the past seven years, David Macdonald has provided economic analysis in areas as diverse as international agribusiness and Canadian health care. He has worked with the Polaris Institute, the Rideau Institute, the Green Party of Canada as well as Labour and community groups helping each to gain a progressive perspective on complex economic issues. In 2009, he coordinated the Canadian Center for Policy Alternative's Alternative Federal Budget and Stimulus Plan. He remains a research associate with the CCPA.

LINDA MCQUAIG is a Canadian journalist and author. She has worked for the *Globe and Mail*, *Macleans*, and the *National Post*, and is currently a columnist for the *Toronto Star*. She is the author of several books, including *Shooting the Hippo*, *The Cult of Impotence*, *All You Can Eat*, and *It's the Crude, Dude: War, Big Oil and the Fight for the Planet*. Her most recent is *Holding the Bully's Coat: Canada and the US Empire*. Her article first appeared in the CCPA Bulletin, June 2007.

DOMINIC MORISSETTE is a photographer and cinematographer. His 2003 film *Les derniers chasseurs du petit havre*, about Nova Scotian fisherman, won a Jutra nomination for best documentary. He has given video and photography workshops in Afghanistan, and co-ordinated the communications campaign for candidates in the Afghan 2004 presidential election. His 2007 film *Afghan Chronicles* tells the story of the Killid Media press group.

MICHAEL NEUMANN is a professor of philosophy at Trent University in Ontario. He received his Ph.D. in philosophy from the University of Toronto in 1975. He is a regular commentator on the online newsletter *CounterPunch* and is a contributor to the *CounterPunch* anthology *The Politics of Anti-Semitism*. He is also the author of *What's Left: Radical Politics and the Radical Psyche*, *The Rule of Law: Politicizing Ethics*, and *The Case Against Israel*.

RICHARD J PRESTON is professor Emeritus of Anthropology at McMaster University. He has published extensively on the culture of the Cree people of the coastal James Bay and on cultural psychiatry. He is active with the Committee as a Response to the Manley

Report, part of the Canadian "Department of Peace" Initiative, a coalition of citizen's collectives founded in 2003 to campaign for the creation of a Federal Department of Peace, with the Minister of Peace as a senior cabinet minister. His article was presented to the Manley Commission.

STEVEN STAPLES is president of the Rideau Institute, an independent research, advocacy, and consulting group based in Ottawa. He is the former director of Security Programs of the Polaris Institute. He is a long-time peace activist from Vancouver, the former chair of the International Network on Disarmament and Globalization (INDG) and the author of *Missile Defence: Round One*. He is co-editor of this book.

ROSE MARIE WHALLEY is a Montreal-based activist, a 40-year veteran of the peace movement. She is involved on issues of war and peace, human and women's rights, as well as aging conditions. She traveled to Afghanistan as an independent researcher. Her eyewitness account was presented as a brief at Public Hearings for the Withdrawal of Canadian Troops from Afghanistan, 9 February 2008, Montreal.

JOHN W. WARNOCK is an author and retired professor of sociology and political economy at the University of Regina. He has been active for three decades in human rights, farm, and environmental organizations. He is the author of the recently published *Creating a Failed State: The U.S. and Canada in Afghanistan*. He is the author of many other books, including *Partner to Behemoth*, *Profit Hungry: The Food Industry in Canada*, and *The Politics of Hunger: the Global Food System*.

ALSO AVAILABLE from BLACK ROSE BOOKS

THE SCRAMBLE FOR AFRICA
Darfur—Intervention and the USA
Steven Fake and Kevin Funk

As massive human suffering continues to engulf the Darfur region of Sudan, the crisis has garnered a rhetorical circus of saber-rattling and hand wringing from Western politicians, media, and activists. Yet such bluster has not halted the violence.

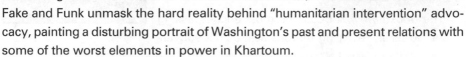

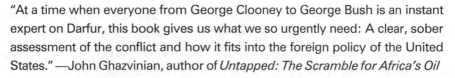

In a careful, yet scathing, indictment of this constellation of holier-than-thou government leaders, corporate media outlets, and spoon-fed NGOs, Steven Fake and Kevin Funk reveal the myriad ways in which the West has failed Darfur.

Eschewing liberal fantasies of Western benevolence, Fake and Funk unmask the hard reality behind "humanitarian intervention" advocacy, painting a disturbing portrait of Washington's past and present relations with some of the worst elements in power in Khartoum.

> "At a time when everyone from George Clooney to George Bush is an instant expert on Darfur, this book gives us what we so urgently need: A clear, sober assessment of the conflict and how it fits into the foreign policy of the United States." —John Ghazvinian, author of *Untapped: The Scramble for Africa's Oil*

> "A devastating critique...well-researched, easy to read, and utterly convincing." —Richard Falk, Princeton University

> "The authors avoid easy answers, and provide a quality analysis with compelling arguments." —Jan Pronk, Special Representative of the Secretary-General and Head of Mission for the United Nations Mission in Sudan, 2004-06

> "A commanding exposé of the duplicitous and damaging role played by U.S. leaders and others in a dark drama. Well-written, well focused, deeply informed." —Michael Parenti, author of *Contrary Notions* and *Against Empire*

STEVEN FAKE and KEVIN FUNK earned degrees in Journalism and Political Science from the University of Pittsburgh.

2008: 344 pages
Paperback ISBN: 078-1-55164-322-9 $19.99
Hardcover ISBN: 978-1-55164-323-6 $39.99

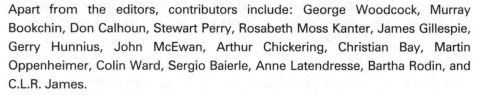

OF RELATED INTEREST

WORLD SOCIAL FORUM
Challenging Empires, Second Edition
Jai Sen, Peter Waterman, editors

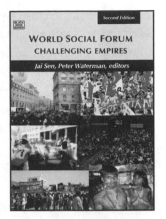

This comprehensive volume provides a glimpse into the wide-ranging discussions, debates and arguments which have gone into making the World Social Forum (WSF) one of the more prominent platforms of alternative ideas and practices in the present world.

Building on the First Edition, this Second Edition has been revised and updated to include coverage of those Social Forums that took place as recently as the summer of 2007.

"An excellent effort at combining both information and critical reflection on the World Social Forum phenomenon." —Massimo De Angelis

"A critical self-consideration of the WSF process by a variety of people." —Milan Rai, *The New Standard*

"A stellar collection of essays." —Immanuel Wallerstein, Fernand Braudel Center

Contributors include: Michael Albert, Sonia E. Alvarez, Samir Amin, Pierre Beaudet, Walden Bello, Jeremy Brecher, Tim Costello, Brendan Smith, Johanna Brenner, Dorval Brunelle, Sally Burch, Irene León, Boaventura de Sousa Santos, Emma Dowling, Jean Naga, Nawal El Saadawi, Arturo Escobar, Linden Farrer, David Graeber, Andrej Grubacic, Michael Leon Guerrero, Tammy Bang Luu, Cindy Wiesner, P.J. James, Michael Löwy, Muto Ichiyo, Michal Osterweil, Judy Rebick, Teivo Teivainen, Achin Vanaik, Gina Vargas, and Chico Whitaker, as well as Jai Sen and Peter Waterman.

JAI SEN is an independent researcher living in New Delhi who has contributed to a number of works documenting the World Social Forum. PETER WATERMAN is the author of *Globalisation, Social Movements, and the New Internationalisms* and of *Recovering Internationalism, Creating the New Global Solidarity*.

2008: 488 pages
Paperback ISBN: 978-1-55164-308-3 $24.99
Hardcover ISBN: 978-1-55164-309-0 $44.99

PIRATES AND EMPERORS

International Terrorism in the Real World, revised edition
Noam Chomsky

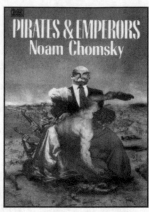

This work deals exclusively with terrorism—both State and "retail,"—with special attention to the scandal surrounding the Iranian arms deal. With meticulous research and documentation, Chomsky demonstrates the true motifs of U.S. foreign policy and the role of the media in ensuring public ignorance of these motifs. He looks behind the rhetoric for a real and comprehensive view of the role of the U.S. government, giving special attention to the disinformation campaign surrounding the bombing of Libya.

"Chomsky sees very little difference between such 'pirates' as the Shiite militiamen who hijacked a TWA flight to Beirut in 1985 and the 'emperor'—Washington—in its backing of the Nicaraguan contras or what he claims was its behind-the-scenes support for Israel's 1982 invasion of Lebanon...*Pirates and Emperors* raises provocative questions about U.S. diplomacy." —*MacLean's Magazine*

"Chomsky is the best and the brightest...and speaks out against dishonesty and hypocrasy with courage and effectiveness." —*Canadian Dimension*

"Disturbing reading and, as always, indispensable stuff." —*Ubyssey*

"Chomsky succeeds in rolling back the decade's mist of conservative ideology to reveal scenes of state terrorism, Orwellian Newspeak in the U.S. State Department, and continental annexation." —*The Whig-Standard*

NOAM CHOMSKY is Professor of Linguistics and Philosophy, and Institute Professor at MIT. He is the recipient of honorary degrees from several universities, and is the author of numerous books and articles on contemporary issues.

1987: 215 pages
Paperback ISBN: 0-895431-20-4 $19.99
Hardcover ISBN: 0-895431-21-2 $48.99

THE DIPLOMACY OF WAR
The Case of Korea
Graeme S. Mount, with Andre Laferriere

In 1950, North Korea invaded South Korea. Sixteen nations fought on behalf of South Korea; two (China and North Korea itself) on behalf of North Korea. By the time the fighting stopped, three years later, nearly two million military, and an estimated three million civilians had lost their lives, with one-half of Korean industry, and one-third of Korean homes destroyed. For two of the three years that the war was under way, both sides were trying to negotiate a peace.

The great strength of this book is in the wealth of detail with which the authors chart the course of policy- making in each of the Commonwealth capitals, the very limited coordination between them, and the way in which their individual strategic needs inevitably led to differing policy positions on Korea.

> "Fifty years on, the relationship of coalition with superpower is as relevant as ever." —Peter Londey, Historian, Australian War Memorial, Canberra

> "A praiseworthy addition to the published material on the Korean War. Interesting, readable, and exceedingly well documented. I found it fascinating." —John Melady, author of *Korea: Canada's Forgotten War*

> "Both assesses previous histories and presents its own judicious findings. It makes complex diplomatic history accessible." —Hank Nelson, Professor Emeritus, Australian National University, Canberra

GRAEME S. MOUNT is the author of *Chile and the Nazis: From Hitler to Pinochet* and *895 Days That Changed the World: The Presidency of Gerald R. Ford* (both available from Black Rose Books). ANDRE LAFERRIERE teaches history at the William G. Davis Sr. Public School in Brampton, Ontario.

2004: 244 pages
Paperback ISBN: 1-55164-238-7 $24.99
Hardcover ISBN: 1-55164-239-5 $53.99

OF RELATED INTEREST

THE CONCISE GUIDE TO GLOBAL HUMAN RIGHTS
Daniel Fischlin, Martha Nandorfy, prologue by Vandana Shiva

Much more than a simple 'guide to global human rights,' this book is an urgently needed and sophisticated reflection on the vital nature of human rights in the 21st century.

> "In a world facing the growing challenges of globalized apartheid and pandemic poverty, human rights will determine the future of every one of us and our sustainability as a species. This book allows us to reclaim our hope in that future." —Roger Clark, former Secretary General of Amnesty International

> "An excellent road map...It should be used by human rights activists and students alike." —Micheline Ishay, *The History of Human Rights: From Ancient Times to the Era of Globalization*

> "A must read." —Dr. Upendra Baxi, University of Warwick

DANIEL FISCHLIN and MARTHA NANDORFY are co-authors of the groundbreaking book *Eduardo Galeano: Through the Looking Glass* (Black Rose Books).

2006: 288 pages
Paperback ISBN: 1-55164-294-8 $24.99
Hardcover ISBN: 1-55164-295-6 $53.99

---

send for a free catalogue of all our titles

C.P. 1258, Succ. Place du Parc
Montréal, Québec
H2X 4A7 Canada

or visit our website at http://www.blackrosebooks.net

to order books

In Canada: (phone) 1-800-565-9523 (fax) 1-800-221-9985
email: utpbooks@utpress.utoronto.ca

In United States: (phone) 1-800-283-3572 (fax) 1-800-351-5073

In UK & Europe: (phone) London 44 (0)20 8986-4854 (fax) 44 (0)20 8533-5821
email: order@centralbooks.com

Printed by the workers of

for Black Rose Books